The Well-Fed Self-Publisher: A Well-Praised Book!

D0424795

"One of the few books that doesn't just tell you how to churn out a book, but how to succeed as a publisher. After more than 20 years publishing in the same niche as Peter, I still found many new ideas. Great way to shortcut the learning curve."

Shel Horowitz, Author
Grassroots Marketing for Authors and Publishers
www.frugalmarketing.com

"Finally, a book that shows self-publishers how to <u>make</u> money instead of simply <u>spending</u> it. Peter Bowerman, who's learned, firsthand, how to thrive financially as a self-publisher, generously shares his proven methods in this down-to-earth, first-person narrative. Self-publishers will find a dazzling array of examples, contacts, and plenty of ways to become well-fed."

Bob Erdmann, President, Columbine Communications & Publications
Publishing Consultant with Four Decades of Experience
Two-term President, *Publishers Marketing Association*
www.bob-erdmann.com

"Most authors have little to gain and much to lose by not taking advantage of self-publishing. Peter shows you in crystal-clear detail how to write, package and market your book—often with better results than what a big publisher could produce. A goldmine of creative ideas that will save you time, money, and migraines."

Joan Stewart, Publisher
The Publicity Hound's Tips of the Week

"GREAT book. This guide tells it like it is. I've read plenty of self-publishing books, and figured I'd pretty much seen it all, but I kept coming across ideas that leaped out at me, and kept saying, 'I've got to try that!' It gives the serious self-publisher all the information needed to turn a dream into a success, but makes it clear that this is no business for the dilettante!"

Moira Allen, Author
Starting Your Career as a Freelance Writer
Editor, **www.writing-world.com**

"Peter tells it like it is. While the nitty-gritty elements of self-publishing add up to serious business, Peter makes learning the ins and outs of the process fun. From the whys and hows to the 'sure-you-can' pep talks, this excellent book guides you along the complex yet fulfilling publishing path."

Kate Siegel Bandos
KSB Promotions ("Visibility Specialists")
www.ksbpromotions.com

"Easy to read and informative, Bowerman reveals the secrets of how you can turn your self-published book into a profitable, full-time living—secrets that can mean the difference between making huge profits or expensive mistakes."

Marisa D'Vari, Author
Building Buzz: How to Reach and Impress Your Target Audience (and four others).

"Peter Bowerman shows how you can write, publish, market, and sell your books in generally less time than it does for you to send out a query and wait to hear from a publisher, AND make more money per book sale, too!"

Priscilla Y. Huff, Author
Make Your Business Survive and Thrive! 100+ Proven Marketing Methods to Help You Beat the Odds and Build a Successful Small or Home-Based Enterprise

"I SO enjoyed this book. I've self-published several books, and the advice in this great book keeps it real. Things I've learned along the way, challenges I've faced...it's all captured here. I'm getting behind on my projects because I can't stop reading it."

Peggy Duncan, Author,
Conquer Email Overload with Better Habits, Etiquette, and Outlook 2003
www.PeggyDuncan.com.

"Don't submit a book manuscript anywhere until you read this book. Bowerman reveals exactly why so many authors are receiving poor deals from book publishers. And not being one to leave you without sound advice, his book provides a practical and proven blueprint for self-publishing success."

Gary McLaren, Editor
Worldwide Freelance Writer
www.worldwidefreelance.com

"When it came time write my first hard-copy book—after years of developing a solid platform for my subject—I knew self-publishing was the way to go. This book was my ticket into a publishing world that had previously looked like an invitation-only banquet. The book's insightful ideas and no-nonsense advice were critical to the successful presentation, production, and promotion of my first title. It should be a FIRST read for anyone thinking of publishing themselves."

Michael A. Stelzner, Author
Writing White Papers: How to Capture Readers and Keep Them Engaged
www.WritingWhitePapers.com

"Unless a book has huge promotional budget and is backed by a heavyweight publisher, it'll be a tough road. Peter Bowerman has found a way to fit between the cracks and come out a winner. He shows you exactly how to snag your fare share of sales. Let the other books collect dust; with this one, you'll have those books moving out the door in no time."

Keith Pascal, Author,
Coin Snatching: The Reputation Builder
www.CoinSnatching.com

The Well-Fed Self-Publisher:

How to Turn One Book into a Full-Time Living

Peter Bowerman

Fanove Publishing—Atlanta, Georgia
2007

This book includes information from many sources and gathered from many personal experiences. It is published for general reference and is not intended to be a substitute for independent verification by readers when necessary and appropriate. The book is sold with the understanding that the neither the author nor publisher is engaged in rendering any legal, psychological or accounting advice. The publisher and author disclaim any personal liability, directly or indirectly, for advice or information presented within. Although the author and publisher have prepared this manuscript with utmost care and diligence and have made every effort to ensure the accuracy and completeness of the information contained within, we assume no responsibility for errors, inaccuracies, omissions or inconsistencies.

Publisher's Cataloging In Publication

Bowerman, Peter

The well-fed self-publisher: how to turn one book into a full-time living/Peter Bowerman – 1st ed.

p.   cm.

Includes index.

LCCN: 2005911130

ISBN-13: 978-0-9670598-6-0

ISBN-10: 0-9670598-6-0

1. Authorship—Marketing.   2. Authorship.   I. Title

PN161.B69 2007   808.02

ATTN: QUANTITY DISCOUNTS ARE AVAILABLE TO YOUR COMPANY, EDUCATIONAL INSTITUTION OR WRITING ORGANIZATION

for reselling, educational purposes, subscription incentives, gifts or fundraising campaigns.

For more information, please contact the publisher at
Fanove Publishing, 3713 Stonewall Circle, Atlanta, Georgia 30339
770/438-7200—peter@wellfedwriter.com

Dedication

To all the Davids out there,
staring down Goliath.

He ain't so tough....

Table of Contents

$11K in Two Months—for Starters
Yes, Virginia, a Full-Time Living, with a Part-Time Effort
Self-Publishing (SP) Success: A Process, Not an Aptitude
Self-Publishing: A First Choice
Five Reasons to Read this Book FIRST
A Radical Approach = A Dramatically Simplified Process
You Have ONE Job, and One Job Only
My Promise: ALL the "How-to" Detail

Chapter One

Clueless Publishers: "You Can't Do What We Won't Do"
Everything a Publisher Does, You Can Do Better
The Antidote to Predictable Promotion
Making Review Copies Work FAR Harder
Extra! Extra! Author Rescues Book from Publisher!
The Internet: The Great Equalizer for the Little Guy
The Huge Advantage a Self-Publisher Has Over the Big Boys
Authors: A Publisher's Necessary Nuisance?
In Praise of Lots of Cheap Books
SP: Well-Deserved Bad Reputations, But Things Are Looking Up
A Romantic Tale of How It Works for Fiction, Too
The Downsides: It's ALL You, Baby, BUT…
Publishers Demand Major Involvement, for Chump Change
Becoming a Creative Force AND a Businessperson

Chapter Two

Muzzling the Mean, Menacing "Marketing" (and "Sales") Monster
My Creds: Nearly 30 Years of Sales & Marketing Experience
Developing the Marketing Mindset—Easier than You Think
What Marketing IS and ISN'T
Sales: Bad Experiences, Bad Associations
It's About Hardcore, High-Pressure Sales—NOT!
Guess What? You ARE Selling (Gasp!)

Acknowledgements

My sincere thanks to:

Geoff Whyte, my positively brilliant, incredibly insightful editor from Down Under. Far more than an editor, he was a true partner on this book, constantly challenging me to make it a stronger work. Hire him. He's that good (and amazingly reasonable!). **www.whyteink.com.au**

Chris DiNatale for creating yet another magnificent cover, to add to the growing pile of design gems (ebook covers, flyers, and more) you've cranked for years to make me look good. And for being my professional cohort in crime for the last 12 years **www.dinataledesign.com**.

Chris Papas, my web guru since 1999, a masterful captain at the helm of my Internet presence, watching bemused as this thing continues to get happily out of hand. **www.mm-ltd.com**

Shawn Morningstar, a creative typesetting force (and a delight to work with), who once again, breathed her fun, energetic energy and spirit into the interior "look" of this book. Thanks for capturing—once more—exactly what I was looking for.

Florrie Kichler, my good friend (and thriving publisher; **www.patriapress.com**) and "first reader" of this book. Thanks for looking out for me since the beginning with countless amazingly helpful suggestions, links, FYIs, and more. I owe you, big time.

Shelley, Beth, Sylvia, Evelyn, Susan, and the whole BookMasters gang for doing what you do so well and making my life infinitely simpler and more enjoyable (typesetting, printing, fulfillment, and more: **www.bookmasters.com**).

Ron Pramschufer, 35-year industry veteran, for his big-hearted generosity. I asked him for a blurb. He gave me a full critique, and his myriad suggestions absolutely made this a better book (and kept me from looking like a dummy…). You didn't have to, but I'm glad you did. **www.publishingbasics.com** and **www.selfpublishing.com**.

Mom and Sis for sharing the progress and triumphs with tons of love and support.

Dan Poynter, the original trailblazer. Thank you for so generously showing the way. **www.parapublishing.com**

Finally, all my readers, around the globe—past, present, and future. Thanks for your support. May all your writing be well-fed.

Peter Bowerman
June 2006

Introduction

On September 1st 2004, I released my second book, *The Well-Fed Writer: Back For Seconds*. For the first month, it was only available on my web site. It wasn't in the bookstores or on Amazon yet (*Writer's Digest Book Club* had copies, but that just helped the overall promotional efforts).

I had been promoting the book's upcoming release to my monthly ezine subscribers for a good six to eight months, building the buzz and anticipation. Given that direct purchases from me netted far and away the most profit, I wanted to grab as many of those sales as possible. Well, things went pretty well…

That first day, I sold $2,000 worth of books, and ended up with over $11,000 in sales for the first two months, of which roughly 80% was clear profit. These results were the culmination of a marketing strategy launched over four years earlier. Not always precise, well orchestrated, or even planned much in advance in many cases, but substantial enough for long enough to make good results downright inevitable.

A Full-Time Income…

This is the potential of self-publishing. And that was just one book through one outlet. Bookstore and Amazon sales, once they kick in, drive healthy sales numbers by themselves, and on a steadier, more ongoing basis. All told, *my first book essentially provided me with a full-time living for the better part of five years.*

That's what we're talking about here. Not struggling as a self-publisher, or even just making some nice "mad money" on the side. I'm talking about the potential of a *full-time living.* Which is why I've extended the "Well-Fed" brand to this book: self-publishing has absolutely been a "well-fed" venture for me.

Yes, I still took on some commercial writing jobs (the field that was the subject of my first two books) to stay in the flow, but I didn't need the work to make ends meet. Now we're not talking "picking-out-chateaux-in-the-South-of-France" kind of money, but the book paid all my bills (including a couple of print runs each year), allowed me to stay the course in funding my retirement account, stay completely out of debt, and take a few nice vacations each year. Would that work for you?

...With Part-Time Effort

I did all that with an effort, which, while formidable, was most definitely front-loaded. Once the machine is up and running, it definitely doesn't require a full-time effort, though if you did work it to that extent, who knows where it could take you? This sort of financial return is possible because you don't have to sell zillions of copies of your book to make a living from it. When your profit per book (after all expenses) is three, four, five, or more times what you could make with a conventional publisher, you can generate a nice income stream with much lower sales numbers.

And we're talking about the best kind of income stream—a *passive* one. You get nice checks every month, even though you're not working nearly as hard as you did at the outset. Increased income gives us options, and *passive* income truly offers up the potential of a quality of life you likely can't imagine right now. But trust me, it's nice.

Time for a Life?

What's absolutely possible, as a result of these income streams, is to be able to carve out some time and space of your own. Depending on your circumstances, that could mean freedom from the 9 to 5 grind, pursuing other personal projects, 'smelling roses' time, or whatever else beckons. I'm guessing that sounds good.

Yet, this wonderfully tantalizing discussion doesn't even touch on the deep sense of satisfaction and accomplishment one gets from building something real and substantive out of nothing more than an idea. Not to mention touching thousands of lives and perhaps making a profound difference in those lives. All of which transcends the money (but hey, we'll take that, too...)

Yes, these were my results. Yours may be different. I'm not you. My book isn't yours. Everyone's monthly obligations differ. But, I'm living proof that it absolutely can be done. Many authors have done it. There's nothing particularly mysterious, difficult, or overly complicated about the process. It just takes hard work, creativity, enthusiasm, persistence, and yes, some money. We'll get into the specifics of all that in the coming pages. But throw yourself into it, and you could end up with a pretty nice life.

Understand this: **Success as a self-publisher is far more a function of a** *process* **than an** *aptitude.* It's far less about some way you have to *be* than it is about a bunch of things you have to *do.* And when we're talking about actions, we're talking about something you have total control over.

Fact or Fiction?

"The only reason to self-publish is because you can't land a publisher."

Every time I hear that, I've gotta smile. The unspoken implication being: the preferred route is to land a publisher. Well, call me crazy, but I disagree. For me, self-publishing is the *first* choice. I actually did not explore the conventional publishing route with anything more than half-hearted zeal. Yet, given the subsequent success of my books, especially the first, I have zero doubt that I could have attracted any number of conventional publishers had I decided to go that route. But I knew pretty early on in the process that I wanted to keep control over the project and process, keep the rights to my work, and most importantly, keep most of the profits.

Self-Publishing: The Perception

Self-publishing. One simple, hyphenated word with a boatload of baggage. What comes to mind when you hear it? Last resort? Desperation? Shoddy production quality? Ugly book covers? Pipe dreams? Poverty? Vanity? The realm of the amateur? Well, it's certainly meant all that for many people, but I'm living proof that there's a new definition out there, one with rising profits as well as rising industry respect. And as it gets progressively harder to land a deal with a conventional publisher, more and more of those writers and aspiring writers with a book inside them are starting to (cautiously) glance in this direction.

All of which raises a key point: this book pre-supposes that your goal is commercial success. Not just, "I'd *like* it to be a commercial success." Everyone wants that. If you're just interested in writing a book as the proverbial labor of love, with no concern whatsoever about whether a dime ever flows your way, great. *And,* this book won't be for you. If that *is* your situation, you'd be better off publishing conventionally or via print-on-demand (POD),—see Chapter Twelve—where your upfront financial obligations are lower or maybe non-existent. As will be, in all likelihood, your profits.

This book isn't about how to write a book; there are plenty of books out there on that subject (Hint: the secret is turning off the TV, working on it a little bit every day, and stringing enough of those days together. Voila! A book. There. I just saved you heavens-knows how much money and time on books and seminars that'd tell you the same thing).

My Goal: Your Success

The focus of this work is to help you create a powerfully "packaged" book, aesthetically speaking, and to give you the tools to help you maximize your marketing, promotion, and publicity efforts in order to turn a handsome profit on your masterpiece. Simply put…

I'll show you how to create a book indistinguishable in quality from one produced by a reputable publishing company; how to do a far better job of marketing and promoting that book than a publisher ever could; and how to make far more money than you ever would with that publisher. And by doing it all yourself, you control the timetable (potentially shaving 12 to 18 months off production). Plus, you retain all the rights, allowing you to leverage the brand you've created into a host of profitable "spinoff" businesses—each with its own income stream.

This book is for those who want to turn their passionate creative efforts into real "pay-the-mortgage" money. I can't absolutely guarantee it will happen with your book, because I don't know anything about you: how driven you are, the genre of your book, your relative level of marketing savvy, business experience, etc. But what I can do is show you what's worked for me.

I mention genre because, obviously, my self-publishing experience is in the non-fiction realm. While general non-fiction lends itself well to self-publishing, a non-fiction how-to book (like mine) is, arguably, the genre best suited for self-publishing. Why? For starters, the buying public has an insatiable appetite for information, and if you can provide the how-to content people want, package it in a compelling way, and are creative and aggressive about getting the word out, you'll do well.

Secondly, in terms of the "getting-the-word-out" process, with non-fiction how-to, it's relatively easy to identify and pursue specific target audiences, a subject to which we'll devote plenty of real estate in this book. Fiction is a different story, and frankly, much more difficult, as we'll explore in the next chapter.

Why This Book?

There are some real classics out there on self-publishing (see Appendix A, especially the first four listings under *Books,* all of which you should read as well). What does mine offer that the others don't? Plenty—in perspective, approach, content, and style. And I'm saving the best for last. For starters…

1) Sales & Marketing Coaching

The very concepts of "sales" and "marketing" are often downright terrifying to creative types. But as readers of my first two books can attest, I specialize in muzzling the mean, menacing, marketing (and sales) monster, which I've devoted all of Chapter Two in this book to doing.

Okay, so I probably won't turn you into phenomenal marketing whizzes in the course of one book (*not* necessary to succeed here). But I promise to demystify some intimidating concepts so you can maximize your ability to market your book successfully—minus any irrational fears of the process.

What qualifies me to make these claims? I bring two invaluable perspectives—and close to three decades of experience—to the table. I was a professional sales and marketing person for 15 years, and I've been a full-time professional freelance marketing copywriter for close to the same period (overlapping with self-publishing since the late 90s). Everything I've learned in those two fields absolutely applies in a BIG way to self-publishing.

Like it or not, it's all about marketing. It's all about being persuasive, about putting your best foot forward, determining what sets a company and its products apart (in our case, our books), and how to showcase that in all our written marketing materials. That means book titles, press releases, book sales sheets, online promo copy, email marketing pitches, and about a gajillion other things.

It's about making personal contacts. About identifying an "audience" and crafting the right message to reach a particular audience—whether it's readers, reviewers, media folks, bookstores, wholesalers, distributors, or any other group you need to persuade along the way. It's about speaking to what your audience values, not talking about yourself and your book. It's about figuring out what your book does better than others and letting the world know (like I'm doing here...).

It's about the power of simple, repeatable systems to virtually automate a marketing process. About developing the confidence to *not* put big-name industry players on a pedestal, and to know that you have every right to be in the game, too. It's about teaming up with others to move a project forward. It's about realizing that it's a numbers game and that you need to make the law of averages work for you, not against you. It's about using a web site as the linchpin of a marketing campaign. All of which we'll discuss.

2) One Big "Real World" Case Study

If you're contemplating self-publishing, but don't know much about it, I assert that this book is the best place to start. Why? Well, some books, while gloriously comprehensive, seem to want to offer up everything you possibly *could* do to market your book, the end result being that you feel so overwhelmed, you want to crawl into bed, pull the covers over your head, pop your thumb in your mouth, and not emerge for a week.

More importantly, that approach often feels theoretical. Given that there's no way one author could possibly do anywhere near everything listed in those books, it bears little resemblance to a real-world scenario (NOTE: John Kremer, author of *1001 Ways to Market Your Books,* makes it clear that one person can only realistically do five or ten of the 1001 well, and that you just need to find those best suited to you and your book).

By contrast, this book concentrates on the things you *need* to do, and more specifically, the things I *did* do to achieve the success I had. And by the way, Appendix C contains a time line, starting from before you begin writing your book right through to after the final version has been printed. It'll tell you exactly *what* you need to do and *when*, so you stay on track throughout the whole process.

Rest assured, I'll offer plenty of ideas beyond the basics, while getting into a level of detail *not* found in other books. As I learned from my first two titles, readers want you to spell things out. *Don't tell me I need to have a press release. Show me how to create a good one. Don't just mention buying shipping envelopes for my books. Tell me what kind, the company, the model number, and how to reach them. Don't just talk about the value of putting an ezine together. Give me some tips, dos and don'ts, and resources.*

Speaking of that, whenever you see this icon ([e]) throughout the book, it means that the item just discussed appears in my separate ebook, *The Well-Fed SP Biz-in-a-Box*, an overstuffed compilation of virtually every piece of written marketing material I crafted in the course of my successful book marketing campaign. It's available as a separate purchase (and for a ridiculously reasonable price). See p. 265 for full details.

3) Focus on Profit AND Process

Many books in this arena focus on the *process*: all the steps involved in producing, marketing, and promoting a book. That's fine, but wouldn't a focus on SP'ing *profitably* be more compelling? Yet, in order to do that, you'd have to have had successful books. Well, I have (as have a few others, of course, but certainly not all). Read this book, and you'll get all the how-to "process" stuff, but delivered through the filter of someone who's made a healthy living with his books. I say that counts for something.

4) A Fun Book

Then there's my writing style—which was, according to readers of my first two books, one of the biggest pluses of those works. Countless times, I heard virtually the same comment: *I feel like you're sitting across the table from me over coffee, chatting.* This is a fun book as well. I say that's important when you're just getting your feet wet in this big, new, deep, scary pool. Plus, I'm "fresh from the fight"—steeped in all this, right now, as you read these words. But, I say, the most important plus of this book is the approach. Read on…

5) A Radical Strategy

A little background. In my second book—*TWFW: Back For Seconds*—I discussed adopting a healthier approach to cold phone prospecting for work (i.e., "cold calling"), one that revolved around the concept of *Actions vs. Results*. As I saw it, focusing on *results* (i.e., the positive outcome of prospecting calls: "hot leads" or writing jobs) was a surefire way to create major anxiety. Why? Because you really don't have any control over whether any given round of calling will yield those results.

By contrast, I asserted that the writer who simply set a goal of making, say, 50 calls a day, would have a far less stressful day on the job. Why? Because he has total control over the *action* of making 50 calls, with nary a thought spent on the *results* of those calls. Once he makes 50, he's done for the day. Goal accomplished. The clincher, of course, was that focusing on *action* (assuming a pretty high volume of action, which lets the Law of Averages work for you) would absolutely guarantee the *results*. Knock on enough doors, you'll get the business. Well, same goes for the self-publisher.

Thanks to some brilliant 11th hour facilitation by my editor, Geoff Whyte, it occurred to me that, as a self-publisher, I'd essentially taken the same *actions* approach. There were three parts to this:

a) ONE Job: Early on, I realized that, as a self-publisher, once you physically produce a book, you have *one* job and one job only: **Build the Demand for Your Book.** You want to farm out everything that doesn't have to do with marketing, promotion, and publicity (i.e., warehousing, fulfillment, shipping, web site, etc.), and perhaps even a few that do. All of which we'll explore later.

b) Targeted Audience: I realized early on that, with a "niche" book, pursuing mainstream media attention (the standard book promotion strategy and far better suited to books with broad appeal) would be, by and large, a waste of my finite time.

Instead, I determined that, by identifying my target audiences and pursuing the gatekeepers (to those most-likely buyers) in order to land reviews, blurbs, mentions, interviews, radio shows, green lights to write articles, etc.—the "demand-building" activities that drive people to my site, bookstores, and Amazon—I'd maximize the results of any given contact. As we'll explore later, this can be a more effective strategy even if you *do* have a mainstream book.

c) Massive Action: I approached this undertaking with a simple hypothesis: if I reached enough of the right people (as described above) with my story, and got enough review copies out there, I'd build that demand, and book sales would fall into place. Which is how it worked out.

What was my definition of *enough*? I thought in big numbers: 350-400+ review copies. Yes, that sounds daunting, but keep in mind two things: 1) we're talking three-plus years here, and 2) if you're hitting it hard at the outset, you can easily get one-third to one-half of that number out in the first few months.

I say it was a pretty potent trifecta. I knew what my *one* job was, zeroed in on the "key influencers" most likely to welcome my overtures, and did a massive amount of it. It reduced a self-publisher's responsibility to **One Big Targeted Job,** not a whole laundry list of energy- and focus-diffusing tasks. Just as importantly, it all added up to a situation where *I was in control of enough things to ensure my success.*

That's in contrast to, say, someone who's trying to handle all aspects of the SP process, not doing enough promotion (likely *because* they're trying to do it all), and hitting up fickle mainstream media who, more often than not, couldn't care less about us little guys. And that, ladies and gentlemen, is the story of *so* many SP'ers out there. Lots of frustration, little control, and littler success.

Incidentally, this strategy of mine is also a stark counterpoint to another "out-of-control" scenario: that of an author who goes with a conventional publisher who determines how the book will be marketed and how much time and money they'll devote to that process (read: little and little) until they move on to the next "flavor of the month." *And* they have the rights to your book. Ouch.

(Note: Succeeding financially with the above formula presupposes that you've produced your book cost-effectively enough that you can make money after all expenses, discounts to wholesale/distribution entities, shipping, etc. But that's easy enough to do if you follow the rules. More on this in Chapter Three).

Think BIG

Piggybacking on the three-point strategy above, I say one of the biggest reasons I've been financially successful in this venture is that I don't have a "small potatoes" mentality. A disclaimer: I *know* that not every book is like mine and can follow the exact steps set out in this book. So, please don't hear what follows as belittling any given person's efforts to promote their book. You've got to do what works for you. I'm just trying, as much as possible, to help people set their sights higher.

Since I began my SP adventure in 1999, I've read or heard countless accounts of self-publisher "success" in publishing newsletters and in writer's group meetings and conferences. Often, this "coup" was something like getting a local independent bookstore to carry a few copies of their book. Or perhaps convincing a local library to stock a few free books. Or sharing their excitement over one review in some mid-profile publication. Nothing wrong with any of that.

Majoring in Minors

But I say that celebrating *any* validation from the larger world, no matter how modest, is thinking small—it's a "starving self-publisher" mentality very much akin to the "starving writer" version. In both cases, it's as if they feel, perhaps unconsciously, that all they deserve is the scraps. That, by definition, the road they've chosen is one on which they're destined to be unappreciated, unacknowledged, and poorly compensated.

The very act of celebrating every minor triumph, in my humble opinion, affirms some fundamental belief that you don't *really* belong there—that you've pulled off this coup thanks to a bit of rare generosity from the larger world that saw fit to throw you a bone. Lose that mindset, and realize you have every right to be there.

More importantly, per the earlier discussion about keeping in control of the process, this "small" mindset shifts that control back into the hands of others and away from yourself. Which just perpetuates the idea that you're at the mercy of forces beyond your control. NOT so. I say, keep your eyes on your #1 job, choose the avenues where you're most likely to be welcomed, take a LOT of action, put the blinders on, and keep at it. You'll be amazed at how far you can go.

Of course, I also suspect there's a perceived payoff to the struggle: that suffering for the sake of art (pearls before swine?) is a noble, romantic calling. Not for this boy.

I approached this adventure with success in mind. But, know this: I didn't set some ambitious goal for book sales, and had no grand strategic plan when I started. That said, I did feel that any outcome was possible, and focused on getting the highest return from my actions, given the limited 24-hour day and other commitments I had.

Laser-Focused Activity

As mentioned, I focused on reaching "key influencers" with *demand-building* activities. Maybe I missed out on a big opportunity, but convincing a small independent bookstore to carry my book or a library to stock a few free copies didn't seem like as good a use of my time as landing a review on a web site with thousands of visitors a month. Sure, if I were visiting some town, I'd stop in the library and perhaps donate a book if they didn't carry it, but I knew that was one tiny brick in a much larger wall.

Friends on Your Side

If you're seriously considering the self-publishing route, one of the first things you need to do is join both of the big independent self-publishing organizations: PMA, the Independent Book Publishers Association (**www.pma-online.org**), and Small Publishers Association of North America (SPAN—**www.spannet.org**). PMA is much bigger, but both are worth joining.

You'll find a wealth of resources, cooperative marketing programs, helpful articles, tips on promotional vehicles, and much more in their monthly newsletters. Each organization holds an annual self-publishing "college"—two to three days of seminars with experts (again, PMA's version is much bigger). PMA also sponsors the highly prestigious annual *Benjamin Franklin Awards*, which recognize excellence in independent publishing.

I'm Just Like You

Let me leave you with this. I've had some pretty atypical success as a self-publisher, hence this book. Yes, I had some experience and talent in the areas of marketing and writing that contributed to my success. But, I assert that anyone can learn how to do any of this, and I'll do my best in the coming pages to give you all the tools you need to do just that.

If you're reading this book, I'd say chances are we're more alike than different. I'm a typical human being. I've got a healthy lazy streak and don't like to work any harder than I have to. I'm sporadic in my marketing efforts. I don't always follow up when I should. I don't always get it right, and don't have it all figured out by any stretch of the imagination. I'm still pretty inefficient in the way I do some things, and I'm still doing too many things myself. I continue to feel my way through the process, and have a long way to go until this machine is running like a Swiss watch.

Yet, despite all these imperfections, I've built something that paid all my bills for a long time. Which means I've done a lot of things right. And which also means that you don't have to do everything right to be successful.

So, a bit intrigued by the possibilities? Let's go take a look at why self-publishing makes so much sense, and why conventional publishing is making less and less…

NOTE: *Virtually none of the many vendor resources mentioned throughout the book were even contacted in advance to let them know I was including them. They are here because they've done a great job for me, or because of positive feedback from my independent publishing colleagues.*

The notation "SP" is used throughout to refer to self-publishing.

The terms "self-publishing" and "independent publishing" are used interchangeably throughout the book.

Chapter 1

Got this unguarded off-the-cuff email (excerpted) from a reader about his experiences with a publisher:

Did an appearance on ABC's 'The View' back in August. Unfortunately, that was two months before the book came out. Out of sight, out of mind, I guess, and an example of poor planning on the part of my publisher. Never go on national TV and promote a book if it's not in bookstores.

The publisher also sent out 300 advance copies with press kits in November but there's been no follow-through. They won't give me their list so I can follow-through with a call or email since the publisher's contact list is "proprietary." In the meantime, I'm sending out my own press releases and getting some radio spots and a couple of plugs in the Chicago Tribune.

This isn't the first time I've gone through this. I managed to hawk my last book by using aggressive press releases, telephone calls, and emails. Wound up on ESPN2's 'Cold Pizza' and on the Fox News Channel's 'Fox News Live'- twice. What I've learned is that you—the author—control most of a book's promotional successes and failures. If you can't market yourself and your book, don't bother writing one. Sure, I'll try self-publishing. Heck, I'm doing just about all the work already with a traditional publisher.

Well, now. Isn't that a pretty picture? Sad to say, this is all too often the reality with a publisher. Poor planning, little support, no follow up, and counter-intuitive rules. And for all the promotional effort he put in—because the publisher couldn't or wouldn't—he got, maybe, a dollar a book. Whoopee. Sign me up. But realistically, what choice did he have at that point?

UPFRONT DISCLAIMER

I have no firsthand conventional publishing experience (being an SP'er from Day One). Seven-plus years of immersion in the industry, while noteworthy, isn't exactly a lifetime. Hence, my perspective—and this book—is, by definition, one-sided. I apologize in advance if my tone is occasionally pointed against traditional publishing. I do not for a second think that all publishers are greedy, evil incompetents. Most are honest, reputable, have their authors' best interests at heart, and are just trying to make a living. Others, like in any industry, are less so. Just as importantly, the publishing business is driven by certain economic realities that preclude doing an optimal marketing job for every new title. If you want your book to be a success, you'll have to play an integral role in the process. And if that's the case, isn't self-publishing worth a look? Sure, self-publishing isn't for everyone. As you read the pages that come, you'll know if it's a fit for you.

Get Clear on This

I assert that everything a publisher does in the course of creating, distributing, promoting, marketing, and publicizing your book is something you can do yourself, and in virtually every case, as well or better (especially the marketing).

Yes, a reputable publishing company can more easily get books into bookstores than you can. That said, there's one language all bookstores understand: book sales. Convince them you'll work overtime to move books off their shelves, and their doors will open. I did, and they did.

Conventional Publishing Today

In case you've been in a cave for a decade or so, it's become increasingly difficult to land a publisher, especially for fiction authors, with non-fiction not far behind. It's simple economics: exponentially more authors want to get in print than there are spaces in publishing companies' stables. Many of the larger players only take on celebrities and proven talents. Bottom line, publishers only accept a small fraction of manuscripts that come their way, and even then, only those they feel have a real chance of commercial success. And even the ones they choose aren't "sure things"; most fail anyway.

It's Come to This…

Sometime back, I was talking to Bob Bly, THE Man in the freelance writing world. Bob is an icon in my field, having written about 60 books on all aspects of writing, business, marketing, sales, you name it. The man's prolific, everyone knows him, he has a huge following, an email list 70,000 strong, etc. Talk about a "platform."

A few years back, Bob was approached, through his agent, by a major publisher who wanted a generic book on sales. Bob had written two books on sales before, one of which sold over 50,000 copies. Bob worked up a proposal, the publishing company contact loved it, said she'd take it to the board. The verdict? Thumbs down. *He doesn't have enough of a sales "platform"* (i.e., a built-in audience for the topic to which he can sell a book, and quickly becoming a requirement in the publishing world these days). Whoa. Bob Bly doesn't have enough of a platform? That's pretty heavy.

Because publishers are in the driver's seat, they can be very selective, and as we'll discuss shortly, take on only those authors who come to them with both a book and a plan for marketing it. In return for mandatory involvement in the marketing process, you're rewarded with princely royalty rates of around six percent of sales (and often *net* sales, after discounts)—roughly a buck a book, give or take a dime.

But, even if you do get taken on, I wouldn't suggest deifying the average conventional publisher as being so much smarter than you about how to get books (specifically *your* book) out into the public eye. We saw a graphic illustration of that a few paragraphs back.

From where I sit, and from being heavily steeped in the whole general publishing milieu since the late 90s, I've been gathering tons of evidence on how the average publishing company operates. Without a doubt, there are plenty of very savvy publishing companies who know very well what they're doing, but much of what I've seen isn't very impressive.

What Were They Thinking?

Some publishers rule the production process with an iron fist, and too often, it shows. I had a friend a few years back who had a non-fiction reference book published by a small company, and she asked me to write the foreword. As they were finalizing the content, my friend reviewed the manuscript one last time and presented the publisher with a list of desired edits. She was told, simply, *We don't have time to make the changes; we have to go to print.* Sure, editing has to end somewhere, but the idea of telling an author, no, you can't have the book the way you want it, grates.

Once it was published, she sent me a finished copy, which I hoped against hope wasn't the final edition. The cover was thin paper, only incrementally thicker than the text pages themselves. Pages were already coming loose from the binding. There was zero professional typesetting; the content looked like one big text file. On dozens of pages, new section headings sat forlornly at the bottom of the page, instead of breaking to the next page to go with the text that followed. Exceptionally sloppy, and hugely disappointing.

In my foreword, they'd left out the hyphen in all references to "Well-Fed", so it read "WellFed". A ten-second visit to my web site would've ensured they got it right. All in all, it looked like they'd done as little as they could possibly get away with and still pass it off as a "published" book. It screamed "LOW BUDGET!" And to top it all off, this shoddily produced effort, a mere 150 pages in length, was priced at $19.95!! If this wasn't a grisly combination absolutely designed to sell less books, I don't know what would be.

Predictable Promotion

Then there's the "shotgun" approach to promotion and publicity that's the order of the day with most publishing companies, even the big ones. Heck, *especially* the big ones! Poorly written press releases, mass emailed to mainstream media outlets, with little or no follow-up. See Chapter Two for a great story about one author's frustration with his publishing company's cookie-cutter press release and how a simple rewrite on his part transformed the phones from dead quiet to ringing off the hook.

And let's not forget the somewhat mystifying approach to sending review copies. Over the years, out of the blue, I've received probably a dozen unsolicited review copies as a result of casual affiliations with certain associations or lists. The books arrive, typically with nothing more than a brief cover letter. Given that I was neither expecting nor interested in them, what're the chances that I'll actually review them? Slim or fat.

The sad part about this is that, undoubtedly, they think and believe—and tell their authors—that they're launching a carefully planned strategic promotional campaign, including sending review copies to targeted industry movers, shakers, and "influencers."

Every *single* one of the roughly five hundred plus review copies I've sent out since I began has gone to someone I communicated with in advance. Every single one was expected. Yes, that approach takes more time (though not as much as you'd imagine), but believe me, it yields far superior "bang for the book."

Saved From a Publisher

In the *News You Can Use* section of the November 2005 issue of *SPAN Connection* (put out by SPAN, the Small Publishers Association of North America, one of the two main independent publishing associations; **www.spannet.org**) was this tidbit:

RELENTLESS MARKETING LESSON FROM A PUBLISHING WINNER.
*If life's a race, competitor Burt Levy has it beat. A self-published version of this race car driver's first novel, **The Last Open Road**, sold out its first two printings (12,000) and was picked up by ABC Press [an established, reputable press everyone's heard of] in 1998, where it got stalled in the slow marketing lane.*

At the same time, Levy continued to outsell bookstores by going the nontraditional route—positioning his title with track vendors, museum gift shops, specialty catalogs, and event signings. Since ABC's weak marketing efforts had the book in a sales ditch, Levy decided to salvage it. He bought back the rights and continued his campaign on the racing circuit. Levy's marketing push has driven sales for **The Last Open Road** *plus two more titles over the million-dollar mark and into victory lane.*

The piece went on to discuss one of Levy's innovative marketing strategies: A thirty-two page full-color advertising/sponsorship section in the back of the book (designed as a car magazine from the same era as the book). Tapping his network, he raised $55,000 in eight weeks, paying off ABC Press, funding his printing costs, and making his advertisers very happy (check out a similar story at the end of Chapter Three). As Levy so accurately puts it, "You have to be relentless, because nobody's going to do it for you."

So, this "household name" publisher dropped the ball, big time, on Levy's book, to the point where he had to buy it back if he wanted anything to happen with it!

Five Months vs. 18-24 Months

Another distinct advantage a self-publisher has over conventional publishing is the time it takes to bring a book to market. It's not at all unusual for a publishing house to take 18 to 24 months from the time the project is signed on until finished books are in hand. Sure, there are exceptions for extremely time-sensitive topics, but, by and large, the traditional publishing world juuuuuust taaaaakes iiiiiiits sweeeeet tiiiiime.

As a self-publisher, *you* control the timetable and make things move when *you* say. Good example... I sent my second book off to my editor on April 8th, and I had actual final books in hand by about the 26th of August: *less than five months later.* That included editing, typesetting, indexing, a pre-pub "galley" print run, (to send to early reviewers and get testimonial blurbs for the final edition), final corrections, and final offset print run. Not too shabby. And a rare occurrence in the conventional publishing world.

The Internet: The Great Equalizer

The Internet has dramatically changed the promotional possibilities for book publishers, but most publishing companies haven't begun to truly tap into these strategies to promote their books more effectively.

Ten years ago, I probably wouldn't have even considered this route, but the Internet has made self-publishing exponentially more feasible than it once was. In the process, it's become far easier for the little guy to compete on a level playing field with the big publishing houses.

Case in point. When I applied to be accepted into Ingram (the main wholesaler for bookstores, both chains and independents), I filled out their Marketing Strategy Questionnaire, listing some fifty to sixty web-based entities in the writing, at-home Mom, and home-based business communities I'd already contacted and who'd all committed to reviewing my book.

This showed them I was serious about promoting my book. They rewarded me with a "Full Publisher Contract," giving my title wider distribution—something usually reserved for larger publishers, not one-book yahoos like me. Making so many contacts, and receiving their replies so quickly and easily, was made possible by the Internet. That made me stand out to Ingram. Playing field leveled.

Self-publishing is still a pretty mammoth task, but being wired and even reasonably net-savvy means being productive to a level that self-publishers of preceding generations could only imagine in their wildest fantasies. We'll explore how to maximize the power of this truly amazing tool in the coming pages.

The SP Advantages

A self-publishing author has a luxury (and arguably, it's a *necessity* if commercial success is your aim) that most conventional publishers don't enjoy because of time and personnel constraints: the ability to focus on one's title, and find the most effective ways to promote that title. As opposed to simply applying a standard promotional template to the book, hitting only mainstream media (already subject to a daily hyper-bombardment of releases), sending out review copies indiscriminately, and in all likelihood, doing little or no follow-through. By contrast, as a self-publisher, I go where the traffic is lighter, the reception is warmer, and the people speak my language.

Truthfully, it's not hard to see how the conventional publishing model often shoots itself in the foot. You saw in the chapter opening how a publisher's contention that their review copy list was "proprietary" prevented the author from doing some crucial follow-up—follow-up that *wasn't* being done by the publisher. *We don't have time to do it and we won't let you do it.* Yeah. *That* makes sense. And incidentally, I know intimately, from extensive personal experience, that the importance of follow-up on media efforts and review copies cannot be overstated. Simply put, it makes all the difference in the world.

Authors: The Necessary Nuisance?

A few years back, I was reading the February 2002 issue of PMA, the Independent Book Publishers Association's newsletter (now called *Independent*), and I came across several reflections on the business of running a small publishing company that made me sad for authors. In one article was this quote:

You can do the math on the hypothetical $10 book. The chain gets a 50% discount (at the low end), leaving $5. The distributor gets, say, 30% of the net sale, so now there's only $3.50 left. If you owe the author a 10% royalty on net receipts, you're down to $3.

That's the publisher who gets the $3. How much did the author get? Fifty cents. On a $10 retail book.

In another piece in the same issue, "Report on Sales Representation and Distribution Options for Independent Publishers," the writer, talking to bigger publishing companies, offered up this observation:

It's difficult to be profitable using distributors unless you can maintain high sales, low returns, manage your royalties to keep them low...

"...manage your royalties to keep them low..." That's pretty grim. Now, I'm not naïve. I understand that this is how the book business works—arguably, how it *has* to work. Yet, these snippets, and a zillion others like it, dramatically underscore where a book fits in: simply as a vehicle to profitability to be secured at the lowest cost possible. (*Note: while the above hints at the downside of working with distributors, which we'll discuss in Chapter Six, remember, the writer was talking to bigger publishers who have more overhead and a less efficient (and effective) business model than a one-person shop would.*)

No Rose-Colored Glasses

Sure, overwhelmingly, authors aren't being deceived or coerced into bad deals. I understand Econ 101, which dictates that when the supply of authors and books is far greater than the ability of the market to profitably absorb them, publishers are in the driver's seat. I get that they can't put all their chips down on one book (like a self-publisher can), and that they have to be promoting a bunch of books at once, meaning that any given book can only expect to receive so much money and attention.

Publishers are just trying to make a living, and I don't begrudge them a dime. I suppose for me, self-publishing was about my unwillingness to be nothing more than cog in a much bigger wheel. Plus, I had some skills in marketing and promotion that I was willing to put to work to carve out my own little enterprise. And I can help you to do the same.

Little Respect

The bigger the publishing company, the better the chances that their...shall we say, *lesser* authors will be treated none too respectfully. This scenario was spelled out by a multiple-book author friend of mine in a "venting" email not too long ago (company names changed):

Off-the-record, I am very disappointed (as are a number of other authors I know that were published by XYZ) how Humungo Publishing is treating us. No welcoming note since they purchased XYZ three years ago, no response to our questions, nothing!

Don't they know that we authors network information amongst ourselves? My agent approached them with three proposals, and by my contract, they have 30 days to respond, but they keep dragging their feet. That's why I am planning to self-publish a children's adventure series on my own. Grrrrrrrrrrr!

Again, the publisher is in the driver's seat. Those authors need the publisher (or perceive that they do) more than the other way around.

Authors: A Publisher's First Customer

Then there's the policy held by many publishers of selling authors their own books for 50% of the retail price. Again, I understand it's one of the ways that publishing companies stay profitable, but it sounds awfully close to cutting off your nose to spite your face. Don't you think this practice might be just a teensy bit of a disincentive for an author to do their own marketing and send out review copies? And yet, relying on the publisher to send out those copies (and follow up) is almost certainly a worse bet.

That particular reality was brought home to me when I spoke to an author with whom I wanted to swap books. He had to get his publisher to send me a copy of his book and, frankly, didn't have much confidence it would happen. "The publisher *may* get it to you," he said wryly. "You never know. They're so inefficient." Meanwhile, I go grab a book from my personal stash, replenished by a simple email to my printer whenever I need more, and at a cost of roughly $2.50 each (including all design, editing, typesetting, indexing, printing, and shipping costs), and it's out the door.

A funny story. A few years back, I was part of a panel on publishing at a weekend writers conference. I was the token pure self-publisher, the other folks having gone the conventional route, POD (print-on-demand), or both, with various books. I talked about having gotten my unit printing costs down to about $1.50, and the gentleman next to me, who'd gone with a publisher, was just blown away, given that his publisher had so charitably offered to sell him his own $17 (retail) book for $8.50 a copy.

I saw him several times during the day, and every time he passed me, he'd mutter, all the while shaking his head with a semi-stunned look on his face, "$1.50 a book...all that money gone..."

Beaucoup Cheap Books

Incidentally, that's one of the key cases to be made against conventional publishing (and POD publishing as well, as I'll discuss later): if you want your book to be a commercial success, you need an abundant supply of inexpensive books in order to send out a *lot* of review copies. You just can't do that if you're paying $7 to $10 each for those books.

Yes, that $2.50 per book cost I refer to as a self-publisher pre-supposes that you've shelled out a decent chunk of change up front, but realistically, if you want your book to be successful, you're going to have to spend some money (or time, and you best start realizing that time *is* money) in either scenario, and if you can't or won't, don't expect much of a return. If you can, what's smarter—to shell out good money to eventually receive a piddling royalty, or to retain all the profits after expenses?

Remember, in a conventional publishing scenario, you'll receive a royalty of roughly $1.00 to $1.50 per book on a $20 retail book. By self-publishing, sure, you foot the bills, but you can end up making four to five times that amount per book, and after you've paid your bills, it's *all clear profit*. And that's on bookstore and Amazon sales. Sales off your own web site can easily earn *twice* that amount. Put it all together, and there's virtually no way you *couldn't* do a better job than a publisher.

As I see it, if you *do* have the time and inclination to promote your baby, the only compelling reason for not going the SP route is that you simply don't have the upfront cash to produce your book (i.e. edit, design, typeset, index, and print it; and we'll get into the nitty-gritty of that in the next chapter). But even if that is the case, those non-trivial financial hits can be softened by shorter initial print runs, bartering strategies for services, short-term loans, etc. Only you can decide how important your book's success is to you. But, you've come this far. Why not give it every possible chance?

Well-Deserved Reputations

Let's deal with the nagging perceptions that exist in the publishing world and were hinted at earlier: that if you self-publish, it's simply because you couldn't find a publisher interested in your work; and that self-published books just aren't to be taken as seriously as ones bearing the imprint of an established publishing house. Bluntly put, these perceptions exist for good reason: a frighteningly high percentage of self-published books *are* indeed amateurish—in content, design, and production quality.

It never ceases to amaze me how self-publishing authors can put years of their lives and copious amounts of blood, sweat, and tears into the creation of their masterpieces, and then put so *little* thought, energy, time, and creativity into the physical appearance, design, cover, and even the title of their book. It's categorically impossible to overstate the difference a good cover and title can make.

Arguably (and yes, somewhat bizarrely), given the logistical reality of the book business, it's more important than the book itself. Assuming the same amount of marketing, a mediocre book with a fabulous cover and title will likely do much better than a fabulous book with mediocre packaging. Yes, that's sad, and perhaps not fair, but knowing it's the reality means there's no excuse for not addressing it.

Out of Their League

A few years back, I spoke at a writers conference put on by a statewide writers organization. They had two book tables. The first, larger one, run by a local bookstore, was selling books by presenters which, almost exclusively, had been published by conventional publishers (mine, of course, one of the few exceptions). Overwhelmingly, they were beautiful, colorful, professional, compelling, and evocative.

On an adjoining, smaller table were network members' books that had been self-published. The contrast was so tragically stark as to bring tears to your eyes. Table #2 looked like the local sixth-grade play compared to Table #1's Broadway show. The saddest thing? It just wouldn't have taken much at all to have both tables looking the same.

Which, incidentally, underscores where conventional publishers truly shine: for the most part, they create a high quality product, aesthetically speaking. That said, it's simply not that hard to duplicate.

The Rise of Self-Publishing

Okay, so these negative perceptions against self-published books do exist. As does the institutionalized reluctance on the part of the publishing industry to take self-published books seriously. Yet these mindsets can be overcome with a commitment to quality, creativity, tenacity, and professionalism together with a few street smarts. I've done it. As have plenty of others. Know this: a good chunk of the battle is simply learning the lay of the land.

You've heard the old saw about how, once you buy a new car, you suddenly see that car everywhere, never having noticed them before your purchase. Same thing here. Once you decide to self-publish, or at least explore the possibility, a whole new world comes into focus. You'll discover a wealth of resources—entire industries!—dedicated to the myriad needs of independent publishers (a broad term, incidentally, that covers the one-book self-publisher up to the smaller publishing house): editors, cover designers, typesetters, indexers, printers, PR/marketing consultants, web designers, associations, publications, publicists, conferences, contests, and much, much more.

Self-publishing is absolutely on the rise, driven largely by the power and reach of the Internet. The quality of self-published books is also on the rise and with it the respect—often grudging—of the mainstream publishing world.

The Benjamin Franklin Awards, hosted annually by PMA, the Independent Book Publishers Association, celebrate the best efforts of independent publishers during the preceding year.

And you'd better believe the show is scouted by the bigger publishing houses; they know that the quality of the nominees' and winners' books is excellent. Sure they're there at the awards night (he said, cynically). *After* the books are proven! But, as mentioned earlier, self-publishing done well is one of the surest ways to attract a publisher, *if* that's your goal (never was mine). Speaking of which…

Fiction Facts

One of the best examples in the fiction arena is *Lip Service*, by M.J. Rose (2000), the former creative director of Harlequin Books' NY ad agency. When a bunch of top publishers rejected her romantic/erotic psychological thriller, she decided to self-publish it, in both ebook and hard-copy formats. She launched a massive grassroots Internet marketing campaign, not unlike mine, offering review copies to literally hundreds of literary, mystery, romance and erotica sites.

In the wake of hundreds of positive reviews, she sold several thousand books, making it the highest-ranked small press novel on Amazon. The book became the first ebook and the first self-published novel chosen by the Literary Guild/Doubleday Book Club, as well as the first ebook to be published by a top New York publishing house.

At press time, she had sold over 75,000 copies of *Lip Service*, and has since conventionally published five more novels and two non-fiction titles (see Appendix A). She also runs a marketing service for authors (**www.AuthorBuzz.com**). For more, check out **www.mjrose.com**.

The Truth About Fiction

All the above said, for the most part, the exception proves the rule for self-publishing fiction. The unvarnished truth? It's a tough road for any novelist, but especially a self-publishing one. For starters, self-publishing novelists, typically with little or no *impartial* screening (i.e., an agent or some other emotionally unattached sounding board) of their work, end up flooding the market with non-edited dreck that's been both written and launched into the world too fast and too soon. It's hard enough to get publicity for good fiction, much less bad stuff.

The Truth About Fiction (*continued*)

Secondly, there are far more novels self-published than traditionally published each year, and with the traditional media far more favorably inclined to the latter, its no mystery which will win the battle for the finite opportunities for exposure. And even the online venues, once the near-exclusive domain of the littler fish, have been getting more and more attention from traditional publishers. By contrast, there are far more outlets for non-fiction self-publishers to be heard – both online and offline.

Plus, with fiction, readers buy *names*, not subjects. Look at the book covers of the big name novelists. What's in bigger type, the title or the authors name? Non-fiction? With few notable exceptions, people buy *subjects*, not names. Bottom line, there's far more really good novels out there not seeing the light of day than non-fiction titles. I'd love to claim that the approach I discuss in this book easily translates to fiction, but I'd be telling tales if I did. I don't ever want to say it can't be done, but it's a pretty high mountain.

The SP Downsides

Why did I self-publish? Probably because I'm a true control freak, and self-publishing puts me firmly behind the wheel of my projects. Moreover, I realized that no publisher could do a better job with my book than I could. Immodest? Not really. It's more a function of an inescapable truth: *no one will care about your book as much as you do.*

Of course, the flip side of being in control of everything is that you're *responsible* for everything: total accountability for financing, production, marketing, promotion, and publicity rests with you and you alone.

The "Adult" Conversation

This is as good a time as any for the "adult conversation." Self-publishing is an enormous undertaking. No way around it. Whatever you'd count on a publishing company to handle, you've got to do yourself. *And* pay for it all, as well. It really is a marathon, not a sprint. Once you finish reading this book, and perhaps a few other suggested titles, you'll end up with a "To-Do List" longer than The Great Wall of China. And yes, your efforts are definitely front-loaded. You'll be working far harder and longer in the beginning.

While going through a traditional publisher *will* free you from the financial and production burdens, if you're thinking—scratch that, *fantasizing*—that you'll find a publisher who will allow you to simply drop off your manuscript with a cheery '*Thanks! Off to write my next book!*' while they take care of that whole "icky marketing thingy," think again. Acclaimed authors such as Grisham, King, Cornwell, Clancy, Siddons, and a handful of other luminaries might enjoy that luxury, but certainly not you and I.

Publishers Expect Involvement

So, even with a conventional publisher, unless you're a proven talent, you'll have to be far more involved in the marketing of your book than you ever imagined or hoped. Why? Because your publisher will be far *less* involved in the marketing of your book than you ever imagined or hoped. Why? Because they don't have the time, personnel, or resources to devote to crafting an effective, focused, and sustained marketing plan for your book. Why? (I know, I'm starting to sound like a five-year-old…) Because yours is just one of a whole bunch of books in their stable. And if another hot property comes walking in their door, you could easily be relegated to the B- or C-list in a New York minute.

Which could result in every author's nightmare scenario: your book is now orphaned and neglected, AND the publisher still has the rights. No fun. Which supports the argument for always including a clause in any contract with a publisher to have the rights revert back to the author after a certain period, or if the publisher, in essence, abandons the book.

Controlling the Long Haul

Most traditional small publishers (the kind you'd likely be approaching as a new author, or one with a niche title) would consider sales of ten to twelve thousand books to be a successful title. At that point, they'd likely turn their attention to the next promising acquisition, and your baby would get relegated to the "backlist". They might still do a bit of occasional promotion, but nothing like the early days. So, your book could be considered a "success" by publishing standards, and *still* never realize its full potential.

Remember, for them, you're one of many. But, as a self-publisher, you can focus exclusively on your book, and squeeze far more potential from it than a regular publisher is ever likely to manage (my first book is well past the forty thousand copies-in-print milestone, and is still selling nicely). You can explore and experiment with different promotional avenues, reach another tier of niche audiences, revisit first-tier audiences with fresh approaches, and more—all initiatives a publisher is unlikely to have the time or resources to pursue.

Below Minimum Wage

Sure, as a conventionally published author, you could certainly keep the pressure up and keep the marketing engine running through your own personal efforts, something the publisher would welcome, if not expect. But how excited would you be to continue what would undoubtedly be a big job when you knew you were making teeny-weeny change, like, say, 6% of net proceeds per book?

Speaking of all the work you'll be expected to do, I read a great article on self-promotion by the author of *How to be Your Own Publicist*, Jessica Hatchigan, (**www.hatchigan.com**) in the September 2003 issue of *The Writer* magazine (**www.writermag.com**) called "Bestsellers are made, not born." She points out one of the pitfalls of dealing with a publishing house:

Unfortunately, authors who receive modest advances for their books—and that's most authors—can expect scandalously little in marketing support from most publishers. One insider recently told me that many publishing houses today, because their profit margins are so thin, don't even bother to send out review copies of their newbie authors' books.

Wanted: Multi-talented Authors

Three-book business author and university professor emeritus Charles Ehin (**www.unmanagement.com**) reflected on the rude awakening he received as an author who was expected to handle much of his own marketing, an undertaking that didn't always have pleasant outcomes:

I had no idea how much the publisher expected me to do in order to promote and market the book. Besides book signings and creating a web site, I even hired a publicist (no less recommended by a friend) who promised a great review by The New York Times, appearance on The Larry King Show (if not that, then at least some other major TV program), and national speaking engagements. In the end I was short $3,000 and had nothing to show for it. I soon found out, unfortunately, that is not out of the ordinary.

In Guerrilla Marketing for Consultants, by Jay Conrad Levinson and Michael W. McLaughlin, the authors outline a book proposal for an author who plans on approaching publishers (pp. 149-50). Item Six in their list of things to include in any proposal was this:

Your plan to promote the book: *Agents and publishers place the lion's share of the promotion burden on the author, so show how you'll support the marketing of your book to meet the forecast you've set earlier in your proposal. Many agents and publishers view this section as the most important part of the proposal. A great book idea with a lackluster promotion plan will come back to you for revision.*

This stands to reason. Again, supply and demand. If someone's got a promising book and no marketing savvy, while another author has both... If a publisher expects me to be an integral part of the marketing of my book, then the case for conventional publishing becomes weaker still, given the anemic royalty rates for authors.

In the February 2005 issue of the PMA, the Independent Book Publishers Association newsletter (now called *Independent*), then-PMA President Kent Sturgis (president of Epicenter Press in Kenmore, Washington) wrote a piece in his monthly column titled "The 10 Most Important Publishing Lessons I've Learned." The #1 lesson was "Put the author to work" (and take special note of the last line):

The best authors are those who are strongly committed to the success of their books and willingly and energetically promote them...I find myself increasingly reluctant to work with authors who believe their work is done when the manuscript has been completed. I understand that self-promotion is difficult for some people. But this business is so competitive that it makes no sense for us to acquire a title that will not realize its full potential without the author's help. I confess I have no problem working with an author who wants to make a contribution to the promotion budget, though we rarely suggest it and never require it.

Incidentally, some of the other headings from Sturgis's "Publishing Lessons" included "Agonize over the title," "Do not economize on design," and "Hire freelancers carefully"—all sentiments with which I heartily concur, and all subjects we'll discuss later.

Less Writer, More Businessperson

If you want to succeed in a creative field these days, you'd better be good at something else besides the creativity or you're not going to make it. Unless, of course, you have a prodigious talent and/or you're surrounded by dealmakers looking out for your best interests. Good luck.

Writers need to start thinking less like writers and more like businesspeople. You've got a choice. You can be an "artist," focused solely on the creative process. In that case—again, unless your talent is extraordinary—chances are excellent that writing will only be a sideline hobby and a relatively unprofitable one at that. And that's okay, if that's okay with you. Or you can become both—not always easy or fun, but definitely worth it—a creative force *and* a businessperson.

In my humble opinion, developing the requisite "marketing mindset" to pull off the SP thing is not that difficult, and certainly not beyond the capability of a reasonably intelligent person. In the next chapter, we'll take on the (not-so) scary "marketing" beast. Readers of my first two books will no doubt experience a bout of *déjà vu*, because much of the marketing information in those books is revisited here.

In those books, I had a similarly daunting task: talking with writers (i.e. "creative types") who wanted to tap into the lucrative commercial writing market, and to do so, had to move beyond their enormous (and largely irrational) fears of the marketing process, and become businesspeople (gasp!).

So, are we ready to get our heads right for the marketing job ahead? Hey, come back here! This won't hurt a bit...

"In the modern world of business, it is useless to be a creative original thinker unless you can also sell what you create. Management cannot be expected to recognize a good idea unless it is presented to them by a good salesman."

David Ogilvy (Grandfather of advertising)

Chapter 2

Say "marketing" or "sales" to a roomful of right-brained author types and watch the sweat beads pop. The breathing gets shallow, and the eyes dart furtively toward the exits—calculating the distance from their seat to the door and beyond—*anywhere* they don't have to listen to this conversation anymore. Alas, so much unnecessary angst.

As mentioned earlier, the S&M discussion (it just *seems* like the other sometimes…) was a centerpiece of my second book, *TWFW: Back For Seconds.* Given the absolutely crucial and all-encompassing role it plays in any successful book marketing campaign, I figured we'd better get comfortable with it here as well. After all, what good is it knowing you'll have to do a lot of "marketing" if you can't even get past the word without having an anxiety attack?

As you'll recall from the introduction, I was in various sales and marketing positions (starting with door-to-door book sales for two summers in college) for 15 years. And that was before I even started my commercial writing (1994) and self-publishing (1999) careers, both of which have involved major sales and marketing efforts, believe me. We're pushing roughly three decades of experience here.

Let's start this new journey with something I'm guessing most of us can relate to. I received this email from a reader some time back—one of many in the same vein:

You're succeeding in a business I've sort of ambled through for the past five years. Like many writers and other types of artists, I have the skills and the talent—but HATE MARKETING MYSELF. [His caps, not mine.]

17

Develop the "Marketing Mindset"

As I received more and more correspondence like the above, I began to realize that "SALES and MARKETING" was indeed *The Boogeyman* for many creative types. It's the thing that wakes people up at night, gasping and sweating, and makes them chew their fingernails to the quick. More importantly, it keeps them from actively chasing their dream, from perhaps pursuing the self-publishing route that's calling to them. Hence my goal in this book, to not only give you a blueprint for marketing your book, but to start a richer discussion about developing a marketing *mindset*, so that your book marketing campaign will be even more effective.

"Why Do We Write Anything?"

In my seminars, when I get to the topic of marketing, I start out with the question above, and get all the usual answers: *To inform. Educate. Inspire. Motivate. Encourage. Entertain. Move. Touch.*

All true. Yet, there's a far more basic reason why we write anything. Care to guess? How about this: *To have it read.* I know, you're rolling your eyes, but frankly, none of the others are even possible until this happens. That's what this chapter is about—boosting the odds that someone will actually want to read what you've written, which, of course is what needs to happen if you want to get your books stocked, reviewed, sold, and read. It all starts there. (Check out the special section, *Seven Tips for a Far More Readable Book,* at the end of this chapter.)

Sales vs. Marketing

For the record, "sales" and "marketing" are different things. Both involve making connections with prospective customers. "Sales" generally refers to *direct contact*—where the point is to make a sale. For authors, direct sales will probably only occur at book signings, talks, seminars, etc.—where you're engaging people and their questions and concerns—with the goal of having them walk away with a signed book tucked under their arm. But, of course, while it does cover direct selling, it obviously also refers to all the other sales channels—wholesale, retail, web, etc.

Marketing, on the other hand, is more about general "awareness-building," which, in our case, usually means all those activities that **Build Demand** and drive people to our web sites, the bookstores, Amazon, and any other place people buy books. Heard of "viral marketing"? It's really just a new way of talking about "word-of-mouth" selling and making multiple impressions on buyers—crucial contributors to a book's success. We'll discuss all the above in the coming pages. Let's discuss marketing first...

What "Marketing" IS

Marketing refers more to efforts to build awareness in less personal ways among your target audience—about your subject, about your book as it *relates* to that subject, and why they should care about it. We're talking about writing articles, sending out review copies, doing radio and TV interviews, link swaps, and a bunch more.

For many, marketing looms as a shadowy, elusive, overly complicated beast. With teeth. Let's muzzle it, shall we? I humbly offer up my simple definition of book marketing:

Successful marketing of a book simply involves letting your various audiences (wholesalers, booksellers, reviewers, and book buyers) know you're out there—on a consistent basis, in a variety of ways, and with a message they can hear through the clutter.

If you can effectively reach enough of the people who can stock, sell, review, publicize, and buy your book, and do that on an ongoing basis, you'll be a successful marketer.

The good news? Despite the fear they inspire, sales and marketing as concepts really aren't that hard to grasp and implement successfully. More good news? Once you're in the game, it's simply a matter of employing the same proven strategies over and over again. Even more good news? None of it is out of your control. Do enough of it, and you'll get the results. Period. It's not easy, but it's simple. None of it is beyond the capability of any reasonably intelligent person. Add in the power of the Internet to dramatically streamline and simplify your marketing efforts, and it'll take your breath away (as we'll see in the coming chapters).

What Marketing ISN'T

Marketing on this level isn't some arcane, wildly esoteric and obscure puzzle, the solution to which only reveals itself to Harvard or Wharton MBA grads after exhaustive, mind-numbing research and analysis. Sure, that kind of marketing does exist, replete with all the vernacular: demographics, psychographics, market share, etc. For all intents and purposes, it only comes into play with much larger publishers, not little guys like us. That's that. This is this. And ne'er the twain need meet. So relax. Check out the reading list in Appendix A. It's amazing how up-to-speed you can get by reading a handful of books.

Dare to Be Seen

As a single guy, I occasionally surf over to one of the online dating sites. The clichés are rampant. Here are zillions of people, looking for the most important relationship of their lives, and barely one in a hundred takes the time to craft a message that is even remotely creative and original.

Virtually every ad lists such unique gems as *I love moonlight walks on the beach*...(FYI, that's "moonlit") *romantic, candlelight dinners*...(FYI, that's "candlelit"), *snuggling in front of a fire*... and, my favorite one to hate, *a man who's as comfortable in a tux as blue jeans*... just like EVERYONE else's.

I always want to ask: Do you think you'll attract the opposite sex by blending in with everything around you? That's called *camouflage*. People in the armed forces do this when their lives depend on *not* being noticed or standing out in any way. If you want to be seen, you have to draw attention to yourself.

Precious few book publishers consistently send out review copies, press releases, offers to have their authors write articles for sites or speak to groups, etc. If you do, you'll absolutely elevate yourself above the din. Getting noticed isn't all that hard if you're one of the few who make the effort to stand out.

Business-Building is NOT Immodesty

I know—you hate drawing attention to yourself. It's...immodest. Listen. There's not a darned thing immodest about drawing attention to yourself when you have a good, high-quality contribution to make to the book marketplace (that's why you wrote the book in the first place, right?). Yes, this last point assumes you've done the research and soul-searching required to determine that—in the case of a non-fiction title—there *is* indeed a market for a book on your subject *and* that yours offers something different and valuable that sets it apart from others like it. Or, in the case of a novel, that your labor of love offers a unique voice and story that will resonate with an audience.

Fact is, you're living in a certain place, driving a certain car, wearing certain clothes, dining at certain restaurants, and vacationing in certain places because some company successfully marketed something to you. Or to the friend who made the recommendation to you. And you're probably glad they did.

There are a lot of writers around the world—seasoned and aspiring—along with other target audiences I've reached out to, who are glad I made it my business to let them know about my book. They acknowledge the difference I've made for them by sending me emails, subscribing to my ezine, and most importantly, continuing to buy my products. Marketing isn't a dirty word. It's life. And, I daresay, on balance—its excesses notwithstanding—it's something we consumers are glad of.

Hate to say it, but you'd better be willing to draw some attention to yourself or you'll need to find another line of work. You're not selling some Veg-o-Muncher on late-night TV. You're not some smarmy car salesman. You're an author with a book the world needs to hear about, and you have every right to tell your story.

Keep Showing Up

Want to know the simple key to publishing success? *Keep showing up.* Assuming you've got a good and worthwhile book, one that's proven to be both readable and popular, it's all about multiple impressions (a concept we'll revisit many times before we're through here). The self-publishers who build thriving businesses would likely be the first to tell you that they're no smarter than the next guy. They just keep showing up in front of their myriad audiences in a variety of ways. And keep knocking on new doors. It's that simple.

Okay, that's a bit about marketing. How about the "sales" thing?

Before You Freak...

I can hear you now: "I'm not a salesperson and I don't *want* to be one! I couldn't sell a Big Mac to a starving man." Relax. You don't ever have to be—nor should you be—a "salesperson," *in the way you likely envision the concept.* By the way, I have every confidence you could. Sell a Big Mac to a starving man, that is…

And that's sort of the point. This isn't about hardcore, high-pressure sales. No one appreciates that, and more importantly, it's never appropriate. This is about reaching those people who are in the market for your book.

Years back, I read an article about being a successful public speaker that, well, spoke to me. While it readily acknowledged the value of all the techniques for honing speaking skills that one might learn in, say, a Toastmasters group, it also pointed to a more surefire determiner of success in this arena: *Know your subject intimately, and be passionate about sharing it with others.*

Think about that in the context of "selling" your books. If you went as far as actually writing a book on your subject, can we safely assume you felt passionately about telling a story? So, forget about "selling" books; just tell your story.

Bad Associations

So, how did sales become such a dirty word? Somewhere along the line, for many of us, "sales" of anything got wired to high-pressure techniques, pushy salespeople, slick sales practices, etc. Why did this happen? Because, at some point, we've been the target of salespeople who embodied all the negative stereotypes. Maybe it was someone selling cars, time-share vacations, encyclopedias, aluminum siding, whatever. Perhaps some obnoxious telemarketers got thrown into that broad "sales" bin as well. However, wherever, whenever, and at whoever's hands it happened, it happened.

Sales: Meeting Needs

Well, guess what? That's not what "sales" is. In our case, "sales" is nothing more than matching your product or service with a prospective buyer's needs and desires. Early on in the SP process, those prospective "buyers" are wholesalers, distributors, and bookstores. It's sales, just not what you may have thought of as sales.

With this group, you're focused on "selling" them on your commitment to your book: how you're going to leave no stone unturned, as evidenced by a tangible "hold-in-your-hand" marketing plan (e). They want to know that you'll be an integral part of the promotion process, that if they agree to take you on in their warehouses and on their bookshelves, you're going to be working very hard to make sure those books don't hang around for long. Very simple. Don't make it any more complicated than that.

"MAKE ME CARE"

Your next market is potential reviewers—whether for mainstream media, targeted web-based entities, radio and TV producers, or any other audience relevant to your book. Here, your "sale" is something different altogether. With these folks, you're selling them on why the subject of your book (and by extension, the book itself) would be of interest to their audiences. They want to know: *Why should I care? Why should my readers care? What's in it for either of us?*

But, remember, these folks need content. Running a newspaper, web site, newsletter, magazine, or radio or TV station means having a constant need to feed info-hungry audiences with fresh content. They don't want to make that gathering process any more difficult than it needs to be. They *want* to like what they're hearing from folks like you. And as we discuss the marketing and publicity angles of this process in the coming chapters, we'll explore ways to make it easy for these folks to say yes.

Your final audience, of course, is book buyers, whose needs and desires could be financial security, how-to information, escapism, feeding a romantic spirit, mastering a particular skill, diagnosing an illness, reaffirming their faith, understanding history, studying a foreign land prior to a trip, succeeding in a relationship, pondering their place in the cosmos, being a better parent, or any one of about a bazillion other possibilities.

You ARE Selling

Bottom line, if you build a successful book marketing campaign, and get your book into a wholesaler's or distributor's warehouse, or onto a bookstore's or book buyer's bookshelf, one thing's for certain: whether or not you thought of yourself as selling something, you did. Those entities *bought* you and your book because of what you had to offer, the case you made for it, and because you were able to *satisfy their needs.*

Into the Mind of the Marketer

I saw a great series of billboards in Atlanta recently. It was for Apartments.com, an online clearinghouse for apartments that allows you to search for exactly what you want in any state. They could have devoted their billboard space to talking about *themselves* (like most companies do) and all the great things *they* offer: unmatched customer service, big selection, easy online access, etc. (I can picture big checked boxes, right?). They *could* have. But they didn't.

The first billboard had just one short sentence (their tag line, actually) across the middle: *You want what you want.* Then, simply their logo and the Apartments.com name. Nothing more. A thing of simplicity and beauty. In one five-word sentence, they nailed THE hot button for their audience: personal taste and choice in an apartment. Heck, they managed to use the magic word "you" twice in a five-word sentence. They know what people want to hear.

People want to be talked *to*, not talked *at*. They want to know that what matters to them matters to the entity that's trying to reach out to them.

It's ALL About the Customer

In the process of letting apartment shoppers know that they understood what was important to them, they disappeared from the process. Meaning, it wasn't about them at all. It was about those customers and what they wanted. The company was simply there to help make their dreams come true.

This example is a good way to introduce the three fundamental principles of sales and marketing I'll be sharing in this chapter—principles that you'll want to keep front and center during your ongoing book marketing/promotion/ publicity campaigns:

1) The Audience—Always understand who your audience is and what language will best get through to them.

2) The Features/Benefits Equation—Focus on driving home what you know is important to your audience, *not* just talking about you and your book.

3) The Unique Selling Proposition (USP)—Figure out what sets your book apart in the marketplace and drive that difference home—early and often. At the very least, if your book delivers something valuable that others do too, but those others aren't showcasing the fact, then claim that piece of promotional real estate as your own.

All Three in Common...

What do these three principles have in common? Each one is already a part of your frame of reference as a consumer:

- (AUDIENCE) You buy products that have been sold to you by advertising that knows how to speak to someone like you to get your attention.

- **(FEATURES/BENEFITS)** You respond to marketing that focuses on the benefits that are important to *you*—and how Company A's product delivers those benefits—as opposed to just listing all the features of their product.

- **(USP)** You buy products because they do something better (or different) than those of competitors.

You're already intimately familiar with these principles, following them automatically and giving them little or no real thought. All we're trying to do here is make you a bit more conscious of the process now that you're on the other side of the table.

Effective Writing

As an SP'er engaged in the process of promoting your masterpiece, you'll be crafting a pretty steady stream of promotional materials: press releases, marketing proposals to wholesalers, distributors, and booksellers, email pitches to book review targets, queries to publications (print- or web-based) to submit articles, notes to groups and organizations soliciting invitations to speak (*and* the materials that accompany the promotion of such events), and much more (again, to simplify that process, see p. 265).

My goal here is not to turn you into crack copywriters. I just want you to understand what's important in this process (your audiences and what they want) and what's *not* (you and your book).

Sales = Making it Easy

Developing a marketing mindset means always looking at things through the eyes of your target audience. This orientation manifests in tons of little ways. For example (and we'll expand on each of these examples, and others, later):

- You want someone to post an Amazon review (after they gushed on about your book in an email), so in order to make it as easy as possible for them, you send them the actual Amazon link to your book, not expecting them to take the time to find it themselves.

- When sending out review copies (and the emails announcing their impending arrival), you include a prominent link to your "Media Resources" section, which includes everything a potential reviewer might need to put a review together. Again, boost the likelihood that it'll happen.

- You want some "key influencer" to promote an upcoming event of yours to their community, so you send an actual ready-to-go promo blurb, as if written by them, so that it's just a simple cut-'n-paste to get it handled. You know what you want them to say to their group, so write it yourself. I promise you, they'll appreciate it.

- You contact a journalist to get some publicity, and you include a link to "News Pegs" in your *Media Resources* section (more on this in Chapter Eight). You want that publicity? Then don't count on them to figure out the angle here. Make their job easier, and spell it out for them.

In all these cases, you're thinking about them, their reality, their pressures, and the fact that you're *not* a high priority in their world. And because you're not, you need to make it as easy as humanly possible for them to do what you're asking them to do. OK, so let's explore each of these three cornerstones in more depth...

"Who's the Audience?"

Think about it. Don't you talk to your mother differently than your friends? Your co-workers differently than your boss? Somebody who *has* something you want differently than someone who *wants* something you have? Consciously or unconsciously, you're always thinking about your audience.

This is absolutely THE first question you need to ask yourself whenever you're about to put together any promotional copy. When you buy a product you heard about through some form of advertising, it's because something spoke to *you*. Someone knew what to say to make *you* sit up and take notice— which is exactly what will happen when a message is well crafted. You're no different from anyone else out there.

Want some surprising news? As simple and logical as this formula is, it's amazing—and tragic—how much marketing material, put together by authors *and* prestigious publishing houses, is poorly written and doesn't consider the intended audience. If you can get it right, you'll set yourself apart.

Different Audience, Different Thrust

I have some key audiences for my *Well-Fed Writer* books: writers, at-home-Moms, home-based business seekers, and the 55+ crowd, for starters. While all these audiences appreciate the key benefits provided by the commercial writing field (good money, freedom, flexibility, etc.), each is likely to rank those benefits differently in order of importance.

Writers, of course, love to hear about the income and the freedom the field offers. At-home-Moms perk up at the idea of the flexibility (doing it on their own terms and schedule) while still making good money. The home-based biz crowd—big surprise—likes the home-based aspect. The 55+ segment, while resonating with all the above, also likes that their age doesn't work against them as it might in the corporate world, and that they can leverage their long years of experience into a lucrative income.

Bottom line, there's no "one-size-fits-all" marketing pitch I can make to all these groups. I have to talk to each of them specifically, and to the things *they* care about. Logical. And it's not hard. In the case of my email pitch (offering a free review copy in order to land a review, interview, blurb, mention, article placement, etc.), I have a standard form (see Appendix B for basic format), which I then adapt for the different audiences (e).

The Features/Benefits Equation

Some time back, I was contacted by an author who wanted me to review a press release for their new book. Yikes. It was full of superlative adjectives about the book, hyperbolic gushing-on about the author, and other unforgivable self-indulgences. In short, every transgression against the rules of proper publicity known to man, all of which would earn it a quick trip to the circular file. So common (and I'll help you avoid all that).

The Features/Benefits Equation is an absolute cornerstone of sales and marketing. And, as you'll see in the broad array of examples and analogies in the coming pages, it's a concept with which we're already intimately acquainted.

Basic Definitions

In our publishing context, *features* are all about a book and its author. *Benefits* are about your target audiences—what's important to them, and how your book addresses those issues. Always begin with benefits, follow with features. The more you make it about you and your book, the more likely your intended audience will ignore you.

A few years back, BellSouth, the Southeastern telecommunications giant, had an epiphany. Until then, its marketing campaigns focused largely on *technology*. Their ads were replete with high-tech images showcasing the latest calling feature, network innovation, gadget, bell, whistle, etc. (*features*). Technology was cool. Then one day, someone woke up and said, *People don't give a rat's heiney about technology*. Exactly. What people care about is *how* that technology can enhance the quality of their lives—free them from the confines of an office, give them more time for leisure, or help keep them in touch with their loved ones (*benefits*).

They soon launched a new ad campaign built around the tagline: ">>>connect>>>create something™." It was perfect—all about benefits. The new TV ads were rich in touchy-feely images, graphically showcasing the *benefits* of technology: business success, family closeness, romantic connection, etc. And nary a feature in sight. They got what was important to people—their lives, *not* bits and bytes.

A Book Example

Okay, using my first book as an example, you think people care that Peter Bowerman leveraged a sales and marketing career into a new career in the lucrative field of commercial writing and then wrote a book about it? That the book covers X, Y and Z subjects? Yawn. That's all about me and my book.

If you were a prospect for my book, I'd wager good money that you'd care far more about the fact that there's this lucrative field called commercial writing, where you can make the kind of money (i.e., $50-125 an hour) you've always dreamed of making. A field that can provide a great income while letting you work from your home, have more time for life, loved ones, and leisure. A field that gives you the opportunity to finally fulfill your dream of being a writer for a living. Sound better? Course it does. Because that's all about you—your favorite thing in the whole world!

See the difference? When I start talking about you (my buyer) and what you care about, it's far more interesting and compelling. Just as importantly, once I get your attention with things I know mean something to you, *then* I can tell you a bit about me: And it just so happens that Peter Bowerman, seasoned commercial writer, has written a few award winning books on the subject—providing all the how-to detail you need to get your own personal commercial freelancing show on the road.

The Features/Benefits equation isn't just something that plays out in business settings. It's a fundamental part of human nature. You live it every day.

Potent Press Releases

In the course of promoting my self-published book, I've gotten a lot of practice writing press releases. Given how inundated my target audience (media people) is with releases, it's always an uphill battle to get noticed.

Here's the plain truth about journalists: They couldn't care less that you've written a book (unless you're Stephen King, Tom Clancy, John Grisham, et al.). The rest of us? *Fugedaboudit.* Send them a press release announcing you've written a book and you'll be lucky if they wipe their nose with it before tossing it. A release about a book and its author is...*features*.

That reporter wants benefits: *I SO don't care about your book. Tell me why that book is important to my readers/viewers, why they should care, why it addresses some need of theirs, some trend or topical subject.* Not the book, but the *angle* represented by the book. Those are the *benefits*. Jane Journalist's job is to write stories that resonate with her readers (and earn her kudos) so her good reputation and solid standing in the industry are affirmed. Cynically speaking—albeit realistically—a journalist, fundamentally, is asking, *"What's in it for me? How will writing a story about your subject make me look good?"*

EXAMPLE: USING THEIR HEAD

Was talking with Mark Levy recently, a very talented and accomplished author, marketing consultant, *and* professional magician (**www.levyinnovation.com**). He shared a funny story with me that underscored the features/benefits equation. Not to mention the inherent limitations in the ability of the big publishing houses to promote your work (making an even more attractive case for self-publishing).

He and his partner Mac King had written a magic book called *Tricks With Your Head*, outlining a whole bunch of routines using one's own head as the main prop. Their BIG HOUSEHOLD NAME publishing company (who will, undeservedly, remain nameless) created a press release with this positively scintillating headline:

NEW BOOK: TRICKS WITH YOUR HEAD

I know this may come as a total shock, but that little gem created ZERO interest in the media. Dead phones. Empty email boxes. In addition to being tragically boring, it focused on the very thing media folks couldn't care less about: *Someone Has Written a Book* (unless of course, that someone is a household name, in which case, it probably would be news).

So, Mark and Mac put their heads together (sorry) and rewrote the release starting with the headline. Since the topic of their book didn't easily lend itself to piggybacking on hot trends, they appealed directly to the absolutely reliable journalist hot button: a topic that's wildly different, unique, one-of-a-kind. Here's what they came up with:

HOW TO STICK A FORK IN YOUR EYE (AND WHY YOU'D WANT TO...)

The result? Over 150 radio interviews and much more. They spoke to what journalists wanted, and answered the question—*Why should I care?*

A "Love-ly" Example

What's one of the most common complaints you hear from both women and men about the opposite sex on the first few dates? *They spent the whole time talking about themselves!* That's *features*. How can that other party feel special, important or even relevant to the first when he or she can't even enter the conversation? It's the equivalent of you going on about yourself and your book.

It's only when one party shows interest in the other—through appropriate body language, asking questions, and *listening* to the answers—that the other person feels acknowledged, important, and included. When that happens, that other person has seen the *benefits* to him or her of hanging out with this person, not just the *features* of this person. This is the equivalent of you talking about what's important to a prospect (i.e., *not* your book).

USP—The Unique Selling Proposition

Every book is unique in some way. Once you determine the audience for your book, zero in on its *Unique Selling Proposition* (USP)—THE thing that sets that book apart in a marketplace full of competitors. What does it do that others don't? Obviously, this is more important with non-fiction than fiction, but even with the latter, your various audiences (from both the business and book buying ends) still want to know what makes it stand out in its genre.

When I decided to write this book, I knew I was facing far more bookshelf competition in the SP arena—including some pretty seminal works—than I had in the realm of commercial writing, the subject of my first two titles. As such, I had to figure out how to best position my book to address the inevitable question: "Why should I buy *this* book?"

I didn't agonize over it too much in the early stages of writing the thing, but rather, waited until the manuscript started taking shape to see what set it apart from others. I came up with several key "market differentiators," which we discussed in the introduction:

- **Sales and Marketing Discussion**

- **One Big "Real-World" Case Study**

- **Focus on Profit AND Process**

- **Personal, Engaging Writing Style**

- **A Radically Different Approach to Marketing**

Once you determine your book's USPs, make sure they show up in your back cover copy and in most everything else you send out. Drive the message home. Identifying your USP also provides more clarity as to what your mission is, and what piece of the marketplace you're claiming.

Do You Have a Viable Book?

Let's put some of these sales and marketing distinctions to work right out of the gate for a *most* important task: *determining the viability of your book idea.*

"Crazy" Lives...

We've all known people who talk about their "crazy" lives, which, 99 out of 100, is just a life like most other lives, or, at the very least, certainly not some Oprah-worthy existence. They exclaim, "I should write a book; no one would believe it." Yeah, and no offense, but I'd wager no one would buy it, either. What *we* think is absolutely fascinating about our life is rarely so for others. So, Rule #1 of the SP game, and part and parcel of the whole S&M discussion here is this:

WRITE A BOOK PEOPLE WILL WANT TO READ.

Painfully obvious, right? Total no-brainer? Well, as we've all discovered, few things are no-brainers, especially this one. A corollary to this rule is: Don't let ego or vanity ("Hooowee, I'm going to be an author!") cloud your judgment and keep you from asking yourself the tough questions to determine if your proposed subject matter is indeed salable. Remember: a garage full of books is an amazingly ego-boosting sight for about two hours. Tops.

Don't Go "Book Blind"!

Put another way, don't succumb to what I'll call "book blindness," a common affliction of first-time self-publishers and even some more experienced folks: when you become so enamored with the idea that you've written a book and you're so intimately attuned to how much blood, sweat and tears went into its creation (and by extension, how "incredible" you *know* it is) that you lose sight of the fact that your market doesn't know any of this and needs to be sold on *all* of it. That means content, cover, title, subtitle, editing, and everything else that contributes to a successful title—in the *market's* opinion, not yours.

What's the Payoff?

Let's look at a clear-cut example of a book people want to read: a Top 10 title on *The New York Times* best-seller list. What makes such a book so popular? With non-fiction titles, the subject is undoubtedly topical and compelling, and the information is sufficiently valuable to enough people to translate to commercial success.

With fiction though, it's likely the draw of a marquee author. What makes those authors so popular? Well, you could safely say that their books strike a common chord in enough readers with compelling story-telling, rich character development, recurring themes or heroes/heroines (in the case of a series), authentic depictions of human nature, etc.

Simply put, for a book to become a best seller, enough people have to feel there's a *payoff*: a feeling that's pleasurable or familiar, something they can relate to on some fundamental level, etc. Will your book deliver that crucial payoff?

Tune in to WRII-FM

All writing, if it's to be effective (i.e., get through to your reader), must always consider the audience, as we just discussed. Throughout the entire self-publishing process, you'll need to keep your reader/listener/viewer constantly in mind. Choosing the right (read *marketable*) subject matter for your book is just the first time you'll do that.

Along the way, you'll do it on countless other occasions, as you craft: 1) email pitches to potential reviewers; 2) press releases to particular publications or associations that have specific "hot buttons"; 3) articles for print/online publications which look for specific content; 4) promotional copy, commentary and content for book signings, discussions, seminars, speeches, radio/TV interviews, other public appearances, and much more.

We need to tune our marketing minds into "WRII-FM," that unspoken question in the mind of the reader of any printed material: "**W**hat's **R**eally **I**n **I**t **F**or **M**e?" If the answer is, "nothing" or "not enough," then it's on to the next book on the bookshelf, email in the inbox, or article in the magazine.

How's Yours Different?

So let's assume for a moment that you've determined that your subject matter would be sufficiently compelling to enough people to make you more than a few bucks. Next stop? The bookstore, both physical and virtual. Head on over to Barnes & Noble or Borders, or visit Amazon.com. See how many other books there are on your subject. It might be a great topic, but if there are 20 titles that deal with it already, do we really need a 21st?

As we discussed in the section on USP in the previous chapter, is there something unique about your book that will make it stand out from the herd? If there are indeed twenty others, then yours had better be pretty darn special, and to someone other than you. Think long and hard on this one, given the healthy potential investment to bring a book to market (we'll break this down in more detail later in the chapter).

Step out of your own shoes and into those of your prospective reader. Assuming there is indeed a healthy market for this topic, will that audience (or at least enough of them) perceive that your book is appreciably superior in ways that are important to them (translation: deliver a bigger payoff) from all the others on the market, to the point that they'll choose yours?

Plenty of Room

In the case of my first book, there was literally one book on the market on the subject of commercial writing: *Secrets of a Freelance Writer,* by Bob Bly. It's a very good book; in fact it was the book that got me started in the commercial writing business. Still, it was just one book. Bob's book is solid, substantive, and straightforward. Mine was going to be just as meaty in its own right but more fun, whimsical, and irreverent—starting with the title itself, *The Well-Fed Writer,* and continuing on from there.

So, clearly, I felt comfortable that there was more than enough room for another book on the subject, especially one with a different tone and approach. Most importantly, the subject matter was very compelling. I knew there were zillions of struggling or "wannabe" writers out there who would be more than a little intrigued by a book that showed them, step-by-step, how to make a handsome full-time living as a writer.

This flew in the face of the conventional wisdom, which held that all writers, except best-selling authors, starve. Moreover, it was a book that met them where they were ("audience" again), and assumed nothing other than that they knew they were decent writers, and they wanted to find a way to make a full-time living at it.

A Book Proposal?

Here's a great way to gel your thinking about the market viability of your book. About the time I'd finished my first book, and before I'd definitely decided to self-publish it, I put together a book proposal (see Appendix B), which, of course, is the first step to pitching agents and/or publishers. But, as one of my readers—and a fellow writer and author—reminded me in an email recently, even if you've already made the decision to go the SP route, a book proposal is a wonderful way to get a reality check. Listen to Heather Allard:

When I started writing my book on new motherhood, I thought it was such a fabulous idea, as I had just lived through it. My female friends, family and neighbors expressed the same enthusiasm for the book's mission. It was through the writing of my proposal that I discovered that, indeed, there WAS a market for this book. Through Internet research, I found out that one million women become mothers for the first time each year—a revelation that made me feel like I wasn't just stabbing in the dark.

I then researched my competition on Amazon.com and BN.com (I find BN.com a better tool for research), what they were offering, what their sales were, etc. So, before you tackle your marketing/public relations/sales opportunities, writing a well-researched proposal can make you very intimate with the business side of your book. Which is something a lot of writers can tend to gloss over—that writing and selling books is just that—a HUGE BUSINESS."

Great point. So put together a formal book proposal, even if you think you'll probably end up self-publishing. It ensures that you'll think this thing through thoroughly before taking the (financial) plunge. That means figuring out what the book would cover, why there's a market for it, who would buy it, why they would buy it, what your competition is, what your expected costs will be, and much more.

Incidentally, in the solid reference I mentioned earlier, *Guerrilla Marketing For Consultants* (Jay Conrad Levinson and Michael W. McLaughlin; John Wiley & Sons, Inc., Hoboken, New Jersey; 2005), on p. 149-150, the authors provide a list of the seven things any book proposal should include. While the list assumes you're planning on approaching a publisher as opposed to self-publishing, it's a good checklist even if you're planning on going the SP route (though some of it won't be necessary for SP'ers). And there's that point #6 again:

1) The idea: What is the subject and how will it grab readers? What's new or different about your treatment?

2) The market for the book: Who will buy the book? How large is the potential market for it? How many books do you estimate you can sell?

3) Comparable/competitive books: Who else is writing on your subject? What are the strengths and weaknesses of those books and what will your book add to the subject? What books complement your proposed book and how will yours add to what's been written?

4) Potential spin-offs: What other avenues exist for publishing your material: book summaries, audiotapes, or companion field guides?

5) Your qualifications to write the book: Agents and publishers will look at how qualified you are to complete the book and how aggressively you will push it into the market. Demonstrate your expertise by identifying a problem and showing readers how to solve it.

6) Your plan to promote the book: Agents and publishers place the lion's share of the promotion burden on the author, so show how you'll support the marketing of your book to meet the forecast you've set earlier in your proposal. Many agents and publishers view this section as the most important part of the proposal. A great book idea with a lackluster promotion plan will come back to you for revision.

7) The details: A book proposal must also contain the book's proposed table of contents, a brief summary of each chapter, and one or two sample chapters.

As the authors confirm here, should you go the conventional publishing route, you'll have to demonstrate in advance that you have a plan for promoting your books, *and* that you'll be doing most of the work involved with that plan. Incidentally, a great little book to help you put together a book proposal is *How to Write a Successful Book Proposal in 8 Days or Less*, by Patricia Fry (**www.matilijapress.com**).

Okay, now that we're a bit more comfortable in our marketing skin, and we've determined that we do indeed have a book to write that has an audience out there, let's turn to the whole process of physically creating a book...

Seven Steps to a More Readable Book

Writing ability. Sure, some people are inherently gifted when it comes to wordsmithing, but anyone can improve their skills by following a few simple guidelines. The suggestions that follow are all about making your writing more clear, concise, conversational, coherent, and compelling, which, not surprisingly, given the focus of this chapter, is all about considering your audience. I've adapted this list from one that appeared in my second book. It just felt like a good fit for this chapter.

Write like you talk (at your best...)

For some inexplicable reason, many verbally articulate people often seem to be taken over by some alien power that compels them to adopt an awkward, stilted, wooden tone when it comes to writing. When people read anything, I say there's a voice in their mind narrating those words to them. As such, read everything you write out loud, and make sure it has an engaging, conversational tone (within reason, depending on the subject matter). If it doesn't, work on it until it does.

I keep this rule front and center when I write, which is probably why my books have earned such high marks for their readability. And don't be afraid to use plenty of contractions; they'll make your copy infinitely lighter and more conversational. It's true. You'll see.

Give your audience credit

Don't overwrite. We all know the good feeling we get when someone we respect highly for his or her intelligence assumes we're just as smart. Want to win over readers? Assume they're bright enough to catch on without spelling it all out like you would to a 10-year-old. It'll flatter them, and a flattered reader is an interested reader.

Sure, there are times when you have to write to a lowest common denominator, and yes, clarity is next to godliness, but don't overdo it. If you're writing a how-to guide, talk to your readers as "you," not "them."

Make every word pull its weight

I once heard an exceptionally useful writing tip: If a word doesn't move the story forward, cut it. Words should not be used to showcase your ability to fill up white space, or as a forum for flexing your linguistic muscles. Words are the building blocks of a story. Don't just have them parading around, impressed with themselves, leaning on their shovels watching other words work, or taking up space in some other way (like I'm probably doing here...).

We could learn a lot from public signage. **"Not Responsible For Lost or Stolen Articles."** The "We're…" upfront is understood. **"Keep Off Grass."** Not "You Need to…" **"Yield."** Not "Yield to Oncoming Traffic."

Make your writing disappear

When you write something, your goal should be to disappear from the process. Readers should just get the idea, without even noticing the words. Words should be the vehicle of a thought or an idea, not a distraction. It's like two workers. One quietly and effectively does his job right the first time, without drawing attention to himself. The other makes a big show of what he's doing, and being more concerned with having everyone know what he's up to, ends up doing a mediocre job.

Cadence is everything

What's wrong with this paragraph?

> The first step of our business process is to understand your goals. We follow that by determining the best avenue to get there. Our solutions always end up being simple, direct and effective. And the feedback we've received has been uniformly positive.

All the sentences are roughly the same length. Big problem. It's too mechanical. This is NOT a good example of "Write Like You Talk!" Mix it up. Short and long. Like I've done in this paragraph.

Start in the middle

You may have noticed that I start off many of the chapters in this book with a story that drops the reader right in the middle of things. It just makes for more compelling reading. This device has become second nature to me, and given how easy a way it is to make writing more interesting, I'm not sure why it's not used more. Once you've grabbed the reader's attention, you can continue on with a more conventional approach. It's more effective, it's more engaging, and it's a heckuva lot more fun to write (and doesn't that sound suspiciously like *benefits* before *features* again?).

Focus on the Reading, Not the Writing

Two meanings: 1) Focus on the sound and flow of the piece as it's being read so it reads naturally, free of excess words, awkward syntax or robotic rhythm, and 2) (more global) Always write with the reader in mind, and try to appeal to *that* particular reader; don't just focus on the words for their own sake.

Chapter 3

A funny story that introduces us to all the nitty-gritty details we need to keep in mind as we put a book together (while reminding us that we learn as we go...). I hope this self-publishing friend won't mind my poking anonymous fun at her naiveté. In 2002, Linda (I'll call her) emailed me about the copyright date of her soon-to-be-printed book. She'd started working on the book in 1996, so that was the copyright date she was going with. Someone had told her she needed to make it the current year, but that sure didn't sound right to her, so she was just double-checking with me. If she didn't hear from me, she added, 1996 was her date, and she was sticking to it.

I immediately emailed her back and told her in no uncertain terms that a 1996 copyright date on a 2002 release—a non-fiction book that relied on facts, figures, and data, to boot—would absolutely doom it right out of the gate. Change made. Happy ending.

Okay, so you've chosen a compelling, marketable topic, done the book proposal to get clear on what piece of book "real estate" you're claiming, and you've written the book (or are steeped in the process). Next? Let's start this process with, arguably, the most important part of your book…

Your Cover

Covers Sell Books

I recently got a copy of a self-published book from a friend who was understandably excited about her new baby, but it *so* looked like a self-published book. This has always mystified me: how is it, given that we're absolutely surrounded with examples of beautifully produced books, that self-publishers still keep coming up with crummy-looking covers? Why, after investing so much time and effort into the writing of their books, do so many authors stop short of the finish line?

As mentioned earlier, it's categorically impossible to overstate the importance of a good cover. Remember: approximately 150,000+ books get published in any given year. Those people considering your title for review, distribution, or purchase will be looking for reasons to cull the herd. The cover is the easiest place to start. FYI, book distributors send their salespeople out to bookstores with suitcases full of, not books, but covers! They can't lug around dozens of books, so many of the buying decisions are made based solely on covers.

Hire a professional designer. *Don't* use your cousin who's artistic, and *don't* let your printer's design department handle it. Most of the covers I've seen done by in-house designers at printing companies look cheesy and amateurish. Can you barter services with a graphic designer? I traded writing for design services with a professional graphic designer who needed copy for her web site and marketing materials, an arrangement that continues to this day.

Study the Best

Got a Barnes & Noble or Borders in the neighborhood? Visit bookstores with your graphic designer and scan the shelves in your genre for cover designs and titles that catch your eye. Note the professionalism that goes into them. Figure out why they appeal to you, and try to capture what works. We non-creative (graphically speaking) folks simply aren't good judges of what's a good cover design and what isn't—an assertion supported by the mountain of really bad book covers out there. So, make sure you always check with the ultimate arbiter of those aesthetics—your local bookstore.

If you choose to ignore everything else in this book, heed this: *take the time and invest the money to create a cover that would have an impartial observer be totally unaware that it's a self-published effort.* A cover so good that when they do find out it's self-published, they're amazed. And understand that doing that will not be some huge triumph. It will simply elevate your book, at least in appearance (which, sad to say, is more than half the game), to a level of parity with all your conventionally published competition out there.

Artwork for All Reasons

Once your designer has created your cover, ask him or her to generate a variety of iterations of the image: large, small, hi-resolution (for print publications), low-resolution (for web-based publications), and even black and white. When it comes time to promote your book on other sites, if you're able to send them the right size artwork, it makes their job a lot easier.

Once you have them in hand, load high- and low-resolution versions onto your web site in your *Media Resources* section (which we'll discuss soon) as downloads, and always mention this fact in your correspondence to the media crowd. If you have a front cover blurb on your book, for clarity's sake, lose it for these smaller images.

If it takes much more than a few mouse clicks for a reporter or a reviewer to get the information they need for a story, it might not happen. Again, it's all about making it as easy as possible for these folks to do business with you. And of course, the easier it is…*All Together Now*…The More Likely They Are To Do It!

Money-Saving Cover Strategies

While a professionally-designed cover could run $1500-2500+, you ought to be able to get one for half that if you hunt. Find a local art or trade school that teaches graphic design, contact the teacher(s), and ask who their most talented students are. Young people starting out are always looking for opportunities to build their "book" (portfolio) with real-world projects, and this fact, coupled with their lack of experience, understandably means they command far lower rates.

Another option is to tap some of the online job sites such as **www.guru.com**, **www.elance.com**, and others. These can be good places to find inexpensive creative resources and almost all will have online portfolios available for viewing.

Given the critical importance of a cover, I don't recommend these as first choices—but if the budget won't accommodate springing for an established pro, it's still a better alternative than using your printer's cover designer. Did I mention your book cover is important?

Your Title & Subtitle

As crucially important as a great-looking cover is a compelling title and subtitle (we're talking mostly about non-fiction titles here; fiction titles can be a little more abstract). In many respects, a title is similar to a corporate tagline, something with which I've had a good bit of experience through my commercial writing career. Examples of famous taglines:

GE. We bring good things to life.®

Delta. We're ready when you are.®

Avis. We try harder.®

Burger King. Have it your way.®

Virginia is for lovers.®

Deliver a "Promise"

What's the common attribute in these and so many others of note? What do they offer? They're *promises*. In each case, it tells you what they'll do for you. They tell you what you can count on. Same with a brand. Think Dove soap. Tiffany's. Mercedes-Benz. IBM. Any doubt as to the promise in those brands? Same thing goes for the creation of a book title.

When I created my title, I knew I needed to offer a promise, and in my humble opinion, I could have done a lot worse than *The Well-Fed Writer*. Of course, I didn't want to stop there; I reinforced, clarified, and elaborated on the promise of the title with the subtitle: *Financial Self-Sufficiency as a Freelance Writer in Six Months or Less*—an additional promise in its own right.

This "promise" idea harks back to the "features/benefits" discussion in the last chapter. A promise is a *benefit*, meaning it's all about the readers and what's important to them. It tells them why they should pick up the book. *The Well-Fed Writer* is a *benefits*-oriented title, and as such, definitely speaks to that reader. If I'd called it "A Guide to Freelance Writing," in addition to being exquisitely dull, it would have been a *features*-oriented title, meaning it was all about the book itself, and what *it* was, not about the reader.

I wanted people to understand what I specifically meant by *The Well-Fed Writer*. Don't make them wonder what your book is all about—make sure they *get it* right away from the title, and then use the subtitle to add a bit more juice, and build on your promise. When crafting your title, brainstorm a bunch of ideas and run them past people. Think clever *and* effective.

Focus on Benefits

Some time back, I was approached by an ebook author to review his book (on writing novels). I couldn't help but feel that his title was a major weakness. The book was about getting past the obstacles that most fiction writers encounter on the way to finishing their books. The original title was:

Writing Your Novel: A Quick and Easy Guide to Getting It Done

Boooooring. I told him he needed to make it more dynamic *and* offer a promise. We chatted about what he was offering in his book, and how he could turn that into a promise. I suggested the following, which I think works a bit better:

UNSTUCK! Kick Down Those Roadblocks and Finish Your Novel Now!

In addition to being more dynamic, someone can look at the title and know instantly what the book is about and the *benefits* they'll get from reading it: in short, the promise.

More recently, I was hired to mentor a new self-publishing author, an ad industry veteran who'd written a book on creativity. While he wanted to tap my expertise on a variety of nuts and bolts issues, in his mind, his title was set in stone:

A Field Guide to Creativity: *One Path and 101 Pointers for Discovering Fresh Ideas*

He already had the cover design and photography done and paid for, so when I told him both needed work, he wasn't exactly overjoyed. I felt a bit like the father telling his daughter that, despite the fact that the wedding was just two weeks away, and all the invitations had gone out and the caterer, florist, photographer and band had all been paid for, her intended betrothed was a loser and it wasn't too late to call it off.

In my mind, the big issue wasn't just that the cover and title were weak (which they were); it was this: here was a book—a really good, interesting, valuable and yes, *creative* book—purporting to help people be more creative, and it just didn't look...creative.

To his credit, he revisited the idea, and while he and I brainstormed a bunch of jazzier titles and images—along with a whole gang of his friends, via email—he ended up coming up with one infinitely better:

ZING! *Five Steps & 101 Tips for Creativity on Command*

Check out the cover design on Amazon; trust me, it's 1000 percent more compelling than his original design.

Know what the #1 best-selling trade paperback of 2002 was, according to *Publishers Weekly*? A cookbook! One that sold 1.8 million copies. Title: *The Fix-It and Forget-It™ Cookbook: Feasting With Your Slow Cooker.* (Authors: Dawn J. Ranck and Phyllis Pellman Good). Now is that a promise or what?

Stellar Subtitles

I remember the exact day and place when *The Well-Fed Writer* came to me for a title. I knew instantly that that piece of the puzzle was now in place. Check. The subtitle took a bit longer, and I suggest putting in sufficient time to come up with a good one.

As mentioned, my first book's subtitle is: *Financial Self-Sufficiency as a Freelance Writer in Six Months or Less.* The subtitle clarifies and strengthens the title. I talk with a lot of people who want to run titles past me, and most of the ones I hear would be great subtitles but they need that catchy "first-glance" moniker preceding it. Good rule of thumb: if the title you've come up with sounds more explanatory than catchy (and more importantly, is more than four or five words, max), it's probably a better subtitle.

I think the subtitle for this book works as well: *How to Turn One Book into a Full-Time Living*. I'd like to think that if I were an author considering the self-publishing route, this title would get my attention and make me take a closer look. We shall see. For some creative tools to assist the process of coming up with a killer title, go visit **www.namingnewsletter.com** and **www.rhymezone.com**.

Your Back Cover Copy

There's an art to writing good back cover copy. Devote some quality time to the process of transforming a relatively small space into a powerful selling tool. If your cover, title and subtitle are clear, catchy, and compelling enough, your potential buyer's next stop for more information is the back cover. And given Amazon's "Look Inside!" feature, a powerfully written back cover is equally valuable for both online and physical marketing.

The Buying Process

At the risk of over-analysis (my strong suit), here's why your back cover copy is so important: think about how you buy a book. You pick it up, look at the cover, and if you like the visuals, title, and subtitle, it's because something resonates in you; something about what you see calls to some desire or longing inside you. That desire could be anything. In the case of a novel (or even non-fiction), it might be to have a transcendent reading experience—to be touched, moved, entertained, transported, etc.

If it's non-fiction, it could be a desire for information about something that is (or sounds) meaningful to you. Or perhaps you want to ease a nagging concern. An amateur chef who would love to perfect his soufflé technique is drawn to a book on the subject. Someone who's looking to explore the potential of real estate investing to enhance her financial picture is attracted to a book that seems to promise a proven path to profitability. A first-time expectant mother, wanting to be a good parent and nervous about what's to come, spots a book on parenting, the cover and title of which speaks to that concern. It's the beginning of a "Hmmmmmm..."

Regardless of the book, if the cover and title intrigue us, a kernel of hope starts to stir. You're daring to imagine that this book will address that desire, uncertainty, or concern.

"Sell Me"

Now, the reader is looking for confirmation of this growing sense of hope. Consciously or unconsciously, they're thinking: "Tell me I'm right. Tell me you can do what I'm hoping you can do." And, in essence—"Tell me what I want to hear." Their next move is to flip the book over, and think—most likely unconsciously—"Okay, sell me." Gee, and you thought it was just a back cover! I bet you had no idea so much was at stake.

Or conversely, as my friend and thriving fellow commercial writer Dana Pulis out in Billings, Montana puts it when counseling clients on creating powerful marketing materials: "Don't give them a reason to put it down." Same goes here.

An Example

Let's take a look at the back cover of my first book. Not that it's the last word in the exercise, but I think it works, and it does so as a marriage of words and graphics. If you don't have it, go to Amazon, look up *The Well-Fed Writer: Financial Self-Sufficiency as a Freelance Writer in Six Months or Less,* click the "Look Inside!" feature, and take a peek at the back side.

1) Upper Left Corner: Category. Check the books in your genre in the bookstore and notice what's most appropriate to put in that spot. Mine? "Freelance Writing" (oddly enough...)

2) Top-Center Headline: a strong attention-getting headline/sub-head that makes a claim, asks a question, or piques your prospect's interest in some other way. My headline/sub-head:

Corporate America Wants Freelancers—Full or Part-Time!
Do You Dream of Being a Well-Paid Freelance Writer and Want to Do It Fast?

3) Sales Copy: Immediately below the headline/sub-head is sales copy, where I let buyers find themselves in my list of target audiences. This is the *benefits*-oriented section of the copy that talks to them and gets their attention.

Once I have that attention in the first section, I move on to the next "chunks" —the *features* section—fleshing out the story by establishing "the opportunity" that exists in the marketplace and outlining how my book can show them exactly what they need to do to capitalize on that opportunity. I like to think that it takes them through the logical mental steps necessary to lead to a book purchase.

Use my example as a template to lay over your book premise. Given that anyone who's gotten to the back cover is presumably in the market for a book like this, we need to maximize this golden "captive audience" opportunity by keeping the persuasive pressure on.

4) Author Bio: Include a brief bio that establishes your credentials to write such a book. You want people to think, "Hmmm...impressive."

5) Testimonials: Initially, I included Bob Bly's killer blurb at the bottom of the back page, moving it to the front on a later printing. You want to include at least one, perhaps more. In my case, because Bob is so well known in the freelance writing arena, I could get away with one. Later, I put another particularly strong one at the bottom of the back cover as well. We'll talk a bit more about blurbs a few pages on.

6) Web Address: A "Duh," perhaps, but make sure you include your URL—prominently. Mine's at the bottom of my bio. If someone chooses not to buy it right there, I've given them the key to more information. My web site can then take them the rest of the way (and perhaps get them to subscribe to my ezine as well).

This book has a similar look to *The Well-Fed Writer* and *TWFW: Back For Seconds*. For me, it's the beginning of a possible brand development. I like to think that this clear, clean, bold cover design is not only visually compelling, but the way it's broken up into sections by color facilitates effective sharing of information in a simple, uncluttered way. This is what a good graphic designer can bring to the table.

Landing the Big-Name Blurb

Put together a blurb target list, email them about a month or so before you plan on sending the galleys out, and ask if they'd be willing to offer a blurb to appear in the book. Tell them you'll be including their notable accomplishments and web site (if applicable).

By the way, in less than a week, using the Internet, I lined up close to 25 commitments (shoot for about 35 to 40, which should yield 25+ workable ones) not only for blurbs, but reviews, interviews and articles (which I'd write). I was getting online responses back in fifteen minutes! Once I had my galleys (which we'll discuss later), these folks got one hot off the press.

I chose what I thought were my two highest-profile blurbs and put one at the bottom of both the front and back covers. Then, I put about 25 more on the first six inside pages. Not necessarily *the* right formula, and you may not need that many inside, but a six-page fountain of good news can make for quite a compelling first impression.

As for landing the marquee blurbs? Ask and ye shall receive. Why not shoot high and go after that author or "expert" whose opinion would really mean something to your audience (and translate to much greater book sales)? What's the worst thing that could happen? They say no. Or never reply. Big deal. But, what if they say yes? What could it mean? So, ask away. These folks are a lot more accessible than you might imagine.

As noted above, I went after Bob Bly, the freelance writing "guru" and author/co-author of 60 books on writing and business. At the time I published my book, he had the only other book on the market that would be competing with mine. What the heck?

Strong Words Sell Books

I approached him through my contact at *Writer's Digest Book Club*—the first club to take on my book. His three-word reply to her request for a testimonial (on my behalf) was: "Be happy to." He ended up writing an absolutely fabulous blurb, which read, in part, "This book is the best information on how to make more money with corporate clients I have ever read. Highly recommended." Wow. You think I sold a few books with those words? You bet, and many buyers, through their email messages, told me just that.

I have a friend who's written a number of books in the psychology and relationship genres, and for his latest one, he landed a blurb from "Dr. Laura" Schlessinger. How'd he pull that off? At a book signing for the controversial talkmistress, he simply asked. All he had was a few chapters at that point, but he left them with her assistant and a few months later, got his blurb. And a pretty good one at that.

Controversial is Good

Funny sidebar. I found out about his mini-PR coup when he called to ask my opinion on whether he should actually use it. Seems many of his friends (not in the book business) told him that using it would be the kiss of death, given the public's mixed feelings about her. Please. Publicity is publicity and even if you don't like her, it's still quite impressive that she officially took note of the book with her comment. More importantly, many people *do* like her, or she wouldn't be as popular as she is.

Just as important—especially with how-to books—are organizations or associations that can offer an endorsement or "seal of approval" for your book. In these cases, while the specific name of the person isn't as crucial as the affiliation, you'll still want to reach the president, executive director, founder, etc. Never underestimate the desire of these folks to see their name in print.

Here's a nifty searchable online database for locating contact info on over 14,000 celebrities: **www.celebrity-addresses.com**. No, you probably won't get their personal email address, though you will find out how to reach their managers, publicists and agents. You'll pay $14 a month, but if you can land some big names quickly and cancel before the month's out, it's definitely worth it.

NOTE: Allow a month or so to hear back from your "blurbers" after sending galleys out. I recently got a review copy from a well-known publisher on a Monday, asking me to provide a blurb by that Wednesday! That's nuts—*and* yet another example of poor planning on the part of the traditional publishing world.

Now that we've got the make-or-break stuff out of the way, let's move on to the crucial minutiae, like…

Numbers, Forms, Registrations, etc.

NOTE: While everything in the coming pages follows a rough sequence, check out Appendix C for the detailed "when-to" of the process.

Your ISBN Number

Every book is assigned a unique 10-digit ISBN (International Standard Book Number) by R.R. Bowker in New Jersey (**www.bowker.com**; Canadian authors need to get theirs through the National Library of Canada). The ISBN appears in several places in the book, most prominently at the top of the bar code on the back of the book, and it makes sure that the right book gets ordered and shipped. The bad news is that it costs $240 to get an ISBN—a $225 processing fee and a $14.95 Publisher Registration Fee (whatever that is). The good news is that, for that fee, you actually receive 10 ISBN numbers.

Of course, you *could* just bite the bullet and spend $800 for 100 numbers—clearly the best value. After all, 100 published books is surely in the cards, no? Seriously, publishing pro Fern Reiss actually recommends you buy 100 numbers, on the theory that buying just 10 marks you as a one-book publisher. I like the way she's thinking, but I assert it's what happens *after* you publish your book to promote it that will set you apart. As such, I'm not sure that fears over a *possible* negative perception justifies shelling out $800 vs. $225. Like you needed convincing...

By the way, if you decide to get your ISBNs from your printer, make sure the ISBN is in *your* name, not theirs. That way, YOU are the "publisher of record."

OPD vs. BBD

Here's as good a place as any to discuss the curious notion of "official publication date" (OPD). It's the date you let the world know that you're officially "releasing" your book, and should be very different from your "bound book date" (BBD)—the date you actually have printed books in your hands. Put at least four or more months between the two dates, giving you plenty of time to build awareness in the traditional media (primarily for mainstream books), in your grassroots Internet communities, *and* among certain key reviewers (who need to see your book *before* your OPD; more on that in Chapter Six).

Truth be known, your OPD is essentially an arbitrary date that no one's going to enforce (the only exception being the pre-OPD reviewers mentioned above, who we'll discuss shortly). Meaning, that *prior* to your OPD, it's perfectly okay to sell your book on your site, at appearances, through book clubs, or even get your books into the bookstores (though, as we'll discuss in Chapter Six, you want to build a strong demand for your book before you approach the bookstores to keep "returns" low). In fact, it's not unusual for a popular book to sell out its first printing before OPD.

ISBN-13 COMING SOON

ISBN numbers are changing to 13 digits. The transition process began on January 1, 2005, and will be complete by January 1, 2007. That means that any book published after 01/01/07 must use the 13-digit ISBN. That's "published" as in your *OPD*, not BBD, meaning if your BBD is in October, but your OPD isn't until February of the next year, you'll have to use 13-digit ISBNs. Already have a block of 10-digit ISBNs? Convert them to 13-digit versions at **www.isbn.org/converterpub.asp**.

This gets a bit confusing, class, so pay close attention here. ISBNs purchased after 01/01/07 will be the 13-digit variety. If you're buying your ISBNs for the first time prior to that date, you'll receive 10-digit numbers, which, again, you'll need to convert *if* your book isn't scheduled to be published (OPD) until after 01/01/07. If you're publishing *prior* to 01/01/07, the bar code company you choose will still put the old 10-digit number on top of the bar code (the 13-digit numbers are already below the bar code; look at any recent book). But, for those pub dates (OPD) prior to 01/01/07, Bowker recommends you include both numbers on your title verso page (a.k.a. your copyright page) stacked and hyphenated as follows:

ISBN-13: 978-1-8736710-0-9
ISBN-10: 1-8736710-0-8

Books published after 01/01/07 only need to have the 13-digit ISBN on back (just provide your bar code supplier with your 13-digit numbers and they'll get it right). Books printed prior to 01/01/07 that have the 10-digit ISBNs above the bar code don't have to be changed until they're reprinted, given that those books already feature the 13-digit numbers below the bar code. In case you're not confused enough yet, visit **www.bowker.com** and look for references to "ISBN-13 Transition" on the home page.

Your Bookland EAN Bar Code

With ISBN in hand, now we need to get our Bookland EAN bar code. You can get both ISBNs and bar codes through Bowker: **www.isbn.org/standards/home/isbn/us/index.asp**. You'll land on a page with several links, including "Bar Code Suppliers" and even a list of printers, which makes it easy to place bar code orders or request print bids.

Several bar code suppliers offer online D-I-Y bar code creation, 24/7, for $10. Such a deal. We want an "ISBN Bookland EAN bar code" (there are many to choose from). Within that category, the basic "ISBN" choice, which reads: "Standard Bookland EAN format: price encoded" will get the job done. Once you have the bar code artwork in its file, pass it on to your cover designer for inclusion on the back cover of your book.

Free Books-In-Print Listing

By the way, once you have your ISBN numbers, you can get your title—upcoming or already released—listed on **www.booksinprint.com**, Bowker's five-million title "database of record for the book industry" (according to the Bowker site). It's a free listing, and you access it through BowkerLink™ (**www.bowkerlink.com**; register first). You can also list for free in the Ulrich's Periodicals database, also accessible through BowkerLink™.

Free *ForeWord* Magazine "Seasonal Announcements"

ForeWord magazine allows you to input free "Seasonal Announcements" for two titles twice annually. Go to **www.forewordmagazine.com**, click FAQs up top, scroll down to the bottom where they talk about registering and go through the process. In a day or so, you'll get a password back. Use that to log in and fill out the listing. Deadlines are May 15th (for Fall/Winter titles) and December 15th (for Spring/Summer).

Sans the SAN Number

At that same link where you apply for your ISBN, you can also apply for something called a SAN (Standard Address Number). Don't bother. I did for my first book, but never saw the value of it. It makes much more sense for bigger publishers with multiple locations and distributors. I contacted both PMA and SPAN, the two big independent publishing associations, and asked them for their take on the SAN. Both said: *Pass.*

The Preassigned Control Number (PCN) Program

The PCN program assigns a Library of Congress Control Number (LCCN) to titles most likely to be acquired by the Library of Congress. We're just covering that base here because we can. To get your LCCN, first go to the *Preassigned Control Number* program page at **http://pcn.loc.gov**, where you can get a preassigned LCCN.

Click the various available links to learn more about the program, and when you're ready, click *Open New Account* to start the process (which is totally electronic). Scroll down and you'll find a link to the application. Fill out the application, and within a few weeks, you'll receive your username and password by email (though, according to their people, that's the longest it would take; more likely within a few days, assuming all is in order).

Once you've received them, return to the site, click the *Log On* button, enter the system with your new codes, and make your formal application for the LCCN number. You'll receive your LCCN number, also by email, and also within two weeks at the outside (and again, more likely within a few days). Once you get your LCCN number, you'll be instructed to send a copy of "the best edition of the book" immediately. Just send it when you finally have it, whether at the galley stage (a pre-pub version we'll discuss shortly) or final copy, to:

Library of Congress
Cataloging in Publication Division
101 Independence Ave., S.E.
Washington, D.C. 20540-4320

With LCCN in hand, you'll start the process of getting your Library of Congress CIP info.

The Library of Congress Cataloging in Publication (CIP) Program

This is a process that a publisher initiates before a book is published. The point of this step? Well, the short version is explained on the home page of this program's web site (**http://cip.loc.gov/cip/**):

A Cataloging in Publication record (aka CIP data) is a bibliographic record prepared by the Library of Congress for a book that has not yet been published. When the book is published, the publisher includes the CIP data on the copyright page thereby facilitating book processing for libraries and book dealers.

Pick up a book right now—any book. Open up to the copyright page and look at that arcane collection of words and numbers. It includes (amongst other things) the CIP data. If you plan to promote your book to the library market, by including the CIP data on the copyright page, you make it easier for librarians to decide to carry your book, because the CIP info makes it easier to catalog your book. Where do most publishers go to get the CIP data for their books? The Library of Congress. In which case, that CIP data is known as LC-CIP. However…

SP Books Need Not Apply

According to the rules of the CIP program, due to limited resources, self-published books are ineligible. Okay, we won't get our noses out of joint, because we have options: hire a third party to do it, or perhaps do it ourselves (with the help of a librarian). In these cases, it'll be known as PCIP, as in *Publishers* CIP.

Here's where there's often some confusion about the CIP and PCN programs. The LC-CIP and PCN programs are mutually exclusive. If you're a conventional publisher and you tap the Library of Congress to prepare your CIP info, you can't participate in the PCN program to secure an LCCN. But, if you're a self-publisher, and you secure your own CIP data (PCIP) through a third party or by yourself, you can participate in both. Don't ask why. Just accept it. Let's look at the third-party route first.

Third Party PCIP Data

Once you receive your LCCN, you can do what I did on my first book (but not my second; see below) and contact Quality Books, Inc. (QBI) in Oregon, Illinois. They're ostensibly a library distributor (helping move your books to libraries) but they can also handle the creation of your PCIP information. Go visit their web site (**www.quality-books.com/pcip.htm**) for all the info on PCIP.

QBI now has an online application process for the PCIP info and it's the *only* way to apply to the program. Go to **www.quality-books.com/pcipintro.php** for complete submission instructions and read them carefully. Files must be sent as *text-only*, no exceptions. Manuscripts can be in virtually any stage of completion, from totally finished right down to just a title page (or reasonable facsimile, given that it's a text file), and at least one of the following: introduction/foreword/preface, table of contents, bibliography, sample chapter (first and/or last chapter), or index.

They'll send you the data by email (usually in less than a week), which you can then forward on to your typesetter, who will put it in place on the copyright page exactly as it appears, with no alterations. Cost: $150 for first editions. Questions: 800-323-4241.

The "Do-It-Yourself" Option

When it came time to put together the PCIP info for my second book, I was all set to use QBI again. I went to their web site and noticed this verbiage on the PCIP info page: *If you are a publisher who is attempting to produce your own CIP block by trying to copy the information from similar titles [or] asking your local librarian to help you...* Huh?

Suddenly it occurred to me that maybe, given that my second book was the same subject and genre, its PCIP data might be awfully similar to the first. I drove down to my library with my first book in hand, huddled with a librarian for all of, literally, two minutes, and found out exactly what I needed to change in the original book's PCIP verbiage to create the new book's iteration. $150 saved.

It gets better. I called up the librarian who helped me with my second book, mentioned the QBI web site verbiage, and asked her if a librarian could indeed help an author with the PCIP info for a *first* book. Her response: "I would think so. After all, it's just basic cataloging information." I just *love* saving money.

Copyrighting Your Book

Technically, any original creation, including a book, is automatically copyrighted by virtue of its creation. Should, however, that copyright be contested for any reason, a formal copyright will offer that extra measure of protection. Given how easy and inexpensive ($30) it is to do, you'll want to take this step.

Visit **www.copyright.gov**, and under *Publications,* click *Forms.* The *Short Form TX* is perfectly adequate for most authors' needs. Just follow the instructions, which include a request to send in two copies of the work. Since you're generally sending the "best" version to date, I usually wait until I have at least galleys, if not the final published version, before filing the form and sending the books.

Your Copyright Date

FYI, if your BBD falls any time after about July in a given year (meaning your OPD is three to four months later), it's perfectly okay to put *next* year as your copyright date. That way, your book stays "new" for longer in the eyes of the book world. Never hurts.

The Lazy Man's Option

Now, let's say you're just not excited about the legwork involved in getting all the aforementioned ducks in a row. If you decide to go with BookMasters (See Appendix A) for your printing, for $580 they'll do all the running around to get your ISBN, Bar Code, LCCN, and copyright info (all in *your* publishing entity's name—more on that later). It's an option. I still think it's pretty easy to handle it yourself (not to mention a bit cheaper), but I'm hip to someone wanting to outsource it. Your call.

Your Copyright Page

Also known as your *title verso* page, this is where all the above data—copyright date, copyright verbiage (ⓔ), PCIP info, etc.—comes together. Again, if you have one of my earlier books (or any book), look at how it's all laid out.

Your Acknowledgements Page

There's no right or wrong way to do an acknowledgements page, but again, take a look at mine to get an idea of how I did it. When praising certain "production partners" such as an editor, typesetter, cover designer, mentor, or anyone else who, in some way, made a contribution to your final product, I always try to include their web site in order to potentially steer work their way. Doesn't take up much additional space, and it's always most appreciated.

For a very funny, irreverent look at one woman's pet peeves about acknowledgement pages in general, check out Emily G's (no last name provided) hilarious screed, *Your Acknowledgement Page Sucks* at **www.blacktable.com/emilyg050721.htm**. At the very least, you'll get a good laugh, though it might also give you a few ideas.

Your Table of Contents

Do yourself—and your prospective buyers—a favor and don't just create a table of contents (TOC) with one-line chapter headings and nothing else. Follow each chapter heading with 10 to 15 bullet points outlining the main topics covered in each chapter. They don't have to correspond exactly with specific subheads in the chapter, but do your best to give someone a good feel for what they'll learn. And have some fun with them.

Again, check out the TOC in my books (or look at them via the "Look Inside!" feature on Amazon). Using this TOC format has three key advantages: 1) it quickly helps a prospective buyer who's checking it out in a bookstore (or on Amazon) to get a better sense of your book (i.e., move closer to buying the book); 2) related to that, it makes for a more robust selling tool when placed on your web site along with a sample chapter and some testimonials; and 3) it just makes the book look richer and more substantive.

Editing

Authors generally don't make very good editors…for their own books. We're too close to it. So hire an editor. On my first book, I was on such a tight timetable (to make good on commitments to deliver books to *Writer's Digest Book Club*) that I didn't go through a formal editing process. I think I managed to get away with it. The way I saw it, I was making a living as a professional writer, so I figured I should be able to handle it.

I did hire one for my second book, and she made some absolutely invaluable observations about the manuscript that unquestionably made a vast improvement to the final product. Try to find one who can do both copyediting (smoothing and/or restructuring your actual text) and proofreading (catching all the typos and grammatical errors).

You might consider doing what I did on this book. I'd contacted one editor I used before on other work (and knew to be good), sent her a chapter from the book, told her how long the final manuscript would be, and asked her to give me an estimate based on that sample chapter. While I didn't ask her to, she went ahead and actually edited that piece to demonstrate the quality of her work.

Based on that, I then contacted a second editor, Geoff, and asked if he'd do the same (and paid him for his time), so I could make a side-by-side comparison.

I ended up going with Geoff for two reasons: he did an excellent job, and having read both my books, was demonstrably more tuned-in (almost eerily so) to my mindset.

Both editors are listed under my recommended A-list resources in Appendix A.

Editor as PM?

Geoff, who's in Australia, incidentally (which highlights the reach and flexibility that the 'net provides), offered up an intriguing thought in one of our back-and-forth emails in the early stages:

Editors come in all shapes and sizes, and provide a remarkable diversity of skills. I think this would be good for prospective self-publishers to know. As you quite rightly say, a good cover and design can make a huge difference. So can quality editing. It's disappointing to pick up a cool-looking book and find the contents are a jumbled mess.

As to the logistics of SP, editors can act as 'project managers' if required, which could also be really helpful for the hesitant wannabe SP. Publishers offer three main things: editing (to knock the work into shape), project management of the process, and distribution. And don't they know how to charge for it! Many of them use freelance editors to do a lot of this now, so SPs can do the same, while hanging on to a whole lot more of their margin per copy.

Something to ponder, eh?

Easier Editing

Part and parcel of any editing process is the inevitable collision between an editor's skills and natural inclinations, and an author's particular writing style. And in my case, using an Aussie editor meant a bit (only minimal) of the "language difference" factor as well. Do the following for a much smoother process: Have your editor edit one chapter. Go through it, make any changes, change back anything you didn't want changed, and then discuss it. Use the discussion to establish some "conventions"—what's okay to do, what he should leave alone, whether you want it spelled "email" or "e-mail", etc. Armed with these distinctions, he won't make the same unwanted changes over and over.

Go "Skype" Yourself

Speaking of...speaking, before our first phone chat, Geoff suggested I download Skype™ (**www.skype.com**), a very cool VOIP (Voice Over Internet Protocol) service which allows you to talk to someone anywhere in the world over the Internet, through your computer, and for free. It's a breeze to download their software, set up an account and username. You just need a headset. I had one already hooked up for some voice-recognition software, so I didn't have to change a thing.

I added Geoff's name to my contact list (he gave me the exact lettering), clicked on it, turned my sound on, slipped on my headset, it starts "ringing" and a few seconds later, we're chatting on a crystal clear connection halfway around the globe, and the bill is never coming. Supremely cool. Check it out.

Typesetting (a.k.a "Interior book design")

I'm using the arguably outdated term "typesetting" here to describe the process of "interior book design," or "interior layout." Those latter terms are probably more accurate, but to draw a clear distinction between "design" as it relates to your book's cover vs. its text, I'll stick with "typesetting."

No, you can't just send your printer a *Word*® document and tell them to crank up the presses. You need to design and lay out that text first, so get a typesetter. For the same reason you don't use your printer to design your cover (i.e, they're likely cranking out cookie cutter designs), find a freelance typesetter who can work closely with you to give you a design that's a match for your book, cover, subject, tone, etc.

While at the bookstore with your designer looking at covers, see what *good* typesetting looks like as well. People can absolutely tell the difference between professional and amateur jobs. Don't imagine for a second that it won't matter. Cut corners, and you'll end up shooting yourself in the foot. If you find something you like, steer your typesetter to the book on Amazon.com and its "Look Inside!" feature.

On my first book, I used a very good typesetter (who was also great to work with; **www.heyneon.com**), but his experience was more in academic book publishing. The result being, I got a solidly done typesetting job, but one that wasn't as creative and fun as my book's content and message. Something I didn't even realize until I found the typesetter for my second book (contact info in Appendix A). This woman had a hefty background in designing manuals for video games. Now we're talking.

If you have both my *Well-Fed Writer* books, take a look at the difference between the two. If not, again, go visit **www.Amazon.com** and look for *The Well-Fed Writer: Financial Self-Sufficiency as a Freelance Writer in Six Months or Less* and *The Well-Fed Writer: Back For Seconds,* and do the "Look Inside!" thing. Typesetters generally charge by the page, usually somewhere in the region of $4-6 a page, but if you hunt around, you can often get it for less (which is especially true if your book is overwhelmingly text; photos, diagrams, and charts all mean more time and more money).

The Right Typesetter for the Job

As I neared the typesetting stage on my second book, I dug in and said *I'm not going to spend a lot for this typesetting job!* I actually asked my indexer if she knew any good typesetters who might be relatively new to the business (read: cheaper). She put a note out (which I wrote, clearly stating I was looking for a "deal") on a bulletin board where indexers and typesetters mingled (quite the wild party, eh?).

With three days, I got a dozen responses, all below market rates. I finally settled on Shawn, the woman I mentioned earlier, who was the best of both worlds: *very* experienced, but going through a slow period and willing to do it for less. I won't say how much less, but just know these things are negotiable.

Good typesetters are true magicians. Shawn fixed all pagination issues and glitches, and so totally imperceptibly, it took my breath away. Real pros can do amazing and wondrous things. Speaking of pagination...

D-I-Y Typesetting

There's a school of thought out there that says, *Don't Pay High Typesetting Rates! Do It Yourself in Microsoft Word!* And the battle rages. Its proponents say it's easy and looks professional. Its detractors howl, *Pffffftttttt! Typesetting in Word is Amateur Hour! I can spot a Word-typeset manuscript at 100 paces!* I'd tend to lean toward the latter camp.

For starters, Word isn't really designed for book typesetting; it's a little too fluid and shifting for the exacting nature of the task. And if there's even a chance it'll compromise the professionalism of the final product, I'm not sure I want to risk it. Plus, if you're not a high-tech type, you'll likely drive yourself into the loony bin trying to figure it all out. However, if you prefer to learn the hard way or feel you're pretty good with *Word*, visit **www.editorium.com**, which caters to D-I-Y typesetters. Another resource for the computer-savvy is a book by good friend, Peggy Duncan, *Just Show Me Which Button to Click! in Word for Authors* (**www.PeggyDuncan.com**).

Indexing

If you're writing a non-fiction book, you'll want to create an index. A book without one will be taken far less seriously by the book trade and *certainly* by librarians, who can generate big, *non-returnable* sales for you. You'll want to create a "galley insert sheet" (ⓔ). On that sheet, I write: "Backmatter: Appendices, Index." Librarians who read those reviews look for this "Index" notation, and are far more likely to take on a book with one than without.

Do what I did and hire it out. On my first book, I tried to create it myself, using the indexing function in Microsoft *Word*. A mistake, for two reasons. For starters, it took me *forever* to do it—many days, enormous frustration, and beaucoup gray hairs. But, adding serious insult to injury, once I turned the manuscript over to my typesetter, given the different operating platform and repagination, my index was worthless and he had to create a new one. Great. So, for this book, I found a professional indexer. (Note: some practitioners do both typesetting and indexing, which could streamline the process).

Indexing is your *final* step—after your typesetter's done. Once you get the index back, send it to your typesetter and have her drop it in. To find an indexer, check out *The American Society of Indexers* (**www.asindexing.org**). Sites for authors in Canada, the UK, and Australia/New Zealand are noted in Appendix A. Or you might like to try the PMA (The Independent Book Publishers Association) resources link on their site (**www.pma-online.org**).

An index can run $750 to 1000, which is cheap, given the hassle it saves you. The going rate is roughly $3 a page, but the person I worked with (Appendix A for contact details) didn't charge full rate for graphics pages, pages with lots of white space, and pages that needed only one listing (e.g., a sample press release that covered two pages only needed one listing and hence was not even counted as one full page). And it's a fast process: you can usually get one turned around in under a week.

Last-Minute Marketing

The very end of your book is the place for a final marketing tool. If you're working on an upcoming book, you might consider including an excerpt from that book at the very end as a "teaser." I plugged this book in my previous effort, *TWFW: Back For Seconds*. Keep your loyal reader base anticipating upcoming works. They want to know. I put my teaser right before my index, and included it in my Table of Contents as an appendix.

Binding and Pricing

Spiral-Bound Books?

The default standard binding for "trade paperback" books (the kind I do) is called "perfect binding." It's how the overwhelming bulk of books in that market segment are bound. Every now and then, someone asks me about spiral binding on books. What's my take? Will it hurt sales?

Here's the scoop, directly from my printer, BookMasters. If you have a book that you want to lie flat when open (e.g., cookbooks, exercise workbooks, etc.), then obviously you'd be exploring some kind of alternative to the normal "perfect" binding found on most trade paperbacks. You've got roughly three choices and it depends on how you plan to market your book.

COMB BINDING

This is the plastic comb-type binding you see commonly, say, on regional cookbooks.

Pluses: You can print on the smooth surface of the binding, which means that when all you see is the spine on a bookshelf, you can read the title. As such, it can be a good option whether you're selling it in bookstores or just through personal sales (talks, seminars, charity fundraisers, etc).

Minuses: when the book lies flat, the facing pages are often uneven. And it can be costly in large numbers, as these books often have to be hand-fed into binding machines.

DOUBLE WIRE-O BINDING

Pluses: This binding actually has two wires threading through each hole, which aligns side-by-side pages more accurately. Fine for personal sales, where bookstores won't be involved.

Minuses: You can't print on this kind of binding, so bookstores seriously frown on carrying books like these. Like the comb binding, books often have to be hand-fed into binding machines, jacking up the costs for larger numbers.

OTABIND™ BINDING

Pluses: Arguably, the best of both worlds. It looks like a "perfect" binding, so spine printing is fine, and bookstores are happy. And it lies flat, just like your different spiral binding options.

Minuses: it costs a little more, but if the "lie-flat" quality is important, it's not obnoxiously expensive.

Pricing Your Book

As with cover design ideas, go visit the bookstores and see what similar books cost. If there are none like yours, then look for books of similar scope. That should give you a good starting point. In my case, I departed a little from the prevailing numbers. For a 300-page book on writing, I was seeing prices in roughly the $14.95 to $17.95 range. Nonetheless, I went ahead and priced mine at $19.95. My thinking was that my offering wasn't just a 300-page book. It was a step-by-step blueprint for a new career, and as such, I could get away with pricing it higher.

"6 x PPB"

You could make the case that that's a clueless point of view and that the cold, cruel market is profoundly indifferent to what *you* think about your book. Perhaps, Econ 101 says a lower price would've sold more books, but how many? You've got to decide how your book fits into what's out there already. That said, there *is* a general rule of thumb: "6 x PPB." Translation: price your book at roughly four to six times the cost of your paper, printing, and binding. While four might work, six is ideal. In my case, my PPB was down to roughly $1.50 a book (5000+ unit print runs), so I was sitting mighty pretty with the formula either way. Needless to say, it starts becoming an issue if you're talking about printing smaller quantities, or books that are more expensive to produce.

Trim Size

As mentioned, most self-publishers (including me) do trade paperbacks. It's far and away the most common edition of books published today in general. Hardback books—with a paperback edition following a year later—are generally reserved for high-profile fiction titles or mainstream non-fiction topics. If you're doing a shorter print run to start (1000-3000), where per units costs are higher, think long and hard about whether going the hard-cover route makes sense, given how much more cost that'll add.

So, what trim size (dimensions) should you go with? Again, it depends on your book, but some standard sizes are 5½ x 8½, 6 x 9, and 8½ x 11 (all in inches, of course), and in the case of specialty books, you might see 4 x 6. While the most common (and least expensive) would be 5½ x 8½, I did my books as 6 x 9. It's only a tiny bit more expensive than 5½ x 8½, but that extra ½" height and width makes it stand out on a shelf just a bit more. And as self-publishers, we're all about standing out, right? You better believe it.

Your Print Runs: Galley and Offset

Galleys

In the process of bringing your book to market, you'll be printing twice: your "galley" run and your main offset print run. A galley is a pre-publication version of the book, also known as an "advance uncorrected proof." You should actually have these words printed on the front and back covers (top or bottom). This is so certain key reviewers, who we'll discuss shortly, and who need to see your book well before it's actually released, won't confuse it with the final printed version, which would make it too late for them. Inside the front cover, you'll tape the "galley insert sheet" we discussed earlier.

The first use for your galleys is to collect advance endorsements (i.e., the "blurbs" we discussed earlier) for your final edition—front and back covers and inside front pages—from key names in your industry. Figure out how many pages up front you want to devote to blurbs and then leave those blank when you print your galleys.

ADVANCE CORRECTED PROOF

Yes, the phrase "advance uncorrected proof" means it can still have typos. However, as I see it, you have to proof it at some point anyway; might as well do it before you print *any* books. Two benefits here. First, you usually only have to slot in the blurbs you receive from your first-line reviewers (and any typos caught in that process) before you're ready for your final offset print run. Second, it's one more way you make your self-published book look like anything but. Remember, we have to work harder than the conventionally published crowd. It's just another little way (like putting four-color final cover artwork on our galleys) we can set ourselves apart.

In Chapter Four, we'll delve further into other uses for those galleys, but suffice it to say, you'll be using them for some pre-promo efforts.

On my first book, I used Publishers' Graphics (**www.pubgraphics.com**) to print my galleys, while on my second, my large-run printer BookMasters (**www.bookmasters.com**) handled my galley run as well. Both did a great job. Some printers specialize in short run printings (I only had 100 galleys printed), others in long runs, and usually—but, obviously, not always—they're not that competitive in the other arena. See Appendix A for contact info on galley printers.

As a rule, galleys are digital, meaning you're going from computer to printing press, skipping the plate-making step used in the offset printing process. This technology, which is at the heart of print-on-demand (POD) technology, allows for the cost-effective printing of far smaller quantities (roughly 50 to 1000) than offset runs. The quality of digital printing is a hair below offset, but certainly good enough for our purposes here.

A month or so before you're ready to print your galleys, you'll verify with your galley printer the format in which they need to receive your files, and let your typesetter and cover designer know (they should know already, but just cover the base). Once you're ready, have those two send their files directly (and separately) to the galley printer. It's usually by snail mail, or a combination of email and snail mail.

GALLEY = FINAL

In theory, galleys can span the gamut in terms of aesthetics and production quality. They can be downright austere, with typed black-and-white covers, or even as primitive as "F&G" (folded and gathered pages). Or they can look identical to the final version—which is what I strongly recommend.

Stephen King or Tom Clancy could print galleys on a stack of cocktail napkins and reviewers would probably be fine with it. As self-publishers, we're already behind the eight ball with the review publications. Overcome their institutionalized reluctance to review self-published books by making your book look like anything *but* a self-published book. That means four-color galleys that basically mirror the appearance of the final edition.

Your Offset Print Run

When it's time to go to print, let's make sure we get the most for our money. Just cruise the aisles of any publishing trade show and you'll quickly realize the competitive reality of the printing business. Lots of companies fiercely vying for their slice of a finite pie. That means only one thing: *printing prices are negotiable.* Do your homework—get multiple quotes.

If you've decided you want to work with a particular company, keep getting quotes from others, and if your #1 is higher, ask them to match or beat it. If they want your business (and believe me, they do), they will.

I found this out the hard way. I shake my head at the memory. I was mentoring a novice self-publisher through the process, someone who was particularly green about many things. But one area on which she absolutely *had* done her homework was printing prices.

Mr. Know-Nothing

She had me look over her final quote from her printer (same as mine)—for a book which was virtually identical to mine in every regard—page length, paper quality, print run, cover stock, etc. Mr. Had-It-All-Figured-Out smugly reviewed this estimate from the "newbie," and his jaw hit the floor. She'd gotten a price for a 5,000-unit run of 10% lower than the price I'd been paying for five printings already! Whoa.

Well, I'll give you two guesses who I called next. I wasn't mad at my printer. They're in business to maximize profits like everyone else, and as such, aren't obligated to offer you the lowest price if you're not pushing them—with rivals' quotes in hand—to do so. But, needless to say, from that point forward, I was paying lower rates.

Moral of the story: get plenty of competing quotes. To dramatically streamline and simplify that process, check out *Printellectual* (**www.Printellectual.com**), billed as "America's best book printing quote collective."

I won't get into the definition of every term on a print quote, but it can certainly look like a foreign language at first glance. If you don't understand something, ask your salesperson to clarify it. That's their job if they want your business.

A Plug for BookMasters

I've been using BookMasters, Inc. in Ohio right from the beginning—for both printing (digital for my "galleys" and offset for main print runs) and fulfillment (physical warehousing and shipping of product, which we'll discuss in Chapter Six).

Eight "By-the-Ways" on the Printing Process

1) The "Paper Weight" Question I've gone with 60-pound paper (noted as 60#) as opposed to 50#, but there's not a huge difference between the two. #60 has more heft, cost, and weight, which is a consideration, shipping-wise. Ask to get samples of both and decide for yourself. Bottom line, most books are printed with 50# paper.

2) What Finish? Cover finishes can be either glossy or matte. Ask to see samples of both. I went with a matte finish, and personally think matte looks far more elegant for many books. Cost is the same. Make sure that you specify "lay-flat" film lamination. Don't let the printer substitute UV coating as "equal" to film lamination.

3) Print to the Proof When you get your galleys, make sure the colors are as vibrant as your original proof. If they don't seems as vivid, make sure you get your printer to "print to the proof" to preserve the original intensity. It won't cost any more to do so.

4) Timeframes From the time you send in your manuscript (a hard copy plus the final files from your typesetter and cover designer) to the time you're holding finished books in your hand will be roughly four to five weeks, but figure on six. Plan accordingly.

5) Proof Stage It'll take one to two days after turning in your manuscript and files for your printer to make sure that all is in order. If all is well, seven to ten days later, you'll get a proof—the final draft generated from the page plates that have been burned. You'll be asked to approve that draft, and it's at that point that the actual printing will begin.

6) Draw the Line It's a publishing law of nature that the moment your content is finalized, you start thinking of things to add, alter, or delete. But at the "blueline" stage, any edits mean a plate change, and plate changes = money. Unless it's an outright typo or some other glaring error, resist the urge to edit at this stage. It'll get very expensive.

7) Shrink From This Your print quote will likely encourage you to shrinkwrap each copy of your book (about 20 cents each). Unnecessary expense.

8) Personal Stash Once your print run is finished, if you've decided to use a fulfillment company to handle the warehousing and shipping of your books (strongly recommended as we'll explore further in a later chapter), have them send you 250 to 300 or so copies of your book for ongoing promotional purposes, review copies, personal stash, event sales, signed copy requests, contest prizes, etc. If you're hitting the promotion trail hard and consistently, you'll be amazed at how quickly you'll go through that first shipment.

Offering galley and offset printing, fulfillment and distribution makes BookMasters a relative rarity in the business (and can dramatically simplify your life). One nice plus of using them for both printing and fulfillment: no shipping cost in getting books from the printing plant to the warehouse.

Sure, in *any* relationship going on since 2000, there will be and has been the occasional and inevitable hiccup, but overwhelmingly, they've done a great job and made my life exponentially easier. Check them out at **www.bookmasters.com** or call 888-537-6727 and ask for Shelley Sapyta (x. 1130).

Sample Book Production Scenarios

In the course of soliciting feedback from readers as I put this book together, many people suggested I include sample cost breakdowns of some typical book projects. Below are a couple of possible scenarios, one for my typical print run of 5000 copies, followed by a more modest proposal if Scenario #1 is a bit rich for your blood.

Look at the first as a worst-case scenario. Yes, it can easily run you roughly $10,000-14,000+ to bring a 5,000-unit print run of a 300-page book to market, but, as mentioned earlier, there are ways to soften the blow (shorter print runs, bartering strategies for services, plain old negotiation, short-term loans, etc.). That's how you should view the second case—what it might be if you get creative. Just remember, the checks on the back end are *all* yours, no sharing necessary.

No Need to Pay "Retail"

Remember, when it comes to editors, typesetters, cover designers, etc., you can always find someone willing to do it for less. Yes, the market-priced professional practitioners out there will want my head on a platter for encouraging you to hunt for cut-rate scenarios. So, let me say this about that: if you have the bucks to spend to get the best, then do so. It's worth it.

But, if your budget doesn't allow that, you'll be on the lookout for less expensive options, whether or not I suggest it. As such, I'd just as soon help you figure out how to do it to maximize the quality of the services you're getting for less outlay. Your best bet is the plethora of online job sites (especially ones either focused on, or with substantial sections devoted to, "creatives"), where good quality service at reduced rates abounds.

In *The Well-Fed Writer: Back For Seconds*, I make the point that the online job sites are generally lousy places to land well-paying copywriting gigs. Reason being, there are always more writers than jobs, which will, as any Econ 101 student can happily explain, drive rates down to nothing. It doesn't necessarily mean that all those writers willing to do it for less are low-quality scribes (low self-respect, perhaps, or light on the experience), just as all those willing to typeset, design, or edit your book for less than market rates are not incompetents. Have a look at **www.guru.com** and **www.elance.com**: and there are others out there.

Needless to say, *caveat emptor*. Get references, check them, request and closely review samples, etc. If you hire a bargain-basement service provider, only to have to hire someone else to redo what the first guy didn't do right the first time, it's no bargain.

Disclaimers

For the first scenario, I've used a typical market rate for editing/proofreading, cover design, typesetting, indexing, and galley printing while in the second, I've assumed you'll find that hungry worker, or negotiate a deal. I've also included—under "Miscellaneous Expenses"—the various fees I discussed earlier in this chapter. Things like ISBN numbers ($240 total for 10 numbers at press time), copyright page CIP Info ($150 if you go through Quality Books, Inc.), bar code artwork ($10-30), copyright fees ($30), Baker & Taylor database fee ($245), etc.

Also, the dollar figures quoted here are only examples. They will likely approximate what typical costs for the different components may run, but get your own quotes to arrive at a meaningful number for your particular situation.

Sample Scenario #1:

Print Run: 5000 units

Pages: 304
60 lb. Paper (Text)
Four-color gloss or matte finish cover

Editing/Proofreading: $1000-1500
Cover Design: $750-1500+
Typesetting: (avg. $6-8 a page) $1000-1400
Indexing: $750
Galley Printing: $600-700 (100 copies)
Main Printing: $8500
Miscellaneous Expenses: $650+
Approximate Total: $11,900-$15,000

Sample Scenario #2:

Print Run: 3000 units
Pages: 304
50 lb. Paper (Text)
Four-color gloss or matte finish cover

Editing/Proofreading: $750-1000
Cover Design: $500-750
Typesetting: $600-800
Indexing: $300-500 (created by typesetter)
Galley Printing: $300-400 (50 copies; shopping around/negotiation)
Main Printing: $5500-6000 (possibly lower with negotiation).
Miscellaneous Expenses: $500+ (D-I-Y/Librarian-assisted PCIP data)
Approximate Total: $8,450-$9,950

On a Shoestring?

If you're unsure of the market for your book, it might be unwise to print 5,000 copies right out of the gate. Why not start with 2,000 or 3,000? And yes, while you'll pay a much higher unit cost for your books than at the 5,000 level, it could mean bringing your biggest line-item cost within the realm of possibility. That said, keep in mind the "6 x PPB" pricing formula discussed earlier. Obviously, smaller print runs mean higher per-unit costs.

One thousand copies still a bit rich? Then consider a short-run printer – a company that specializes in runs of 50 to 1000 books. Find a struggling but talented graphic artist who's starting out (contact local art schools and ask the teachers for the names of some talented students), and get him to do your cover design and typesetting for below-market rates. No, you might not get the quality of an established market-rate practitioner, but if it accomplishes your goal of getting a printed book into your hands cost-effectively, it could be a good place to start.

Safe Numbers

Ron Pramschufer, maestro of **www.publishingbasics.com** (and **www.selfpublishing.com**, his printing arm; check it out for instant online quotes), and 35-year publishing veteran shared this tidbit with me: "According to a Book Industry Study Group (www.bisg.org) report a few years back, the average page count is 256 and the average print run is 3000. *At that page count and quantity, virtually every discount scenario works.*" (italics mine) Bottom line, according to a guy who would know, quantities of 3000+ of an average-length book should keep you good with the "6 x PPB" formula.

As for shorter-run (under 3,000 units) scenarios, let's be frank. There's a decent chance that your unit costs may not fit the "6 x PPB" formula. Meaning that in these cases, while you'll certainly be fine for "back-of-the-room" sales and sales opportunities on your own, making it work in the larger trade distribution scheme of things—where the discounts are hefty—might be challenging. Keep this reality in mind as you move forward with your own particular strategy. Bottom line, the game favors those who jump in with both feet and print higher numbers.

By the way, speaking of Ron Pramschufer, check out **www.selfpublishing.com** site, where you can get instant online print quotes (at press time, as far as he knew, the only one offering this). And his prices are really excellent. He's not out to play back-and-forth price games, so this no-haggle pricing. And apparently, he's getting into the fulfillment game as well. Tell him I sent you and he'll take extra good care of you.

A Marketing Wizard of "Oz"

Speaking of strategies to lower your upfront costs… My editor Geoff shared a story he'd heard from one of his clients in Australia about an author who put together a book of inspiring stories, affirmations, and photos related to the healthcare field (e.g., people overcoming life-threatening situations, etc.). The author then went out and sold advertising in a 16-page pre-release promotional flyer (featuring the cover of the book along with excerpts and testimonials) to likely suspects such as drug companies and private health care organizations. The advertising proceeds completely paid for the hefty initial print run of both book and flyer. Nice.

In addition, this enabled the author to set up a phenomenal circuit of promotional appearances with prequalified audiences eagerly awaiting the book. As a final coup de grace, this marketing-savvy scribe also hooked up with a well-known charitable foundation, and cut a deal to donate a certain percentage of all proceeds to charity, which in turn, opened up BIG markets for the book in the charitable circles.

If you've SP'ed intelligently, and have healthy margins to work with, you can afford to be generous. Remember, 75% of your normal profit on a chunk of business you wouldn't have had otherwise is way better than 100% of far less. All of which begs the question: Would a traditional publisher have the smarts, the inclination, or resources to craft such deals?

Okay, we've got us a book. Now, how do we start using all we learned about sales and marketing (gulp) in Chapter Two and let the world know all about it? Right this way…

Chapter 4

There's a wry observation that circulates in the book biz underscoring the daunting marketing challenges facing self-publishing authors: *Writing the book is the easy part.* Now, don't go screaming into the night. Just see it as a reminder that as self-publishers, we have not chosen an easy road. Potentially highly rewarding? Oh, yes. Easy? No.

That said, here's the good news: without question, the process gets easier over time, *and* it's definitely frontloaded. You'll be working much harder in the beginning as you get the book produced and the marketing machine cranked up, than you will to keep the whole thing humming along. Furthermore, the marketing process isn't very difficult, and certainly not beyond the intelligence of someone who, after all, is smart enough to write a book! But, it's a lot of work. Let's go figure out how to make it easier.

Blanketing Your Audience

A few years back—I'll never forget the day—I was checking my email and I got another book order notification. I had a little information capture mechanism that asked for name, email address (for future mailings) and where they heard about the book. Her answer? "Everywhere!" Music to an author's ears. And proof that I was getting the job done.

That was only the start. I kept hearing different iterations of the same theme. One woman wrote: "I first heard about your book on writersdigest.com, then on writerswrite.com and finally on writersweekly.com. After the third time, I figured I needed to see what it was all about." What does that tell us (besides that I'd been busy)? People need multiple impressions before they take action. Exceptionally useful information.

Another buyer sent me this note:

I attend a Wednesday morning writers group. My first time, I asked the girl next to me, can you really support yourself at this? And she said, "You need to get 'The Well-Fed Writer.'" So, a month later I met another girl and asked her the same question and she gave me the same response. And recently, I gave my copy of your book to a friend and ordered another!

Yee-hah.

Given where this woman, and countless others, heard about my book (on the Internet), you think it'd be a good idea to take full advantage of this amazing tool? In the hugely competitive scramble for attention in the book world, the 'net really can be the great equalizer for the little guy. Not to mention that it's meant dramatically enhanced productivity, allowing for maximum accomplishment and "reach" in minimum time.

NOTE: A Different Approach

As discussed earlier, the marketing approach that I took with my books is a departure from normal book marketing strategies, which emphasize the pursuit of mainstream media (MM) attention. Courting MM absolutely makes sense for authors whose books cover a mainstream subject (love/relationships/sex, religion, diet/health, money/finances, parenting, etc.).

My book wasn't in that bracket, and I offer up my blueprint to those authors who find themselves with a similarly "niche" title. Frankly, if you're an unknown author with a niche subject, the blunt reality is that the mainstream media doesn't care much about you.

Sure, even niche-subject authors should still be on the lookout for topical, relevant "news pegs" that connect your book with a larger subject of broad public interest, so you can make occasional inroads into traditional media channels (more on this in Chapter Eight). Though the further you have to reach with those pegs while still linking to your book, the more newsworthy the peg becomes, and less so your book.

Regardless, given the limited amount of time available for the solo or small-shop self-publisher to handle a never-ending list of tasks, it makes much more sense to chase the attention of very targeted (and hence, more receptive) web-based entities whose members fit one of your book's audience profiles, rather than beat your head against the wall trying to catch the attention of the infinitely more fickle and broad-based MM Monster.

Unless I'm going to a city to do a seminar (in which case I contact the local media, since I'm now *incrementally* more newsworthy, and might get lucky with a bit of coverage), I don't mess with them. But, even if you have a mainstream title, I assert you can get even more promotional mileage out of it by pretending it's a niche book as well (more on this at the end of the chapter: pp. 87-89).

As we covered in the intro, remember your #1 job (**Build the Demand for Your Book**), zero in on the key influencers for your target audiences, and focus on taking massive action.

ID Your Audiences

Okay, let's take my first book as an example: *The Well-Fed Writer: Financial Self-Sufficiency as a Freelance Writer in Six Months or Less*—a step-by-step how-to for establishing a lucrative full- or part-time freelance corporate writing business. With all the downsizing of the past decade, Corporate America is outsourcing plenty of writing projects at hourly rates of $50-100+.

Okay, so who are my audiences? For starters, how about any and all aspiring writers looking to make a handsome living with their pen? You, perhaps? ☺ Add seasoned freelancers (magazine articles, short stories, grants, etc.), looking to diversify into higher-paying work. At-home-Moms, 55+ career-changers and "retirees" (in quotes because no one really retires anymore, do they?), and home-based business seekers—all looking for a flexible, high-paying career that they can pursue from home. There are a lot of sub-audiences as well, such as current or ex-journalists, academics, scientists, engineers, marketing professionals, and more. But I'll focus on writers of all stripes, at-home-Moms and home-based business seekers.

Have you determined your audiences? If you're writing non-fiction, ask yourself, *Who would be the most likely readers of my book?* Or put another way, *To whom would my subject be especially appealing?* Given that you decided to write a book in the first place, after determining that there were audiences for it, chances are you had at least some sense of the demographics of those audiences, right?

Think hard. Some audiences may be obvious to you, but others may only occur to you after digging deep. When I began the process, writers were obvious. Less obvious, but right on the heels of writers, were the Moms and home-biz crowds. Later, I realized that the 55+ crowd and academics (frustrated professors of English, MFA grads, etc.) might find value in my books.

Who Likes What?

How did I arrive at each of these potential markets? By understanding that there were different "points of appeal"—distinct facets to the message in my books, each of which would appeal to different people. Obviously, writers love the idea that they can do what they love and make good money at it. An at-home Mom finds the topic appealing because here's a field where she can leverage her past career experience into a flexible, lucrative, sideline income.

For her, it's about the nature of the opportunity; the writing is secondary. Ditto for the home-based business seeker, who loves the idea that he can work out of his home. The 55+ crowd? Several things: the ability to leverage a career's worth of experience, the flexibility to do it on their own terms, more time for family, etc.

What are your book's "points of appeal"? Spend some time looking at your subject from different angles, and see what you come up with.

Go to Your Market

OK, we've established the audiences. Now what? Well, my email-based marketing campaign had two parts. First was the hunt for blurbs, which we discussed earlier. That "Audience ID" process will determine the folks you approach for those blurbs. Once I had the 25 blurb commitments, out went the galleys to these folks to begin the process of gathering their (hopefully) glowing comments.

First-Line Reviewers

There are a number of publications that need to see your book well before its "official publication date" (OPD). Getting reviewed in one or more of them can get the early buzz going, and end up selling lots of books for you. The main ones are:

Booklist—**www.ala.org/booklist/**

Library Journal—**www.libraryjournal.com**

Publishers Weekly—**www.publishersweekly.com**

ForeWord magazine—**www.forewordmagazine.com**

Kirkus Reviews—**www.kirkusreviews.com**

Incidentally, *ForeWord* is dedicated to independent publishers, so you absolutely need to contact them. All these entities want review copies (galleys OK) 90-120 days prior to your OPD, making an even stronger case for an extended period between your "bound book date" (or BBD; when you have printed books in your possession) and the OPD. Once your book is officially released, it's too late for this group. Don't miss that window.

FYI, on the *Publishers Weekly* site, it says, *"We do not review self-published books unless there is a first printing of 2,000 or greater, and an arrangement with a reputable distributor, in which case we will take the book under consideration."*

Another potential review publication that also needs to see books or galleys early is *Book Page* (**www.bookpage.com/guidelines.html**). These folks also say they don't review self-published books, but I'd say just go for it. Just make sure your publishing company sounds *bona fide* (again, not "Joe Blow Publishing"), and your book looks exceptionally professional in terms of its production quality. They might still bust you, but I'd love to have them figure it out after the review's been printed. Why do they have such a policy? Same reason others do: because they've found most self-published books to be amateurish. And most are. So, be different, and surprise them.

Shortcut to Big Library Sales

Librarians in particular make big use of the above-mentioned publications (except *Book Page*, which isn't library-related). With limited budgets and time, librarians rely heavily on these industry pubs to do their pre-screening for them, often ordering *all* books reviewed. They figure that if a book's made the cut (only 10-15 percent of those submitted get reviewed), even if it's not a fabulous review, it's a noteworthy book that deserves to be on their shelves. And remember: library sales are final. No returns.

Land a review in *Booklist* (the publication of *The American Library Association*), *Library Journal, ForeWord* magazine, or *Publishers Weekly*, and you'll sell a ton of books to the libraries and nicely boost the credibility of your title.

As mentioned, only 10-15 percent of all books submitted get reviewed. But, that's not exactly lottery odds. Especially when you consider that of the 150,000 new books released each year, a huge chunk of them are, without a doubt, of pretty mediocre quality (both the writing and physical aesthetics). It's just not terribly hard to stand out if you do a few things right.

Improve Your Odds

You'll boost your chances of getting reviewed in one of these five publications by doing some things we've already discussed: writing a good book that will appeal to a fairly broad audience, putting some serious thought and expense into your cover and title, and doing four-color galleys virtually indistinguishable from the final edition.

I remember having a lively, upbeat phone chat with a review editor at *Booklist*. She'd received my galley (but didn't have it in front of her) and asked me nonchalantly who my publisher was. I should have simply given her the name of my self-publishing entity, Fanove Publishing, and spoken of it as if it were separate from me.

But she caught me flat-footed, and being the lousy liar that I am, I mumbled— "me." Long pause. "Oh. Really. Well…we rarely, if ever, review self-published books." Yet, they still did. As did *Library Journal* and *ForeWord*. And the fact is, a lot of self-published books have gotten reviewed in these pubs.

Hopefully, you'll be a bit smoother than I was if asked the same question: "Oh, a small publishing house here in (your city)." And if you're Joe Smith, make sure you haven't named your publishing entity Joe Smith Enterprises or JS Publishing. You'll instantly identify yourself as a self-publisher—and an amateur one at that.

Of course, writing a book called *The Well-Fed Self-Publisher* makes it a little hard to hide the fact that it's a self-published book. Now the whole world, including the world of reviewers, knows my secret. The gig's up, I guess.

Why "Fanove" Publishing?

So, how did I come up with the name *Fanove* for my publishing entity? Well, about six months before I finished my first book, I found myself dragging my feet. One day, I was flipping through a fun book, *Le Mot Just* (The Right Word), a compendium of phrases and idioms that we've imported into English from other languages such as Latin, Greek, French and Italian (e.g., ad hoc, quid pro quo, ciao, etc.). While nosing around in the Latin section, I came across *facta non verba*, which, loosely translated, means "actions, not words." In essence, "Stop talking about it and do it!" Well. Pretty fitting for where I was. I simply took the first two letters of each of the three words and voila! *Fanove*. And since I created the word, I get to say how it's pronounced: fah-NOH-vay. ☺

The Book Sense Program

In the same "early review" category is a unique (and potentially very promotionally juicy) program called *Book Sense*. Sponsored by the *American Booksellers Association* (**www.bookweb.org**), *Book Sense* targets independent booksellers, who can be a self-publisher's best friend. If indies like a book, they spread the word. These folks like to see advance copies as well, also before "official" publication, and they'll let you know by email if they're interested in looking at your title.

Cost to participate is $100, though if you join PMA (**www.pma-online.org**) or SPAN (**www.spannet.org**), it only costs $50. Send your check to: American Booksellers Association, 828 S. Broadway, Tarrytown, NY 10591, Attn: Sadie Evans. Or pay by credit card with Sadie at 914-591-2665. For full details, visit: **www.bookweb.org/booksense/publisher/3311.html**.

Getting Reviews—Job #1

Okay, now that you've got the crucial early reviewers out of the way, it's time to focus on the ongoing job of garnering reviews from aaaaaaaaaalll the other review entities out there. After I secured my blurbs, I simply crafted a slightly different email pitch than the one I used for that process, and repeated the pitch process over and over (See Appendix B), soliciting reviews, interviews, promo blurbs, mentions, permissions to write an article, and other placements. I repeated this process roughly 350+ times over a few years.

Yes, I know that sounds scary, but if you hit it hard on the front end, you'll likely be knocking a third or more of those out in the first few months. Remember the "front-loaded" thing.

REVIEWS & ARTICLES SELL BOOKS

Shoot for reviews and article placements—far and away the cheapest and most effective way to build demand and sales. To find targets for all these efforts, go where your various target communities hang out. Scour the Internet for web sites, associations, newsletters, ezines, and newsgroups that cater to folks in your target audiences.

For associations: **www.ipl.org/div/aon**, **www.marketingsource.com/associations**, or **www.weddles.com/associations/index.htm** for starters. Google "Associations" or "Directory of Associations." For links to magazine, newspaper, and ezine directories, check out p. 159 in Chapter Nine. Articles are usually easier to land than reviews, especially in online venues, where they're far hungrier for content than print pubs (and where space isn't an issue). But while you're there, why not suggest a review, interview, mention, or even a book giveaway along with the article?

PLAY "GUESS-THE-SITE"

Try any URLs that sound right. For me? writers.com, writing.com, freelancewriting.com, athomemoms.com, homebusiness.com, etc. Got a parenting book? Try parenting.com, parents.com, raisingkids.com, etc. If you can think of it, chances are, someone else has.

Do straight Google searches as well. I might hunt for "Writers Groups – California," "At-Home Mom Publications," or "Home-Based Business Web Sites." Are you promoting an additional book in your same genre (like I was with my second book)? Google your name and/or earlier related titles. What'll likely show up are reviews and articles. Many you'll already have noted on your list, but there are always some new ones you didn't contact the first time around, but who reviewed your book anyway. How's that? Well, I'll explain in "The Marketing Boomerang" a few pages ahead…

OTHER REVIEWERS

For an exceptionally juicy list of additional review copy targets, visit this link on The Midwest Book Review site: **www.midwestbookreview.com/links/ othr_rev.htm**.

As touched on earlier, while I had a standard pitch letter I used in my marketing (Appendix B), I tailored it to speak to my various audiences (writers, at-home Moms, home-based business seekers, 55+'ers, etc.), each of which had different hot buttons. For example...

Answering Objections in Advance

While writers in general respond to the money/freedom angle, when I'm pitching fiction writing groups and sites on reviewing my book, or general writing conferences (which cater largely to fiction writers) to land presentation gigs, I try to get into their mind and think about how they'd react to a book like mine. Remember *audience*.

Frankly, to this crowd, steeped as they are in the creative world, commercial writing might be viewed, at best, as irrelevant to their world, and, at worst, as the redheaded stepchild of the writing business (read: sellout). So, like any good salesperson, *I answer their objection before it comes up*, so that, hopefully, they'll keep reading. In addition to covering the key points I'd make in any pitch, I'll include verbiage like this:

Let's be honest: most commercial writing isn't as sexy and exciting as other writing of a more literary flavor, but financial realities force many to pursue their writing on the side, after their "day job." Yet, with hourly rates for freelance commercial writing ranging from $50-125+ ($60-80 is typical), this can effectively become that "day job" (as it's been for me for the past twelve years) or at least a healthy supplement. Not to mention vastly superior freedom and flexibility, giving writers the crucial time and "financial space" to pursue our writing passions.

Credible Voices

When I'm addressing the home-based business crowd, I'll tailor that letter with audience-specific verbiage (bold below for emphasis), and include testimonials from some prominent home-based business experts—names that will mean something to them:

*This award-winning book (see email signature) is a very detailed how-to for quickly breaking into the lucrative (avg. hourly rates: $60-80) and surprisingly accessible arena of freelance commercial writing—**a bona fide home-based business opportunity.** As Corporate America has downsized, it has outsourced much of its creative needs, making this particular writing direction more viable and profitable than ever before.*

Upping the Sophistication

For the 55+ crowd, my latest target audience, I solicited stories from active 55+ commercial writers amongst my ezine subscribers about how the commercial writing field has been a fit for their lives. I compiled their wonderful feedback into an article about the field that never mentioned the books until the attribution paragraph right at the end. Check out the article and a host of offshoot pieces at the *Attn: 55+* link at **www.wellfedwriter.com**.

In going after this audience, I crafted a more sophisticated campaign than I had previously, and one that could serve as a stronger template for other targeted promotional efforts. What I did was put together a marketing letter (Ⓔ) to editors of publications—or sections of daily newspapers—catering to the 55+ demographic. Then I secured a list of 150 of these entities from **www.KSBPromotions.com**.

I split up the list, emailed half, snail-mailed the other half, and then reversed it, hitting all the non-responders again with the other contact mode to maximize response rates. I got a decent response, nothing to set the world on fire, though at press time, they're still coming in. Point is, keep trying different strategies, and see what works best.

Talking to Authors

When my second book was released, I sent it off for review by Independent Publisher (**www.independentpublisher.com**), the entity which, by the way, sponsors the annual IPPY Awards honoring independent publishers (that'd be us…). The editor wrote back that he liked it enough to want to feature it in a focused section on writing titles he was running a few months later. He wanted a news release that would resonate with his readers (mostly authors), and after some back and forth, I sent him one with this headline and lead:

NEW BOOK HELPS WRITERS LEVERAGE "PUBLISHED AUTHOR" STATUS INTO LUCRATIVE COMMERCIAL FREELANCING

ATLANTA, GA—July 22, 2004—You've written a book or two, maybe more. So what now? Royalties not quite enough to pay the bills? Well, a new book floats the tantalizing prospect of leveraging your "Published Author" status into high-paying "commercial" freelancing.

FYI, when I got his draft back to review for accuracy, he'd used the release almost verbatim, as well as a half dozen questions from my FAQs link, also verbatim. You'd be amazed at how often a reviewer will just take your written words and run with them. We love that. After all, it's exactly what you want to say about your book, so if they want to use it because it saves them time, we don't mind. And the key is having it in "cut 'n pasteable" electronic format. Do what you have to do to make it easy for a reviewer to say yes.

That might also mean including a "mock review" (great idea from Dan Poynter): a review that *you* write as you'd ideally like to see it written. It's something you can include in your press kit accompanying your review copies. Kind of a borderline surreal concept, but you'll be amazed at how often large chunks of that review, if not the whole thing, will make it into the publication venue. Though, given how busy everyone is these days, maybe it's not amazing at all. Do make up a few versions and rotate them. Given that our goal is multiple impressions, if readers keep seeing the same verbiage showing up in distinct venues, it might start looking suspicious...

Be an RCP (Review Copy Pushover)

Given how "easy" I am about sending someone a review copy, have I likely been scammed out of a free book now and then? No question. But, to send out a review copy costs me less than $5 (including book, mailer, postage and press kit) for the very best form of advertising I could possibly use: the book itself. If I get even one actual bookstore/Amazon sale as a result, it's paid for itself almost twice over. If that sale is off my site, now we're up to a three-fold payback. Plus, another book is out there in someone's hands, with all that word-of-mouth potential.

And take it a step further. Even when someone hasn't asked for a book, think about why sending one might be a smart idea. A few months back, I threw an audaciously self-serving offer out in my monthly newsletter: *Want some cards to spread the word on my work (for your friends, writers groups, etc.)?* And had a few takers. Including a guy who ran a large writers group out west, who also asked me if I'd like to be a presenter at their spring conference, all expenses paid.

I wrote him back, and given that he'd asked for 40 cards (cool "book business cards" described in Chapter Fourteen) to hand out to his group, I asked if he'd like a few signed copies for the next meeting. Of course he did, and it made the card handout *much* juicier. Not only are there goodies (a drawing, maybe?), which had me look like a good guy, but everyone there got to paw through the actual books. Think I sold a few more? So, be prepared to give a little. You may be surprised at where it leads.

Serendipitous Advertising

Let me share an email I got from a buyer of my first book that underscores not only the importance of a good cover and title (yet again), but also the power of getting the books into people's hands. Literally.

In Barnes & Noble, I picked a book off the shelf because the cover was an eye-catching orange and had the words "Well-Fed" and "Writer" in the same title. I take it up to the cafe and give it a real evaluation; I know how to get the most book-bang for my buck. A gentleman stops me, "Where did you get that

book?" "In the writing section," I reply. "Do you think they have any more?"
"I don't know."

A few moments later, another voice, "There's a book called 'The Well-Fed Writer'? Is there another copy?" I had the last copy in the store and I was afraid if I took my eye off it for a moment I'd lose it. I bought it and quickly left the store, hiding it in my black bag. If your sales jump suddenly in New York you can thank me. This pattern of spontaneous inquiries continued on buses, subways, in courthouses, and theatres all over New York. The title is genius.

Think I didn't just love every word of this? It had me thinking about how to get free copies of books into people's hands in return for them reading them in very PUBLIC places, without attracting all the mooches in the world...

Books as Seeds...

At the risk of sounding "new-agey" here, you need to alter your relationship with your books. Develop a split personality. On the one hand, each copy potentially represents (in my case), say, $20. On the other hand, even though, as a self-publisher, you're paying the bills, your book costs very little to produce (about $2.50 in my case, delivered): exceptionally cheap marketing tools.

Yes, they're your babies and precious and all that, but think of them as dandelions in their cottony seed-ball stage. Each book you send out, if the recipient really enjoys it, is like blowing the seeds to the wind in a "promotion explosion." They'll tell others, and often, *many* others. It's absolutely worked that way with mine. This is all part of developing a marketing mindset when it comes to your book. Let word of mouth advertising work its magic for you, and the only way to do that is to have lots of books out there—even free ones. Unless your books are very expensive to produce, don't be stingy.

Let Other Authors Sell You

Then, of course, there are writers of related books. When contacting these folks for blurbs or reviews, get in touch with your inner Sherlock Holmes. Look up their book on Amazon and just drill down from the main book profile page to find a personal email address. Or google the author's name to find their web site (most have one), where you're sure to find their address. Don't count on a blinking marquee on the home page (they're not *trying* to fill up their email in-box), but if you hunt, you should find it. My email address is in a few places on my site, but visitors have to scout around just a bit.

Okay, once you locate all these target sites, find the "Contact Us" link and make your standard pitch for a review, mention, article placement, etc. Again, make up one standard pitch letter, vary it slightly for your different audiences, and cut 'n paste. Yes, with all these web-based resources, you could be compiling lists until the wee hours, but you'll be amazed at how many people you can actually reach, quickly and cheaply.

Over and Over and Over Again...

Remember the idea of multiple impressions we discussed at the beginning of the chapter?

John Kremer, independent publishing guru and author of the seminal work *1001 Ways to Market Your Books,* has this to say about that: *In publicity, there is a rule called the Rule of Seven. It states that if you want your prospects to take action and buy your product or use your service, you need to connect with them at least seven times within an 18-month period.*

Those impressions could be a review, an article—print- or web-based—an interview, store display, a recommendation from a friend, a chat room mention, a book signing, etc. Kremer continues: *Once in a while, you get lucky and make a sale the first time someone sees your book, but it is far more likely that it will take five, ten, or even twenty impressions before someone is moved to buy.* Don't keep count—just assume you're never done getting the word out. Make it a habit and it won't loom so large.

A "BIG One" is Still ONE

Which brings me to another point. I never focus on one review like a triumph. Sure, if I can get one in *Writer's Digest, The Writer,* or some big daily paper, wonderful. But I'm always thinking numbers. I *know* that one review, no matter how big or high-profile, means almost nothing in the big scheme of things. Too many authors languish in poverty and obscurity because they think like writers, not businesspeople. They have an over-inflated sense of the importance of their work to the average person.

Well, guess what? The average person doesn't care about anything except his or her own life. To get people to the point where they actually interrupt their routine to buy your book, you need to have "touched" them multiple times with your promotion efforts. They need to have seen something about your book in a bunch of places (and had it speak to some need/desire in them) until finally, they say *OK, I need to check this thing out.* Isn't that how it usually works when you buy a book?

Back to Earth...

I have a friend who self-published a book a few years back and had gotten the local Atlanta daily newspaper to do a feature on her. In her newbie naïvete, she was sure that this was going to sell her a gazillion books. My comment to her? *That's nice. Should be good for a few hundred books, at best. Now do it about 300-400 times more.*

Prior to our conversation, and based on that *one,* albeit high-profile media hit, she'd decided to do a first print run of 10,000 copies. Knowing what the realistic impact of that story would likely be, I practically begged her to print no more than 5,000 (even that was pushing it). While she was skeptical, she grudgingly agreed. Four months later, she called me up, miserably grateful for my advice. The article hadn't delivered anywhere near the windfall she'd expected (unh-huh), had only resulted in a few hundred sales, and man oh man, it sure was proving hard to move those 5,000 copies…Is there an echo in here?

Authors don't always *get* that achieving success in this business is a marathon, an ongoing, consistent process that you've got to keep up. It's about repeating what works, over and over and over again. To think you'll be successful by getting reviewed in a few places is tragic self-delusion. Again, as mentioned earlier, you'll be working hardest in the beginning, but you still need to keep the process going—steadily and continuously.

Find the "Key Influencers"

For review copy targets, always try to think of those people who are in a position to influence a lot of others. Obviously, that's the thought behind contacting any publication, association, group, etc. to get the word out, yet the relative "reach" among these different venues varies widely. Within any niche, there are usually X# of major players who are there because they've earned the trust and attention of large swaths of your target audience, many of whom, predictably, are members of multiple entities. So, use these "opinion-makers" to help you move toward that "multiple impression" thing.

Marketing and copywriting guru Marcia Yudkin, in the April 28, 2004 issue of her weekly *Marketing Minute* ezine (subscribe at: **www.yudkin.com/ markmin.htm**), discussed this strategy in relation to her own business:

Suppose you have a budget for mailings and limited slots for lunchtime schmoozing. Dollar for dollar, hour for hour, you get the greatest return from your expenditure of money, time and energy when you focus on individuals in a position to recommend you to many, many folks.

Years ago, I sent Marketing Minute postcards to several hundred heads of speakers bureaus. Many who subscribed not only picked up tips for their own business, but also urged speakers they represented to subscribe or call me for consulting. Ditto for directors of Small Business Development Centers, who can recommend my web site, books, and newsletter week in and week out. Ditto for media people.

For your target market, who routinely comes into contact with prime potential clients? Who doesn't do what your company does but has the confidence of those who suffer from the problems you solve? Aim at people who represent a hub of influence!

BIG Opps with Little Guys

There will only be so many major influencers. Then, you're into the mass of lower-profile reviewers. But, these folks are usually a more accessible and more receptive audience. We're talking about the operators of smaller web sites, either on your subject, or with audiences that would find your topic interesting and compelling.

I say the little guys (and gals) appreciate the regard you're paying them. Because they're small, they love to get the content, and will usually bend over backwards to make sure they include all the salient contact info (i.e., your URL), which you absolutely can *not* count on a news reporter to get right or even *care* to get right. They're great links in that wonderful WOM (word-of-mouth) chain.

No, these smaller operators don't reach nearly as many people as a newspaper can but, 1) if they like the book, they'll likely tell a lot of people, and 2) exposure on a web site or in an ezine has a far longer shelf life than a one-day (or even one-week) appearance in a newspaper.

Of course, an appearance in an ezine is vastly preferable to a web site, given that it's "push" marketing: it goes *out* to someone, as opposed to a web site, where you hope people come to it. Even if the web site owners notify their base via email of the new issue, the actual piece showing up in someone's email box is always stronger.

The Gift That Keeps On Giving...

In most cases, a review, mention, blurb, Q&A, article, or interview has a permanent link on a site. Granted, that's of only limited value if someone has to dig down deep to find it, but that's where the glorious Googles of the world come in.

It's no newsflash that in this day and age, search engines are *the* preferred mode of information gathering. Meaning, your prospective buyers are harnessing Google's technology to ferret out all those hidden references to your book tucked away on dozens of sites. This assumes that the key words and phrases related to your book's subject show up in the review—a pretty good bet. Of course, if someone knows your book's title (and if you've been doing your marketing job well, they will), all the better.

A Google-generated list of, say, 20-30 impressive references can quickly move someone from researching to reaching for their wallet. Just for fun, do a Google search for "The Well-Fed Writer" or "Peter Bowerman." It's almost obnoxious. But, I'm guessing you wouldn't mind seeing your book's title showing up in that many places in .39 seconds flat.

Get Those Links

Another plus to dealing with the little guys is their willingness to swap links, which is veeeeery important. It's not just about connecting visitors to your respective sites to each other's sites; it's about climbing up in the search engine rankings. Search engines *love* links between sites, and the bigger the web you've spun between your site and the rest of the WWW, the higher up the search rankings you'll be. So, build that web.

The "One-a-Day" Plan

A simple suggestion for sending out review copies: The One-a-Day Plan. Shoot for sending out one review copy a day. Just one. Over the course of a year, that's 365. And that's a LOT. You'll definitely get things stirred up. John Kremer takes it a step further with his "Five Promotions a Day" suggestion: "All it takes is five promotions a day. Mail a letter. Send out a news release. Phone someone. Take an editor to lunch. Contact the media. It needn't take much time—15 to 20 minutes is enough—but it can make a world of difference to how well your book sells."

I think either plan is a good and sound one. Just do something—consistently. As he points out, it doesn't have to take a lot of time. Again, the "frontloaded" thing I referred to earlier. Once you have the machine up and running, it doesn't have to be a labor-intensive process.

This does *not* mean I'm advocating handing out free books indiscriminately. I did a book show a few years back, sharing a booth with a dozen or so fellow authors and members of a local writers group. I noticed one couple literally handing out copies of their book to anyone walking by who'd take one.

I suggested that maybe this wasn't the best strategy, given that they had absolutely no idea whether the passer-by was even remotely interested in the subject. Their take? Well, a few months earlier, after printing 1000 books, they'd taken out an expensive ad in a magazine that they were sure was going to lead to a windfall. They'd sold a grand total of 50 books. I'm surprised they did that well. I could have told them they were wasting their money. As a rule, unless a publication is laser-targeted to *the* precise audience for your book (and/or it's a book they absolutely *must* have, to do their job better or whatever), advertising is a lousy way to sell books. Why? People don't find advertising credible. Imagine.

In any case, that bad experience was apparently sufficient to trigger the adoption of a bold new strategy, one of just pushing the books out into the world. As they saw it, the books were all paid for, so better to get them out there than have them sitting in their garage. One way of looking at it, I suppose, though I'm not sure I follow the logic. If you ask me, they might as well have just swung by the dumpster when they left home that morning and spent the day doing something pleasant, rather than literally accosting people as they walked by and handing them a book.

No Contact, No Book

Which segues nicely into one of my cardinal rules of review copies: never send a review copy to anyone who isn't expecting one. Just to be crystal clear, *only* send books to people you've specifically sought out and asked if they'd like to receive one, OR someone who's specifically sought you out and asked you for one. Period. Sure, it's more work than mass review copy mailings, but don't fool yourself. An overwhelming percentage of recipients of unsolicited review copies will do nothing with them. Except perhaps make a quarter off it at their next garage sale.

"But," you ask, "what if I just *know* that Mary Earthmother, the editor of *Macrame Monthly* is just going to flip over my book, *Macrame Mu-Mus*, but I can't get her to return my calls or emails. Can't I send her a book?" Sure, absolutely you can send her a book. It's a free country. I'm just sayin'... Seriously, if it's a key review target, definitely cover the base, but know that the "blind sends" should be the exception, not the rule.

Review Copies Around the Globe

Don't be afraid to do a little international marketing, which means sowing review copies hither and yon. I have a nice following for my book in Canada, the UK, Australia and New Zealand. Those countries have plenty of web sites similar to those in the States catering to the same audiences. And given that the strategies I outlined in my book for starting a freelance commercial writing business have proven to be transferable to other countries, I spread the word. As long as people can get the book, and thanks to Amazon, that's usually the case, we're in business.

Of course, make sure you also have ebook versions of your works available for purchase and automatic download off your site. And when doing your international marketing, drive home the point prominently in your cover letter that those electronic versions exist. I have gotten ebook sales from literally every corner of the globe. By the way, while ebooks will likely be the preferred purchase for your international customers, send foreign reviewers an actual book, not an ebook (more on this in Chapter Thirteen).

No Reply Means Nothing

Some time back, I was following up on a review copy sent out to a radio show. I'd sent the book, and then three weeks later sent an email follow-up, but still hadn't heard anything. So, I picked up the phone and called. Got the producer on the second ring, and she said "Because I'm so busy, I almost always end up ignoring the first contact, but I always respond to the second one." She thanked me for following up and booked me on her show for about 10 days later. Follow-up absolutely works.

NOTE: It's not necessary to follow up by *phone* with every review copy recipient you haven't heard from. That could come across as a bit aggressive.

In this case, the fact that it was radio prompted my call. Radio folks expect to hear from potential guests by phone, indeed actually prefer to, since the call is a mini-audition of sorts, giving them a sense of your topic, voice, manner, and energy.

But email follow-up? Absolutely. The importance of this *cannot* be overstated. *The extent to which you diligently follow up on the review copies you send out is the extent to which you will have promotional success.* You simply can't send out review copies to people and expect that they will, unprompted, do a review, blurb, mention, Q&A, or solicit an article. Sure, it does happen, but it's just prudent to assume it won't happen unless you politely nudge them—perhaps, repeatedly—until they do so.

Follow Up, Follow Up, Follow Up...

Now, let's make a distinction here, between those folks *you* approached and those who approached you. For the first group, you should be a little less persistent than you'd be with those who knocked on your door. But regardless, in either case, there have been literally countless times where continued follow-up, often three or four times, resulted in a review. It never would've happened with just one contact, let alone with none.

Here's the thing: many folks fully intend to do a review, but hey, life gets in the way. We can all relate to that. Even that person who absolutely plans on doing a review may not get around to it if there's no reminder. But when there is, it becomes the squeaky wheel, and it's far more likely to happen.

Incidentally, the whole arena of follow-up is where you, as a self-publishing author, can do a *far* better job in maximizing your promotional efforts than a publishing company ever could. Most publishers, I promise you, simply don't have the time or resources to mount any sort of targeted campaign to get the word out on your book, much less follow up consistently with the efforts they *do* make. And that lack of follow-up can be lethal.

The Marketing Boomerang

Do enough marketing and you'll experience the delightful phenomenon I call the "marketing boomerang." In the beginning, you'll be contacting publications, web sites, associations, etc., asking if they want a review copy as you look for a little exposure. After you've done a bunch of that, you'll start getting requests for review copies from people you've never heard of *or* contacted.

Finally, after you achieve a sort of critical mass with your marketing, you'll discover, as I did, to my pleasant surprise, that readers will start contacting you, referring to publications, groups, web sites, etc. where they heard about your book—again, places you never contacted. These entities find your book on their own, buy a copy, and review it on their site or in their publication without ever even contacting you. You gotta love that.

Keep 'em Honest

For those who've approached you for a review copy, you have every right to be very...shall we say, *intentional* about getting that review, mention, blurb, article, etc. I was reminded of this recently when I did several cooperative marketing programs with PMA (The Independent Book Publishers Association: **www.pma-online.org**), where you buy a little space in a mini-catalog. While some are specifically devoted to a category like Business/Career, Children, Cookbooks, Fiction, Finance, Health/Fitness, Political, etc., others are more general, with books across the spectrum, You submit cover artwork together with a 100-word blurb.

One I did—focused on Business/Career books—had this back-page note:

Attention: Reviewers—please note

PMA, the Independent Book Publishers Association, is a non-profit association. The publishers who send you their books for review do so at their own cost with the assumption that you will take the time to read and review their product. It is our intention that this service be a benefit both to our membership, who pays for this mailing, and the reviewers, who receive these products at no cost. We ask that you respect the implied "honor system" here and request only those books that you actually intend to review.

Good for them. And for us. PMA is looking out for their publishers. Certainly, there's a bit of self-interest there. If their publisher clients shell out hundreds of dollars only to get a bunch of mooches glomming free books and never writing a review, chances are pretty good they won't write that check again. But, more importantly, it was an affirmation of our rights as authors and publishers to expect that the *quid pro quo* of sending someone a free book (or when my second book came out, often *both* books) will be honored.

Keep Knocking

So, I don't feel the slightest whiff of compunction when I send one, two, three or more notes to someone to get a review. Neither should you. Don't misunderstand. We're not talking about increasingly snarky exchanges between publisher and "deadbeat" reviewer.

As I write this, I just got a note back from a woman who requested both my books about six weeks ago. My first follow-up went unanswered. My second got a reply, saying, "Thank you for writing. I haven't had a chance to read them through yet, but they are on my agenda." I wrote back, "Thanks for replying—may I touch base again in a few months? Hope you enjoy them!" Her reply: "Sure, I'd be glad to hear from you. Thanks!"

No tension, no bad feelings, just two people communicating intentions (P.S. I got my review). If I hadn't followed up the second time, I bet I wouldn't have.

Note that I got permission to follow up again, which gives me every right to do so. As for that follow-up contact, figure out the best way to remind yourself to shoot off that email on the appointed day—tickler file, note in your Day-Timer (my approach, given my Luddite nature), Rube Goldberg-like contraption, whatever.

My Publicist

As I'll discuss in Chapter Eight as well, I've participated several times in a publicity program put together by Ada, Michigan-based publicists (and all-round good folks) Kate and Doug Bandos of KSB Promotions (**www.KSBPromotions.com**). Thrice a year, they put out *KSB Links*, a glossy pub that goes to about 8,000 media folks. Leads come in to them first, so they can gauge the success of the placement, and occasionally offer advice/cautions when they forward them on to you (e.g., "looks like a mooch…they've requested other review copies and not done reviews…no email address, you decide…," etc.).

For each placement I do, I create a file on my computer (e.g., KSBLinks1-05) and keep track of the leads. Here's a sample note emailed to the requester when I first send out the book (I keep it in the same file, along with the second-contact version as well, so it's a quick cut 'n paste):

Hi Mary,

Peter Bowerman here, author of The Well-Fed Writer and TWFW: Back For Seconds. Got an email from Kate Bandos (KSB Links) with your request for a review copy of The Well-Fed Writer. I sincerely appreciate your interest and I've got a book on the way to you. I'll be in touch in a few weeks. Please contact me if you need anything else. Talk to you soon!

Peter
987/654-3210
www.wellfedwriter.com

P.S. For virtually everything you'd need to EASILY put together a story, mention or blurb about my books, check out my Media Resources link: www.wellfedwriter.com/media.shtml.

For starters, it's just the professional thing to do. Lets them know you're running a tight ship *and* it nicely puts them on notice that you'll be in touch (i.e., that you're not just in the business of sending out free books with nothing expected in return). I also plant the seed in my P.S. about what a piece of cake it's going to be to put that placement together.

When you get a sec, take a quick look at the *Media Resources* link I mention in the P.S. (more detail on this in the next chapter). As I've said, ad nauseam, if you want someone to do something for you, make it easy for them.

Approximately three to four weeks later, whether or not they responded to the initial note, I send this one:

Hi Mary,

Peter Bowerman here, The Well-Fed Writer, following up on the copy of The Well-Fed Writer I sent out to you a few weeks back. Hopefully, you've received it by now and are enjoying it! Let me know if you need anything else from me. And needless to say, I appreciate any help you care to offer in getting word out to your communities. Thanks again for your interest and I look forward to hearing back!

(Same signoff and P.S.)

Okay, now they *know* I'm interested in getting a review, blurb, mention, etc. and didn't just fade away. They know I want to hear back from them. Again, I offer the valuable resources on my web site to make their job easier.

If another month goes by, and still no reply, I send this one:

Hello Mary,

Peter Bowerman here, The Well-Fed Writer, following up again on the copy of The Well-Fed Writer: Back For Seconds I sent out to you. Hopefully, you've enjoyed it. I appreciate your help in getting the word out to your communities. Thanks again for your interest and I look forward to hearing back!

(Same signoff and P.S.)

If I don't hear back from the second follow up, I'll usually try a few more times before giving it up.

Keep It Up

While I sent out about 100 review copies right after getting my finished books, and literally another 250+ more over the next few years, I'm always on the lookout for more contacts in my target communities.

Pay For a Review? Pleeeease...

Some time back, in one independent publishing ezine I get, a woman was crediting her publisher with submitting her first novel to PMA's *Benjamin Franklin Awards* (which she won) and for getting it reviewed, adding, "...paid for, but her review was so enthusiastic, it was worth it!" For starters, she didn't need a publisher to do those things, but so many novice authors think there's this inner sanctum of knowledge possessed only by publishers. I got your inner sanctum of knowledge. Right here. In this book.

More importantly, *paying* for a review? Bad idea. As for the "enthusiastic" review, um, if "reviewers-for-hire" wrote unenthusiastic reviews, why would authors continue to hire them? Sheesh. More importantly, a paid review is a tainted review. Here's a book that won a *Ben Franklin* award! If it's that good, why in heaven's name does she have to pay for a review?

The only exceptions are services like **www.allbookreviews.com** (I'm assuming there are others similar), which do charge ($46/56 for U.S./Canada, at press time), but you get a lot of PR goodies for that fee. And they *do* have a free review option as well; it's just not nearly as expeditious. So, you could say you're paying for the certain, expedited publicity, not the review.

Internet Marketing: Raising the Stakes

When you're ready to take online marketing to a whole new level, pick up Steve O'Keefe's seminal and exhaustive work on the subject: *Complete Guide to Internet Publicity* (Wiley, 2002). Steve is the guru on Internet publicity and his company, Patron Saint Productions (**www.patronsaintpr.com**), offers comprehensive book promotion campaigns, chat tours, blog tours, online seminar tours, and much more.

I had a chance to be on a panel with Steve at *PMA University* in 2005 and he's one dynamic dude, and up to some very exciting things. He found out about my success through the grapevine and asked if I'd join him in his session. Apparently, I was a poster boy for the very strategy he was working, though he's doing it on a much more technologically sophisticated level than I am.

It was actually a bit surreal to see a strategy I'd pretty much made up as I went along (but managed to run with successfully) bulked up on steroids in his hands. Steve also puts out a "seasonal" newsletter called *The Beautiful Plan*, which is worth subscribing to (contact his firm, Patron Saint Productions, at **news@patronsaintpr.com**.

To Another Level...

This whole chapter has showcased the targeted marketing approach I took with my books. As mentioned earlier, the small publisher, given the limitations of time and budget, really does have to pick and choose their promotional battles carefully. More importantly, the targeted approach is what you *need* to do to get noticed.

But even if your book is more mainstream in content and potential appeal, warranting a more mainstream media strategy, I say there's real value, as we saw above, in viewing your promotional campaign through the eyes of a niche book marketer as well. Pretend you've got a niche book, and figure out who some specific key audiences might be, and how you might reach them.

CASE STUDY: Mainstream AND Niche?

"Biggie" Publisher Drops the Ball

In case the earlier "Why Self-Publish?" chapter didn't drive it home enough, make mental note to self: Do NOT put publishing houses on a pedestal as being true founts of wisdom and marketing savvy (as the following story reminds) and hence, infinitely preferable to self-publishing. It ain't necessarily so. Yet *another* reason to take a closer look at self-publishing.

Sometime back, I came across an interesting example of a more mainstream book that could no doubt have benefited from being viewed through the marketing lens of a niche book. I heard about it in a somewhat sad article by *Pasadena Star News* columnist Carolyn Howard-Johnson (**www.carolynhowardjohnson.com**) in the August 2002 edition of SPAN *Connection* (**www.spannet.org**), the independent publishing newsletter. It was about Sylvia Ann Hewlett, a university economist and author of several books on demographic trends related to women and parenting. At the time, her latest book was titled:

Creating a Life: Professional Women and the Quest for Children.

In it, she examined how many career women end up childless after being misled by the stories of Hollywood celebrities having babies well into their 40s (often with the help of unpublicized surrogate mothers and expensive procedures). The book garnered enormous mainstream press, the kind for which most authors would gladly donate a kidney sans anesthesia—*Time*, *60 Minutes*, *The Today Show*, *Good Morning America*, *Oprah* (are you dying yet?). However, despite this veritable avalanche of platinum publicity, two years later the book had only sold 8,000-10,000 copies, despite publisher predictions of 30,000 units. Serious head scratching ensued.

As a sidebar, Howard-Johnson opined that perhaps the flat title was a contributing factor. Ya think? Seriously, I think that title had a lot to do with anemic sales. And I'm surprised (though should I be?) that her publisher, Talk Miramax, while apparently investing a six-figure advance, never questioned this waaaay boooooring, and arguably mismatched (it just doesn't capture the book's content) title for such a hot and controversial topic. Not that anyone asked, but I'd have gone with something like:

MISLED! Career Women and the Tragic Myth of 40-Something Childbirth.

Not necessarily the last word in a title, but certainly more provocative and intriguing than the original. And, far more indicative of the book's content than the other, it delivers a promise of what the reader will learn. I literally came up with this after just 60 seconds of thought. I think it gets attention and leverages the controversy surrounding the issue.

In all fairness, another suggested explanation for why the book tanked was that it was Bad News: The author points out that only a very small percentage of women from the mid-30s upwards get married for the first time, making the chance for children just as slim. Howard-Johnson mentioned discussing the book with her unmarried 37-year-old daughter, who said, "I just flat out don't want to hear this. Why would I slap down the price of a book to get depressed?" Why, indeed?

We can only wonder what might have been possible if they'd paid a bit more attention to "audience." Perhaps the publisher might find the following thoughts intriguing…

Try a Different Audience

Undoubtedly, the mainstream media coverage the book received would have reached a lot of 35+ women (and plenty of others, but with a broad brush), who, frankly, *wouldn't* want to hear it. So, what's the answer? Well, let's think about this logically. If 35+ women aren't a good audience for this book because it's hitting them too late (and too hard where it really hurts…), who would be? Well, using the targeted strategy I just outlined, I'd suggest focusing on women in their 20s, or even young women still in college and high school.

Perhaps we could try to get articles placed in teen magazines, college publications or magazines geared toward younger women. It's about reaching market segments that *can* still do something positive with the message. In addition, how about trying to reach older women, who might have daughters who would be potentially receptive to the message? All we have to do is steer toward the publications that cater to that demographic, say 45- to 60-year-old women, and write the articles to *that* audience.

How about religious groups? This could get a tad more complicated, philosophically, but let's face it, the message of this book is a more traditional one: Marry Earlier. And the teachings of many religions would line up nicely with that sentiment. Religious publications, guest appearances in churches, endorsements from religious leaders, etc. could all be bricks in the wall. Bottom line, I assert that a book like this would do much better by pursuing a much more focused and targeted marketing strategy, precisely *because* the group it's actually speaking about (and by default, targeted to) would have plenty of reasons *not* to want to buy it.

Now, this probably isn't something you should worry about in the early stages—you'll have more than enough to keep you busy. But, it's definitely a worthwhile promotional strategy to pursue further down the line.

Hungry Interns Await

I can hear you wailing: "Where am I going to find the time to do a focused campaign, in *addition* to the general one, which is pretty all-consuming by itself?" I hear you. And here's an idea. First, define those audiences clearly, figure out where to find them on the 'net, and craft exactly what you'll say to them when you do. Once you've got all that done, chances are excellent you can find a young intern (maybe a college student with sights on a career in marketing, PR, or publishing) to handle the grunt work of making those contacts and effectively reaching deeper and wider into your potential buying public. All of which is a great strategy regardless of what type of book you have—niche or not.

These whippersnappers are typically far more Internet-savvy than older generations, and are usually delighted to get $7-10 an hour for the experience. Especially when it means working from home, on their own schedule. I hired an intern the summer before I released my second book (and I'm doing it again for this book) to update my review copy list from the last book, and expand on it by creatively brainstorming other review copy candidates. The ultimate goal was to generate a list containing full contact details of 150-200 people who wanted to get a review copy of the second book.

Aside from the expected few hiccups, I ended up with a good confirmed list of about 125 plus a long list of other possible leads, including some inquiries for conference appearances that yielded multiple bookings. Good results overall.

I set my Girl Friday up with an email address on my wellfedwriter.com domain and, operating out of a separate email program, all emails she sent out came from **hername@wellfedwriter.com**. She'd introduce herself as "the marketing coordinator for Peter Bowerman, author of *The Well-Fed Writer...*" That raised my profile a bit, and her return address made it all fit. And remember, summers are best to hire an intern.

To find interns, put up notices on bulletin boards (real or virtual) in appropriate academic departments (marketing, communications, English, etc.) at local universities. Or check out **www.internweb.com** and **www.internjobs.com**.

I would never dare to suggest that we've truly "covered" the subject of marketing here, given that it's an ongoing, never-ending process, but I think I've given you a few good ideas. And while we're in marketing mode, let's move on to the amazing power of a web site...

Chapter 5

Network Control. Central Command. World HQ. The Bridge of the Starship Enterprise. You get the idea. That's what a web site is to any self-publishing author. Everything starts there and ends up there (or should). Ideally, it should be a combination storefront, PR/marketing department (able to speak and sell to different audiences), information center, knowledge base, resource archive, cashier, info-capture tool, electronic product delivery system, and much more.

Instant Info Access

A web site is mandatory. Period. Don't even think about not having one. It's the linchpin of any Internet marketing push. Mine (**www.wellfedwriter.com**) has a sample chapter, table of contents, reviews, cover art, Q&A, sample radio/TV interview footage, seminar info, ezine signup (and back issues), my commercial writing portfolio, ways to buy my book, ebook, CD series, mentoring services, and much more.

Assume that most people visiting your site will have headed there after hearing about it somewhere, as opposed to stumbling on it. Picture your site as one of many millions of tiny storefronts in the biggest mall in the world. If that were the actual reality, you certainly wouldn't count on them just finding it by chance. You'd need to let them know where you were and why they should come visit, *and*, most importantly, give them reasons to come back.

Don't count on search engines to bring people who initially knew nothing about it to your site. Sure, that will eventually happen, and certainly cover your bases in that arena, but work on building awareness and therefore traffic to your site through your marketing efforts. Keep the site simple, and make it easy for them to get in and out. Focus on conveying information in a logical flow, and dispense with fancy (browser-clogging) graphics. If things take too long to load, trust me, they *will* leave.

Duplicate Yourself

The main benefit of a web site is that it duplicates your effort: it works for you while you're off doing something else. Include your URL on your business cards, in all your promotional materials, in the "signature" of every email you send, in the final "attribution" paragraph of every article you write—print or online—and any place else you can think of.

Do all that, and you instantly connect your market to a wealth of information—at no cost to you or them. You'll be surprised at where interest in your title comes from. That URL translates to the single most expeditious way that's ever existed in history to connect your prospects to buying information. No exaggeration. That's strong stuff. Milk it for all it's worth.

When you email press releases to media folks (or any potential reviewer), by including your URL, you give them instantaneous "click-thru" access to your site and all the things they need to make their job easier (see "Attn: Media" link description ahead), all of which makes it easier for them to say "Yes!"

A Decent Model

Go visit **www.wellfedwriter.com** when you get a moment. Not the last word in web sites, but it gets a few things right. Might give you some ideas. Don't freak out at how much it covers. Where it is today is the result of years of ongoing evolution—*and* it still has a long way to go. You don't have to have a full-blown site from day one. Grow it.

Start this building process roughly six months prior to having printed books in hand (BBD), by adding content to your site as you develop it: sample chapter, table of contents, cover artwork, testimonials, sell copy, etc.

As we'll discuss in more detail in Chapter Thirteen, a potentially lucrative business model is to start with a book and spin off additional books, CDs, ebooks, seminars, teleseminars (and accompanying CDs), ezines, paid mentoring services, and more. You'll find links for all these on my site (explained below). Needless to say, many of these additional directions will mostly apply in the case of a non-fiction title, and specifically a how-to title, but any book can generate spinoffs. Get creative.

Your Email Signature Earning Its Keep?

I recently came across a tip about juicing up the final attribution paragraph of any article you write. (i.e., the one that reads: "Peter Bowerman is the author of The Well-Fed Writer, blah, blah, blah…"). It reminded readers not to just tell people who you are and what you've done; use the space as a "call-to-action", something I'll discuss in Chapter Eleven. I'd been getting it wrong for years, but hey, better late than never.

Then it occurred to me that the same principle applies to an email signature. Heck, here's something that's going out maybe hundreds of times a day, so why not maximize its punch. Let's turn it from a "feature" (all about the sender) to a "benefit" (about the recipient and what he or she might care about). Make it that "call-to-action"—a reason for them to click the link. Another thing I'd gotten wrong forever. Oh, well.

Here's what I was using before I saw the light:

Peter Bowerman, Author:

"The Well-Fed Writer" (award-winning, Book-of-the-Month Club selection, 2000) "The Well-Fed Writer: Back For Seconds" (Now available!)
Details: http://www.wellfedwriter.com/bfs.shtml Subscribe to the
THE WELL-FED E-PUB, the critically acclaimed monthly ezine and companion to The Well-Fed Writer: http://www.wellfedwriter.com/ezine.shtml.
www.copywriter.pro—Freelance Copywriting Services

Whoopee. Yay for me. Here's the new version….

Know anyone who dreams of making a GOOD living as a writer? Steer them to www.wellfedwriter.com for a FREE report, "Why Commercial Writing?" by Peter Bowerman, author of the award winning, Book-of-the-Month Club selection, "The Well-Fed Writer" and its companion, "TWFW: Back For Seconds", how-to standards in the field of lucrative commercial freelancing. Subscribe to THE WELL-FED E-PUB, the critically acclaimed monthly ezine and companion to The Well-Fed Writer: http://www.wellfedwriter.com/ezine.shtml. www.copywriter.pro—Freelance Copywriting Services

Better? I think so. Turns it from dead-end copy into a gateway to possibly far more. And note the first line. If I'd just said *Dream of making a GOOD living as a writer?* and it didn't apply to them, they'd ignore it. By asking them to think of someone else who might fit that bill (a softer, less in-your-face approach anyway), it becomes potential "forwarding" material. If it *does* apply to them, they'll check it out.

Remember this: potential buyers of your book will visit your web site because something intrigued them. But intrigued is not "sold." Hence their site visit. Their message to you? "Tell me more." If you tell them what they need to know, you might sell another book (or ebook, CD, etc.). Or, at the very least, perhaps gain a new subscriber to your newsletter. Provided you serve up solid, valuable information in the newsletter, you'll earn regular permission-based access to them. It's a beautiful thing. So remember that, and cover the necessary bases when you put your site together.

These are the links on my site:

1) Peter Bowerman—Include a picture and brief bio on you and the book. Update it regularly with any awards, prestigious book club placements, number of copies in print, etc. It's a quick way to establish the credentials of both you and your work.

I include my email address here, though not in many other places on the site (I'm not trying to make it *too* easy). Yes, this will result in more emails from readers. But, I've learned first-hand that a more accessible author sells more books. Whether warranted or not, authors occupy a hallowed place in the public's consciousness, but they're often seen as aloof, with no time for the "little people." Be different and it'll pay off.

2) Books—I used to have my book covers right on my home page, with "how to buy" links right up there. Seemed logical. But then I read several articles on web usability saying that you shouldn't do that: sites which made visitors click one or two steps further into the site to get to their products sold more than ones that tried to pitch right from the get-go.

Well, that made sense, too, from the standpoint of making your site less of a bazaar, focused on the quick sale, and more of an *information portal*, geared to building longer—and, ultimately, more profitable—relationships. So, I made the change, and while it's hard to tell if it made a big difference, what I do know is that it forced me to make my site more interesting and compelling, in order to draw a visitor in.

Go to my site and you'll find you have to click on the "Books" link to take you to both book covers, and a choice to click *here* to order, *there* to order both books, or down *here* for more info. The "More Info" choice takes them to another page, offering a sample chapter, table of contents, and testimonials—the basics to move them along the sales cycle. The sample chapter should be five to ten pages long. If you're worried about giving away too much in that short a grab, you don't have much of a story to tell.

3) Ebooks—At press time, I'm selling ten ebooks on my site: ebook versions of all three books, five compilations of my ezine, and two "tool boxes" of goodies for commercial writers and self-publishers. I offer up table of contents "teasers" for all the books, and instant downloads. Ebooks are the closest thing to "found money" out there. Think hard on how you can e-package new and compelling content. Hard money for soft electrons is one of the best deals going. In Chapter Thirteen, see how you can use ebooks—a no-cost product—to drive enhanced sales of physical products.

4) Testimonials—Currently, my site has, literally, a dozen sets of testimonials. Click on the main *Testimonials* link, and you'll get nine sets right there—for my two books, CDs, ezine, mentoring services, and more. Click on the link for my first book, and you'll find three more sets there. Because my book was about commercial writing (freelancing for corporations), a field of writing many of my readers never even knew existed, I felt I first needed to establish that it was indeed a *bona fide* writing arena with promising financial prospects. So, I collected a bunch of quotes from corporate writing buyers, all echoing my contention that good writers were in low supply and high demand.

The second set are some key book reviewers, along with several members of the first group, affirming that my book indeed provided the kind of good information an aspiring commercial writer needed to break into the business. In many ways, I consider these the most relevant to my average reader.

For the third set, I simply collected some of the best reviews from Amazon.com (I currently have 100+ there for my first book) and archived them on my site. We'll explore Amazon further in Chapter Seven.

Under the *Testimonials* link, I include *On-Line Publicity*. I sat down one day and made a list of all the web sites on which any of my reviews, articles, interviews, blurbs, mentions, etc. had appeared. As new ones came online, they joined the list. While what you see here is by no means a complete list, it's still a pretty healthy collection, and one that paints a clear picture of where I've been focusing my efforts—and it's not on mainstream media.

Overwhelmingly, these entries are a product of exceptionally focused and targeted online marketing to my main target audiences. Bottom line, and at the risk of a "Duh," it's always easier to get publicity from entities that are clearly defined audiences for your book, as opposed to more general cross-sections of humanity.

5) Free Ezine Signup—It's here that I've archived back issues of my free monthly ezine, together with links to the packaged ezine compilations and an ezine "signup/unsubscribe" link. To boost signups even more, I put a "subscribe" link on every page of the site.

6) Mentoring—Here I describe my one-on-one paid mentoring program, born of too much of time being sucked up by emailed questions from readers. I offer this coaching service for both commercial writing business start-ups and self-publishing endeavors. I describe both offerings, the arenas in which I can help, how the mentoring process works (including payment details), and a good list of testimonials.

7) CDs—By the time you read this, I may no longer have a link to my 6-CD *Well-Fed Writer Seminar on CD* program, as I'm phasing it out. A few years back, I professionally recorded one of my all-day *Well-Fed Writer* seminars on launching a freelance commercial writing business. On the web link, I included some audio snippets from the program, the CD Content Outline, and some listener testimonials. As I write this, I'm selling that 6-CD set through my site and also promoting it through other writing sites (paying a commission to those site owners for sales from their sites).

8) Teleseminar CDs—I've done several teleseminars with other folks who've set up the programs and had me as a guest. Afterwards, I get a copy of the program to resell through my site, which is what I do here. On the link, I include a rundown of what appears on the CD, and testimonials from either teleseminar participants or buyers of the CD. I'm about to offer up downloads of those same programs in *mp3* format for less—sort of an ebook equivalent of a physical book.

9) Attn: Media—Click on this link, and you'll see the "Media Resources" section off to the left—which includes just about everything that a media person could want—all in one place. Many of these things appear elsewhere on the site as well, but the point is to *not* make the visitor hunt for them.

The whole "make-it-easy" approach acknowledges the reality that your book and its promotion is ultimately your job, and way down the priority list of any potential reviewer. Yes, these people *do* need a steady flow of content (articles, reviews, etc.) to fill up their info vehicles. But it's far safer to assume they really don't care about your book, and that it's your job not only to make them care, but to make it *easy* for them to care. We'll discuss the Media Resources section in more detail in Chapter Eight.

10) FAQs (Frequently Asked Questions)—Whenever I'm approached by anyone doing a story, interview or review, I steer them to the FAQs. Especially in the case of an interview where, in many cases, the interviewer can have their job 50+ percent done right out of the gate. I promise you, they always appreciate it. Making it easy—once again.

11) Seminars/Signings—Always keep your readership abreast of your appearances, wherever they are, and for whatever reason.

12) Links—Make your site worth visiting *and* returning to by adding a "links" section. I have an extensive list of writing links on mine that are always being updated. In this way, you make your site more than just one big promo for your book. Actively seek out web sites and web-based organizations to link to, and then ask them for a reciprocal link. Extend your own "web" far and wide and who knows what you might catch? Remember: the more links you have, the higher you'll end up in the search engine rankings.

13) Home—A cardinal rule of web site navigation: *always* include a link to *"Home"* on every page—either at the top or bottom of your navigation bar. Give people a way to get back to the beginning, no matter where they are. I'm amazed at how many sites get this wrong.

14) Contact Info—While, as you saw, I definitely included contact info in my *Attn: Media* section, that same info is a bit more elusive on the rest of the site. Most web site construction guides will mandate including contact info front and center. Usually, I'd wholeheartedly agree. But if you're writing non-fiction how-to like I am, that could mean a *lot* of questions, making this middle-of-the-road position prudent.

Attracting Niche Audiences

On my site, you'll find other links that are specific to my offering such as *Attn: Moms* and *Attn: 55+*, which target specific audiences that I know are key potential buyers. Poke around in these two to see what I include. Especially the *Attn: 55+* link, which offers up an archive of free articles, ranging in length from 150 to 2100 words, for the taking. As discussed in the previous chapter, I recently did a simple marketing campaign to publications serving this market segment.

In addition, you'll find a *Booksellers* link, which speaks to independent bookstores that might be interested in stocking my book. I offer a bit of marketing copy, along with terms and ordering details.

Merchant Accounts

An integral part of any SP'ers site is a way for people to buy your products, and that means a merchant account. There are a million companies trying to get that business, and it can be hard to sift the good from the shady. I found mine through a PMA web resources listing, so I felt comfortable with them, and have been happy with their service ever since (Electronic Transfer, Inc. of Spokane, Washington; 800-757-5453; **www.electronictransfer.com**).

Electronic Transfer actually cobbles together several companies into a fully integrated solution. Investigate several companies in this arena to give yourself a basis for comparison.

Generally, you'll pay several recurring monthly fees (totaling $10-20) plus a small fixed per-transaction charge, and finally, a percentage (2-3%) of the sale. If you plan on doing a decent amount of business, these work out to be pretty negligible fees (I average roughly $45-50 a month total).

You'll get a detailed statement every month outlining all your sales, what piece was taken out by the company, your fees, etc. (don't forget to deduct those fees as expenses on your taxes each year). Proceeds from sales automatically transfer to your checking account of choice within roughly 48 to 72 hours.

Applying for a merchant account will entail a somewhat comprehensive, hoop-jumping approval process, but having one makes all the difference in the world for an online business. You've got to be able to take credit cards (Note: if you're using a fulfillment company, you could use their merchant account, as I did, but you'll pay more for that than if you had your own—more on this in Chapter Six). Not being a techy type, I had my web guy integrate the merchant account into my system.

PayPal—The Pros & Cons

What about *PayPal*? Isn't that good enough as a payment system? Well, it depends. When I started out, *PayPal* was relatively new, and still a bit clunky. Today, it's a much cleaner and fuller-featured technology. Plus it allows buyers to pay both by credit card and directly from their checking account.

The obvious advantage of *PayPal* (**www.paypal.com**) is that you avoid the normal approval hurdles—applications, background checks, etc.—that you have with the merchant account approval process. Plus, there are no recurring fees, just a percentage of any given sale (which can drop with your business volume). There are good reporting features (which of course, you get with a merchant account as well) so you can keep track of transactions, fees paid, etc., and transferring your balances (which happens automatically with a merchant account) into the bank account of your choice is simply a matter of a few mouse clicks.

The downsides of *PayPal*? As I see it, there's only one, but it's a big one: it doesn't offer the immediate, minimal-step buying process a merchant account does (i.e., click to order, type your info and card number, click to buy). If the buyer doesn't have an account with *PayPal*, they have to open one and go through that process. Maybe that's not a big deal for you. Fine. But know that every additional step a buyer has to go through to purchase something is just one more chance for them to say, *Forget it*. Or *I'll do it later* (but will they?).

If you opt for your own merchant account (which I'd recommend), I'd still absolutely offer the *PayPal* option for buyers. There's a certain percentage of buyers who're *PayPal*-philes (especially young people), and that's their preferred method of payment. Plus, for folks who don't have credit cards, the debit-from-checking-account option makes sure you cover that base.

My "Shopping Cart" System

After years of using a workable but severely limited shopping cart system, I recently bit the bullet, and I'm upgrading to a new one through **www.1shoppingcart.com**. The new system integrates into my web site nicely, and as I had my own merchant account (one of a few dozen providers that mesh with their system), I didn't have to change that. If you don't have a merchant account, they offer that option as well.

My desire to set up an affiliate program (discussed ahead) was the main impetus for hunting around in the first place. I could have just gone for an affiliate program through a good provider like **www.fusionquest.com**, but given the limitations of my existing system, I saw the value of taking the long view and getting into a "scalable" situation.

At the risk of sounding like an ad, *1ShoppingCart* offers a system I can grow into, no matter how big I get. You pay differing levels of monthly fees (roughly $30, $50 or $80) for different capabilities. I chose the upper end because of the affiliate program, but it also provides a complete ebook delivery system and tons of other goodies.

Affiliate Programs

This is the next step in marketing your products. What's an affiliate program? There are a lot of related web sites that would be ideal candidates to steer *their* members, subscribers, and visitors to my site. But they'll be far more willing to do that (via direct web links) if they know they're going to benefit financially by doing so. So, I'll make a deal with them: *Send folks my way, and I'll give you X% of any sale.* That percentage will vary. A book sale will be less than, say, a CD or ebook sale (although with ebooks, you can be more generous, given that there's zero production or shipping costs).

Once you hammer out the arrangement, you need a way to automate the process of keeping track of leads that result in sales. Enter your affiliate program. It's yet another way to extend your marketing reach and tap those incremental sales you wouldn't otherwise snag. If you don't have to do a thing to get X# of additional sales, you probably wouldn't mind sharing the profits a bit.

How Much Affiliate Commission?

So what kind of affiliate commission should you pay for a lead that turns into a book sale? Well, the benchmark commission structure is, of course, that used by Amazon.com. Amazon pays commissions to referring sites that start at 5 percent and rise slooooooowly to a potential high of 7.5 percent. We're talking moving up to 6 percent only when they ship 331+ units a month from a site's referrals! 7.5 percent? Please. Try 9401+ units (at press time).

My thought is a straight 10 percent commission, regardless of sales volume. Should be an easy sell to other sites. In my case, my total unit cost of books is only $2.50 ($20 retail), so I can easily absorb the 10 percent *and* free shipping, and still be nicely profitable.

Web Marketing Tools

I don't for a second consider myself some "web site marketing maximization" expert. I do a few things right, but I could be doing far more (that *triage* thing again…). To get a glimpse into where you could take your web site, check out the marketing features on **www.1shoppingcart.com** and **www.kickstartcart.com**.

Speaking of web site maximization, there's a nifty site called Web Trends (**www.webtrends.com**, and others do the same thing), that can provide the stats for your site, with nice graphical breakdowns. You can see how many people have come to your site, where they went, and where they left from. It helps to determine if your site is really working for you or not. Worth a look.

The Nuts and Bolts

Probably about six months before you finish your book, go ahead and register your domain name. There are a zillion companies that do this (I use **www.godaddy.com**). Make yours something easy to remember, *and* easy to type. If you have a five-word long title, don't try to include it all. Originally, I reserved **www.wellfedselfpublisher.com**, but that seemed awfully clunky, so I shortened it to **www.wellfedsp.com**. I hung on to the first one, in case people tried it as a guess, and if they do, that URL links straight through to the second.

Keep the registration info you get back from your domain company (including the expiration date) in a file on your computer that's easy to remember and find. Make a note in your planner or tickler file to remind yourself to renew it as the expiration date draws near. While you'd think it'd be in a company's financial interest to remind you, they're not always as organized as you'd think. Losing your domain in the middle of a book campaign because you assumed something could be a freakin' disaster.

When in Doubt, Hire it Out

You may ask: "Should I hire someone to create my web site, or do it myself?" To which I'd reply: If you love rolling up your sleeves and diving into a new software program, perhaps you have the temperament to do it. You'll save yourself a bundle. By the way, do-it-yourselfers, the word on the street from many web designers is that *Dreamweaver*™ is the best program for the more technically savvy.

If you're not very techy but still feel the urge, there are several great sites for the low-budget, low-tech, D-I-Y crowd, most notably **www.godaddy.com** (cheap domain names, too), **www.quickbizsites.com**, **www.homestead.com**, and **www.citymax.com**.

If however, you're a techno-phobe like me *and* you have a few bucks to spend, you're probably better off hiring someone. If I'd waited till I learned how to do all this, I'd still be without a site. If you don't know any web designers in your area, you might start by trying the Independent Computer Consultants Association (**www.icca.org**).

Alternately, you might look for hungry, talented students at local art or tech schools who might do it for less. The key is to get it done. Web designers aren't exactly scarce these days, which is driving rates down. At some point, I know I'll probably need to bite the bullet and learn how to do this stuff, both to save money and be able to update my site without having to wait on my web guy to get around to it. Until then, it's *so* worth it to have him handle it. The money I'd theoretically save by doing it myself would be more than eaten up by the lost productivity (given that I'm a techno-moron...) and the loss of the increased sales that I'm getting because I can focus on marketing.

Now that we've got an idea about how to go about harnessing the *awesome* (in the *true* sense of the word, as opposed to the hackneyed, overused, popular culture version...) power of the Internet, let's find out about the various ways our books find their way into the hands of our dear readers...

Chapter 6

Go to any writer's conference or publishing convention and one topic seems to keep surfacing: *distribution*. Plugging into the channels that'll get your books in front of potential buyers. Crucial stuff. More to the point, the inevitable question is:

How Do I Get My Books Into Bookstores?

There's actually a far more important question, but I'm getting ahead of myself...

When I started my publishing adventure in 1999, a few things were different. Some think it's harder now for the little guy, but I disagree. I say, that for the publisher who's decided to follow a strategy like mine and stay focused on **Building Demand**, it's more like six of one, half dozen of another. Before I explain that further, let's get straight on a few basic definitions. FYI, this gets a bit involved, and necessitates jumping around some, so hang with me here. There's a method to my madness...

Wholesalers

Why does the industry need wholesalers? When the thousands of bookstores and libraries out there want to order books, you think they want to deal with a zillion individual publishers? Hardly. With their wish lists of onesies, twosies, tensies, or hundreds, they want to go to one entity to get it all handled. Wholesalers expose your books to the world, and make it easy for the world to get their hands on them.

Wholesalers simply stock books; in industry jargon, they "pick 'n pack." They don't actively sell or promote them through a sales force (like *some* distributors do), though they do offer marketing programs (for extra) to give your books more exposure.

103

Enter the two main wholesalers: Ingram (**www.ingrambook.com**), which is *the* wholesaler for the "trade": all the bookstores—chain and independent alike. Then there's Baker & Taylor (**www.btol.com**), which has traditionally been the major player in the library market. Technically, Ingram is roughly 80/20 (book trade/libraries) while Baker & Taylor is now closer to 50/50. Ingram's a bit more complicated, so let's cover them first.

Door #1 to Ingram: a Distributor

When I started out, with one book in hand, I could walk right into Ingram's front door and deal with them directly. Well, as of June 2001, Ingram instituted a new policy, whereby they no longer dealt with publishers of fewer than 10 titles (since I got started prior to 06/01, I was grandfathered in for future books, and can deal with them directly). But, fret not. There are several ways into Ingram's door—one that's been in place since the 10-book rule, and a second, which is relatively new. If you see bookstore sales as an important component of your overall mix, you need access to Ingram.

The first way is to go through one of their preferred distributors, which are listed at **www.ingrambook.com/new/distributors.asp**. According to Ingram, *Each company listed has a relationship with Ingram. Once you have established an agreement with the service provider of your choice, they will contact Ingram with all pertinent information. Your product will then be added to our database and purchase orders will be placed through the distributor as demand warrants. This will ensure that your product will be available to all customers that Ingram represents.*

Incidentally, BookMasters, my printer/fulfillment company, is on the list, and offers distribution through their associated entity, AtlasBooks (**www.atlasbooks.com/atlasbooks/publishers.htm**). *(Note: I use BookMasters for printing and fulfillment only, not for distribution.)* After we discuss Ingram and Baker & Taylor, and how to gain access to their databases, we'll get into distributors and all the ins and outs of those arrangements.

Door #2 to Ingram: PMA/Ingram Wholesale Acceptance Program

The second way into Ingram, launched in March 2006, is a program sponsored by PMA (the big independent publishing association) and created for their members: the *PMA/Ingram Wholesale Acceptance Program*. A little background. Ever since Ingram implemented their 10-book minimum in 2001, PMA's been trying to figure out how to help smaller publishers get into Ingram's system. Without that connection, unless your book is a very "niche" title (whose success doesn't depend on bookstore sales), *and* you're an extraordinary marketer, your book probably won't go far.

The *P/IWAP* is for publishers who aren't currently being represented by Ingram. You have two opportunities each year to submit your title for consideration— March/April and September/October. Acceptance isn't automatic, so be sure to read the upcoming section on "Wooing Ingram, Distributors & Bookstores." A committee made up of representatives of PMA, Barnes & Noble, Borders, and several divisions of Ingram reviews prospective books. If your book is chosen, here are the terms:

1) Ingram waives the normal $750 set-up fee

2) You sell your books to Ingram at the standard 55 percent discount, and you pay the freight to and from Ingram.

3) Ingram agrees to pay you within 90 days of sale.

4) You agree to pay a $50 per title one-time co-op fee.

5) You participate in the *New Vendor Title Visibility Program*, which will run you $500 (paid upon signing). For that fee, you'll receive a quarter-page print ad and one *ipage* ad (Ingram's e-business web site), a $2,500 combined value. While other advertising opportunities are available with Ingram, the one above is required.

6) You have to sell $20,000 worth of books at "cost" (after returns) over the first two years of your participation in the program (see explanation ahead). If you don't, you'll either be dropped or be allowed to stay on, but at a larger discount.

More details at **www.pma-online.org/benefits/ingramprogram.cfm**.

A Little "Tough Love"

The *P/IWAP*, as it's structured, also addresses what was seen as a glitch of sorts to working with Ingram, pre-2001 (and the 10-book rule). Back when any one-book publisher could hook up with Ingram directly, many publishers assumed that once they had that access, they'd always have it (and Ingram didn't tell them differently). But Ingram is a business like any other, and if a title wasn't moving, they'd drop it. So, one day, out of the blue, publishers of slow-moving titles would get a "Dear John" letter telling them that their book was out of the database. If you depended on that access, it could be the kiss of death.

The new arrangement addresses this in a "tough love" sort of way. As a publisher, you get that critical access to Ingram (at that 55 percent discount), but you have to shell out some bucks to promote your book, and in order to keep that access, you know *exactly* what level of sales volume you need to hit: $20,000 in sales at cost (minus returns).

Translation? Well, let's assume a $15 retail price book. "Cost" on a $15 book is 45 percent of $15 (given the 55 percent discount), or $6.75. $20,000 divided by $6.75 = 2963 books. So, at that price point, you've got to move roughly 1500 books a year through their system to pass muster. And frankly, if you can't do that, then you probably shouldn't be in the business. All in all, pretty darn fair, and its requirements will keep you on your toes.

Baker & Taylor

To get into Baker & Taylor's database and expose your book to the vast library market (and, to a lesser extent, the trade), you simply pay your money, and you're in. Their *Partner Program* will run you $295, though as an added benefit of joining PMA or SPAN, the independent publishing associations, you shave $50 off that fee. Nothing to do cartwheels over, but every little bit helps.

For PMA's version, click **www.pma-online.org/benefits/bakerandtaylor.cfm**. For SPAN's, check out their web site (**www.spannet.org**), click *Membership Benefits* and scroll down to #5 (and check out all the other bennies while you're there). Baker & Taylor has no "10-book minimum" rule, so the little guy can deal with them directly at a standard 55 percent discount. Remember, the library market is enormous, and unlike a bookstore's shelves, once a book is on a library's shelves, they're non-returnable. Use Baker & Taylor to maximize your reach into this crucial book-buying segment.

Other Library Wholesalers

There are a number of other library wholesalers: Brodart (**www.brodart.com**; 800-233-8467), Midwest Library Service (**www.midwestls.com**; 800-325-8833), Emery-Pratt Company (**www.emery-pratt.com**; 800 248-3887), and Ambassador Book Services (**www.absbook.com**; 800-431-8913). According to Brodart, they're very similar to Baker & Taylor (even in size), except that they do field a sales force like some distributors (but unlike a distributor, they don't take over your logistical fulfillment). And their focus is exclusively libraries, while B&T's is split between the library and the trade. Given that no one entity gets exclusivity, you might list with several of these.

Library Distributors

There are two major library distributors—companies that field a sales force, and cater almost exclusively to the library trade: Quality Books (in Oregon, IL—**www.quality-books.com**) and Unique Books (in St. Louis, MO—www.uniquebooksinc.com). You'll be selling to them at that same standard discount: 55 percent.

QBI, according to their site, is "committed to bringing the voices of the vibrant small press community to a larger audience through libraries." UB calls itself, "the premier library distributor of books, DVDs, videos, and audios published by small and independent presses." Sounds like us, no?

Here's what listing with Ingram and Baker & Taylor means: if anyone walks into a bookstore or library anywhere and requests the book, the store or library can easily order it. In the case of libraries, it doesn't mean they *will* order it, but the system is now in place to do so. I promise you though, if a bookstore or library gets enough requests for a book, they'll start stocking it. Without at least one of these "plug-ins," you'll severely hamper your ability to move sizable numbers of books. Now, let's explore what it means to work with a distributor.

Distributors

Okay, so a distributor is one passport into Ingram, and there are some major advantages in working with one:

1) It's one of the single best ways to get your book(s) into the bookstores.

2) They become your warehousing and shipping entity, physically sending product to Ingram, Baker & Taylor, Amazon, etc., and handling invoicing, collections, and book returns processing. It's part of the deal—non-negotiable.

Now, truth be known, most of the distributors on Ingram's list mentioned above won't be interested in working with a one-book publisher (BookMasters is an exception, and there's another one we'll discuss in a few pages). And when you do find one who will, because of the above services they offer (and perhaps others; see sidebar ahead), you'll be netting less profit than you would by going through a wholesaler. How much less?

Pay More, But Get More

Well, both Ingram and B&T buy books from publishers at a 55 percent discount. But if you use a distributor to get to Ingram (Door #1), you'll end up selling books at a discount of roughly 65 percent, give or take a few percent, depending on which distributor they partner with. Though, as we've just seen, distributors offer a lot for that extra premium.

Now, you won't see that 65 percent discount figure on any distributor agreement (like you might see 55 percent on a wholesaler agreement). Why? Because, technically speaking, a distributor doesn't buy books from you; they remain your property (as opposed to wholesalers, who *do* purchase books from you).

A distributor simply warehouses your books until they're purchased by a host of other entities. At that point, the distributor sells and ships them to those entities on your behalf, and takes a piece of that transaction. That piece, combined with the normal 55 percent discounts at which the distributor sells to other entities (Ingram, B&T, Amazon, etc.) adds up to that approximate 65 percent number. *(NOTE: This is where the "6 x PPB" formula discussed in Chapter Three moves front and center. When you're giving up that big a chunk, your production costs become mighty important.)*

Now, while that 10-book publisher doesn't have to go through a distributor to get into Ingram's door, fact is, most of them do because it makes their life a lot simpler, ensures they get into bookstores, and because they do indeed get a lot for the extra they pay. Given their larger stable of titles, even though they're making less on each book, they can still be nicely profitable because of the volume.

All Distributors Are NOT Created Equal

Many distributors (but NOT all) have an outside sales force that promotes your book directly to key bookstore buyers, which absolutely can translate to higher sales (these salespeople make their pitches armed with a case full of…covers! Once again, the "un-overstateable" importance of a book cover). In addition, some distributors send out catalogs featuring your book to thousands of book-buying entities: other smaller wholesalers, distributors, etc.

I had an interesting conversation with Shelley Sapyta, my salesperson at BookMasters, as I was finalizing this chapter. Given how widely the service offerings vary between different distributors, she emphasized how important it was for publishers to do their "distributor research" and ask any prospective distributor what they provide in the sales and marketing department (all will handle the logistical end of things).

Which, of course, means that BookMasters' distribution arm offers sales force, catalogs, and more. They're plugged into 80-plus specialty distributors catering to a broad range of interests (academic, religious, airport stores, general trade, etc.), and can get you in front of these outlets. They can even help authors set up book signings.

Just know that all distributors aren't the same, so make sure you know what you're getting for your money. Granted, chances are, you'll have to sell any distributor on taking you on (and we'll discuss how to do that later), but at least you should be pitching entities that deliver the whole enchilada.

Research Now, Less Misery Later

While there are a good number of reputable distributors out there, there's also a regular rogues gallery in the field. If you decide you want one, do your homework. Hire an attorney to review the paperwork. Anyone in the biz for any length of time has heard plenty of horror stories about distributors. Cheating their authors, screwed-up (either intentionally or through incompetence) royalty statements that require a CPA to decipher, going belly-up with a warehouse full of your books, etc. Say the word "distributor" in a book crowd and you're likely to start a "one-up" contest to see who had the worst experience!

This is where your affiliations with PMA and SPAN can come in handy. A few exploratory calls or emails could expose an apparently "reputable" distributor as a bunch of crooks to be avoided at all costs. You will have just saved yourself the cost of association membership many times over.

CAVEAT "DISTRIBUTEE"

Understand the "locked-in" nature of a distributor arrangement. One of my coaching clients had an unhappy introduction to the "one-company-handles-it-all" reality when she signed on with BookMasters for distribution. She wanted to handle the Amazon piece herself, but found out that, according to the exclusive distribution contract she'd signed, she couldn't. Read the fine print carefully, and understand what you're getting into. And know that the rules can often change at their whim, with little or no advance notice.

A few of the current big players (and "good guys") are IPG (Independent Publishers Group; **www.ipgbook.com**), Publishers Group West (**www.pgw.com**), NBN (National Book Network (www.nbnbooks.com), Consortium (**www.cbsd.com**), and Midpoint Trade Books (**www.midpointtrade.com**), and of course, BookMasters (**www.bookmasters.com**).

Attn: One-Book Publishers

As mentioned earlier, one-book publishers will likely have trouble catching the eye of many of the distributors on Ingram's aforementioned approved list. I recall a brief conversation with a rep of one of the big distributors at BEA (Book Exposition of America, THE big U.S. book show each year; **www.bookexpo.reedexpo.com**) right after I'd released my first book.

I asked what sort of opportunities a small publisher had with their firm, and the guy said something like, "Well, we'll *consider* small publishers with less than 10 books, but..." Okaaaaay. Bu-bye. I was tempted to ask him the policy for those with less than two books just to see if I could get a laugh out of him, but decided to exit with dignity.

But you've got options. Yet another benefit of PMA membership is the *Trade Distribution Program*, something I considered briefly before deciding to stick to my own course. Sponsored by PMA and the distributor IPG, the program is a good way for independent publishers to tap into the big distribution channels.

Here's how it works: twice each year, a committee made up of representatives from IPG and buyers from Barnes & Noble, Borders, Ingram, Baker & Taylor and several independent bookstores, meet and review submissions made by PMA members (books *not* already being carried by the bookstores). If a book is accepted, IPG agrees to offer the publisher a distribution agreement (yes, at an effective 65 percent discount). For more details, check out **www.pma-online.org/benefits/tradedistribution.cfm**.

If you don't have a lot of time to invest in the marketing of your book (worth weighing if you're considering the SP route), it would definitely make more sense to take on a distributor. If you do have the time, you just might not need one.

Wooing Ingram, Distributors, & Bookstores

Okay, because I didn't use a distributor, my initial pitch was to Ingram, and eventually, the bookstores, which will be your path as well if you opt for PMA's *P/IWAP* to access Ingram (remember: acceptance isn't automatic). If you go the distributor route, you'll be making your pitch to those folks, and if they take you on, they'll be your ticket into the bookstores (eliminating the need to pursue the big bookstore chains as I had to).

In the following paragraphs, I'll share how I went about the process (though things were different then), because regardless of your choice, you'll be wooing some entity along the way. It'll underscore the importance developing the "marketing mindset." Chances are, it won't all apply to your situation, so take what you need and ignore the rest.

Per the discussion that opened this chapter, your long-term publishing success is not going to depend on the answer to the question, "How do I get my books into bookstores?" nearly as much as it will on the answer to this question:

"How do I *keep* my books in the bookstores?

In the big scheme of things, it's not terribly hard to get your books into bookstores. It's keeping them from quickly coming *back* to you as returns that's the challenge.

The Revolving Door

I've been told that I have a keen grasp of the obvious. See if you don't agree. Every year, approximately 150,000 books get published. But, as far as I can tell, my local B&N and Borders stores stay the same size. No new wings being added each year. What does that tell us? That, overwhelmingly, books come and go. Only a few hang around for the long haul. Sure, you'll get your shot at "90-days-of-bookstore-fame," but if buyers don't move your books off the shelves, the bookstore will. And back to you, Jack. My books continue to sell, years after they debuted, because I continue to work them.

Okay, so how do you convince a distributor or Ingram to take you on so you can get your humble little gem onto bookstore shelves? Simple. What do wholesalers, distributors, and bookstores all want? To *move books*. So, you simply need to convince them that taking you on will be a good financial decision for them; that they're going to move lots of your books. How do you do that? *Not* by conveying the impression that you want to get your books into the stores, and hope, with fingers crossed, that people will stumble across them. No, you want to demonstrate to them, in detail, that you'll be working your little tail off to *build demand* and drive buyers into bookstores who are *looking* for your book.

Raising Ingram's Eyebrows

As discussed earlier, I landed a *Full Publisher Contract* with Ingram (reserved for larger publishers, and promising wider distribution) by convincing them, through my aggressive marketing plan, that I was going to leave no stone unturned in letting prospective buyers know about my book. Through their response, Ingram sent a clear message: we want to work with, *and* will reward, those publishers—regardless of size—who are committed, through consistent marketing efforts, to promoting their book(s). Makes sense to me.

In the *Marketing Strategy Questionnaire* (**e**) I sent to Ingram (which you can use as an example of a good marketing proposal—regardless of the audience), I showcased not only my impressive marketing efforts up to that point but the big promotional plans I had coming up. This is exactly the kind of information the wholesalers, distributors, and bookstores all want to know about. Show them that you're an author who's intimately involved in the ongoing, active marketing of your title—which spells profits for them—and you make it a much easier decision for them to make.

Bookstores: Not Ideal, But Necessary

All that said, many of the most successful self-publishers rank bookstore sales near the bottom of the scale in importance. SP guru Dan Poynter is fond of saying, "Bookstores are lousy places to sell books!" and he's right. The hoops you have to jump through, the return policies, and the huge discounts you have to give, make them less than ideal.

Duly noted. And sure, I'd love to think—okay, daydream—that I could sell the lion's share of tens of thousands of books right off my web site (where profit margins are giddily high), and gleefully thumb my nose at the big chains. And theoretically, if you do enough ongoing marketing (and you had a true "niche" book), I suppose it could happen.

But if you have a book with even some mainstream appeal, what that fond hope ignores, and what you have very little control over, is people's book buying habits. Regardless of where someone hears about a book—and today, the Internet is a darn good bet—a certain percentage of people still love buying books in bookstores. Not to mention that bookstores are simply the best physical showcases for books. By all means, build that vast zillion-tentacled marketing infrastructure and affiliate network that boosts the chances of those juicy high-profit web site sales, *and* know that you probably still need to be in bookstores.

Speaking of people coming into bookstores looking for your book, I say that there's little point in having your books in bookstores (libraries, maybe) until you've done enough promotion to drive people there. Many authors' egos allow them to tragically delude themselves by positioning the bookstores as some Holy Grail: *If only I can get my books into the bookstores, I'm home free.* Not. As if the mere presence of their books on store shelves means they'll be discovered, and start flying off said shelves. *SO* not.

Heed This Warning

Do not make the fatal mistake of assuming that people will stumble across your book in the bookstore or library, having arrived at either of those venues with zero knowledge of it. Sure, it happens, but you're *far* better off assuming that no one will ever know about it until they hear about it somewhere else (ideally, many somewhere elses), because of some promotional efforts you've made. By all means, get hooked up with Ingram and Baker & Taylor, and make it easy for the bookstores and libraries to get their hands on it.

But, get your book into the big chains before you've established a strong and enduring demand, and you'll end up with a ton of returns *up to a year later, in any condition, for a full refund.* No fun. And whether dealing with a wholesaler, distributor or a fulfillment company (coming in a few pages), returns need to be processed, and "processing" costs money. But it won't happen if you make your *demand-building* efforts consistent and ongoing.

High Returns, Low Fun

Typical industry return rates are 30-plus percent, and I've heard no small number of scary stories of rates as high as 60 percent! An article in the March 2004 edition of *Southern Review of Books* (**http://www.anvilpub.com/ Southern_Review.htm**) had this to say:

In the United States, half the books printed in 2002 and shipped to booksellers were returned to the publishing company to be remaindered or destroyed, according to the Association of American Publishers. It's the result of a wasteful and archaic American system that encourages booksellers to overstock titles they in effect order on consignment from the big publishing houses.

My return rate through roughly 40,000 copies of my first book? Less than five percent. Yes, it's a good book, and yes, it's a niche book, for which returns are often lower. But I say that a key reason for such a preternaturally low return rate is that I focused, first and foremost, on establishing an enduring demand, knowing that once you do that, everything else falls into place: bookstore, library, Amazon, web site, and ebook sales. And assuming you keep up the promotional pressure, your sales will continue to be healthy and your returns low. Make sense?

Too Few Books Out There?

Some might say that a return rate as low as mine means I've got too few books out there. That I'd be better off with a distributor who could move, say, twice that many, and even with a 20 percent return, I'd still be moving a lot more books. Possible. But, when I posed the question at a self-publishing conference at which I was speaking, many of the attendees (generally a lot more experienced than moi) said, "Hey, I'd take that return rate any day." And my numbers were good. So, it's hard to say. I think I'll hang on to it.

Bookstores Will Stock "Movers"

If you've created the demand, which drives enough people into enough Barnes & Nobles or Borders asking for the book, I promise those bookstores will start and keep stocking your book. In my case, I got hooked up with Ingram and B&T, but didn't rush to get my books onto their shelves. Instead, I focused on building demand and a good buzz.

Pretty soon, I started getting *Request For Title Information* faxes from the bookstores. Translation: *We're getting requests for this book, which we don't carry. Tell us about it.* After I got three or four of those, *then* I went through what's known as the "small press review" process (described shortly) with B&N and Borders to get my books into their stores. Build it (i.e., the demand) and they will (not) come (back).

If you end up following a path necessitating pitching the bookstores (unnecessary if you're going the distributor route), don't use the RFTI faxes as *the* litmus test. If you know you've built a healthy buzz through extensive promotional efforts, and you're selling decent numbers through Amazon and your own site, go ahead and start the small press review process with the bookstores. Give them a full rundown of your activities. They want to know, and you want to know. FYI, those early promotional efforts are the ones you can do in the three- to four-month period between your "bound book date" (BBD) and your "official publication date" (OPD) we discussed in Chapter Three.

Of course, when they start ordering your books, they'll always be doing so through the wholesalers or your distributor, never directly from you. Just the way it works.

Bookstore Contacts

When you're ready to contact the bookstores, here's the drill: for Borders, contact "New Vendor Acquisitions" at 734-477-1100 (ext. 1333 for new acquisitions) and listen for the correct prompt to get pre-recorded info on the program. At press time, there was no web-based program information.

For B&N, call 212-633-3388 for pre-recorded instructions on what they'll need in order to consider your book for placement in B&N stores. Basically, you'll need to send a *finished* book (no manuscripts or galleys), along with a Letter of Intent, explaining why you think B&N should carry your book, what makes it special or unique, any reviews you may have received, and most importantly, a current and future marketing plan. In my case, and per my largely web-based marketing plan, I listed all the publications and web sites through which I'd been promoting my book—which was a rather extensive list by that point.

You then send all this to:

Barnes & Noble Small Press Department
122 Fifth Avenue
New York, NY 10011

Check out these two URLs for more info:

www.barnesandnoble.com/help/pub_wewant_tosell.asp and

www.barnesandnobleinc.com/authors/advice/ac_getting.html.

Okay, given that a distributor will handle all the aforementioned physical and financial logistics of getting book orders filled and paid for, if you don't go the formal distributor route, you'll need a way to handle all that without turning your home into a shipping center, and your free time into a fond and distant memory. And that means using a fulfillment company (even if you think you'll try to land a distributor, read on, especially the *Onesie, Twosie Buyers, Too* section ahead).

Fulfillment Companies

I recently had a coaching call with a renowned industry expert on a specialized writing niche who was finishing up a definitive how-to book on his subject. Over several years, he'd built a solid "platform," had a popular web site with beaucoup visitors, and a thriving ezine with 20,000 subscribers. Plus, he had a solid roster of affiliates—related sites ready to promote his products heavily to their audiences in return for a cut.

His upcoming book was unique—nothing like it existed on the market. The book's content was specialized and esoteric, and he had a robust and growing captive audience willing to pay a premium for the information. Given his content and target audience, he knew he'd have few "tire-kickers" as buyers. Those who needed it *really* needed it.

Ideal for Ultra-Niche Books

So, given the "niche" nature of his book, bookstore sales weren't as critical to his success, so there was little need to go the distributor route. Wouldn't it be smarter, he pondered, to maximize high-profit sales through his own site and referrals from his affiliate network, and cover the library market with B&T, than to try to slog it out in the fiercely competitive mainstream book trade marketplace? Sure, he'd cover that base by connecting with Ingram (through PMA's *P/IWAP*) and hooking up with Amazon.

Sounded like a good plan to me. And as such, he was a superb candidate for a fulfillment company. Like me, he had no desire to get into the business of warehousing, inventory, shipping, invoicing, collections, etc. Entities like Bookmasters (my fulfillment company in Ohio; **www.bookmasters.com**) can be a godsend for self-publishers.

If you hire them for both printing and fulfillment as I did (with BookMasters, you can contract them for either or both), here's how it works. Once printed, the printer moves your books over to their warehouse (for a small "receiving" charge of $20-30). You then direct all your customers (i.e., Amazon, Ingram, B & T, smaller niche distributors, etc.) to the fulfillment company (FC). You fill out simple forms with the FC, specifying contract terms for each customer, and provide those terms and the FC's contact information to your customers. The two parties then take it from there. You're out of the loop.

Out of Your Hands

From that point forward, whenever one of those entities wants to order books, they contact the FC, who assembles the order, ships it, invoices the client, and collects the money. All this happens completely independently of my knowledge or involvement, possibly while I'm sleeping.

Every month, I get a check and a statement (they've recently gone to online statements) outlining all sales, including processing of 800 number/web site sales of individual books (for which they can handle the credit card processing), along with details on any returns, miscellaneous charges, and a full itemization of all fulfillment charges. It'd take you forever to learn all this stuff. They can do it in their sleep. Let them. You've got much bigger fish to fry.

Had I tried to do all this myself, I'd have won the battle and lost the war. As discussed, the lost revenue as a result of time spent away from marketing would've quickly and handily outweighed any money saved. As it is, I *really* don't have to do much in the way of accounting, inventory management, invoicing, or all the other admin stuff you'd have to take on if you were handling all the logistics yourself. My life *is* pretty darn simple. Again, not easy, but focused on my role as "marketing/publicity/promotions director."

Onesie-Twosie Buyers, Too

I also use BookMasters to handle all my one- or two-book sales generated through either my web site or the toll-free number (it's their number, which they answer generically, but I use it in my sales materials as if it were mine). If you go with a distributor, they may or may not handle direct personal sales through your web site or a toll-free number, so you may need this service as well. Far easier to hire someone than mess with it yourself.

For sales through the toll-free number (minimal compared to online sales), I'm completely out of the loop. They get the call, process the credit card, pack up the book, and send it out. For those, I'm charged about four bucks and change, plus postage.

For sales through my site, I get the order first, and forward it on to them for processing (unless I've promised someone I'd send their book out personally). On these orders, because I've handled the credit card processing, they're simply doing the packaging and shipping, which runs me less than $1.75 plus postage. If you want to offer online sales but don't have a merchant account yet, you can use their online purchase gateway.

I *could* just have all my online orders going straight through to them and stay out of that loop as well, but given that I'm also selling CDs and other products which I fulfill (for now, at least), I prefer having all orders come to me first, and then forwarding the appropriate ones on to them. When I go on vacation, I add their email address to my merchant account processing profile. In those cases, because they're receiving *all* product orders, I just give them clear instructions to *only* mess with the book orders, and ignore all the rest, which I can usually cover with local help.

If you want to find other fulfillment companies, google "Pick and Pack services," which should bring up other fulfillment service firms. And be sure to check the *Publisher Resource Recommendations* section of Appendix A for ideas in that arena.

A Structure for Life Simplification

Successful self-publishing is never an easy job, but it doesn't have to be an overly complicated one. Boil the process down to its essence:

- Build a web site that provides all the information visitors need to make a buying decision, and give them ways to buy products immediately.
- Get set up with one or more wholesalers and establish your physical distribution system—whether a distributor or fulfillment company.
- *Build the demand for your book* in all the ways we've discussed.

Yes, that last one's an enormous job by itself, but by setting things up according to this strategy, you don't get bogged down in time-devouring administrative minutiae. And once your structure is in place, those marketing efforts can be optimally fruitful.

Nickels and Dimes

Just a heads-up here. As you research both distributors and fulfillment companies, you may initially be struck by all the little charges that come with those arrangements. *Will I ever make any money at this?* you may wonder. In truth, the recurring charges I pay monthly for fulfillment are a non-issue at this point. Yes, they add up, but I make enough money that I don't dwell on them at all. Frankly, it's worth every penny I pay to avoid messing with logistics and to be able to focus on my ONE job.

Summary: Distribution

So, as I see it, you've got several options:

1) Get plugged into both Ingram (through a distributor) and Baker & Taylor, and use that distributor to handle all logistics. **Pluses:** simpler, get it all handled in one place. The distributor *might* offer some sales function—pitching your books to the trade—along with other marketing services. **Minuses:** you'll give up another chunk of money and some control. If you hook up with a bad distributor, it could get ugly.

This scenario makes more sense if you have more of a mainstream book that needs to be in as many traditional distribution venues as possible, and you see bookstore sales as a big component of your sales mix. Perhaps, you don't have the time to do as much marketing and promotion, and choosing the right distributor can pick up some of that slack.

2) Get plugged into both Ingram (through PMA's *P/IWAP*) and Baker & Taylor, and hire a fulfillment company to handle all logistics. **Pluses:** you have more control and give up less money (especially when dealing with Amazon). **Minuses:** The cost savings over a distributor won't be huge, and you won't get any of the sales and marketing services offered by some distributors.

This scenario makes more sense if you have more of a niche book (i.e., like the example I shared earlier), and can envision a healthy chunk of sales coming from your own site and affiliates, while still covering the "trade" base with Ingram and Amazon. And you have the time and inclination to do a lot of your own marketing.

Remember, you can always start with one scenario and switch to another down the road if it makes sense to do so. Nothing is forever.

D-I-Y Fulfillment/Bookkeeping

Both the above scenarios presuppose that you've (wisely) concluded that you need to focus your efforts on *demand-building* activities, and not on logistical/admin functions. If you *haven't* concluded that, then, I suppose that means there's a third option: #2 but without the fulfillment company. Sure, you'd save the money you'd give up to a fulfillment house, but the time you'd end up spending to handle all this (remember, time IS money) would so quickly outweigh that savings, it'll make your head spin.

But hey, it's a free country. If you want to go the D-I-Y route, there are a number of good software programs to help take care of this end. Two good options are *AnyBook* (**www.ronwatters.com/RonSoft5.htm**; roughly $100-400, depending on level chosen) or Myrlyn (**www.myrlyn.com**; $349, or $249 for PMA/SPAN members).

Book Clubs

With galleys in hand, approach the book clubs early, well before your official publication date. Here's the bittersweet reality of book clubs. You do it for the typically hassle-free arrangements, and the priceless promotional value of being able to use, say, *Book-of-the-Month Club* in all your marketing materials, and *not* for the big checks. So how does it work? Well, typically, book clubs will get your files from your printer and print the books themselves, absorbing all production costs.

They then pay you a royalty of roughly six to eight percent of *their* retail price for the book, which is usually 20 to 25 percent below regular retail. In a way, this is pretty close to a conventional publishing scenario, which is where the "hassle-free" part comes in. You do nothing and get checks. Not big checks, mind you; for me it would've been roughly 75 cents a book. But it's some money for basically doing nothing.

A Nice Bonus

In my case, happily, it unfolded a little differently. After estimating the number of books they'd need, and looking at their production costs, they concluded that it wasn't cost-effective to print the books themselves, so they approached me to buy directly from my stock, which happens reasonably often. I made a little profit *and* my royalty on top of that. Bottom line, their orders often paid a healthy chunk of the costs of the next printing, while eating up a much smaller share of the total print run. I'll take it.

As it turned out, the book became a much more successful title for them than they (or I) ever imagined. So the irony was that the numbers they ultimately ended up buying would absolutely have justified printing the book themselves. But who knew?

Book Clubs for Everyone

Again, *Literary Marketplace*—the bible of the publishing industry—has a complete listing of book clubs with contact people. You can flip through the hard copy edition in your library or subscribe online at **www.literarymarketplace.com** for $399 a year or $20 for a week (okay, the library isn't that far...). Or visit *bookspan's* (an umbrella entity encompassing a bunch of book clubs) online list at **www.booksonline.com**. Some examples? *The Military Book Club, Outdoorsman's Edge Book Club, Science Fiction Book Club, Good Cook Book Club,* and dozens more.

Don't be afraid to shoot high. I landed *Writer's Digest Book Club* early enough that I could use it in all my Internet pitches—a phenomenal door-opener. I didn't even consider *Book-of-the-Month Club (BOMC)* and *Quality Paperback Book (QPB)* until I'd landed a few prestigious reviews in *Library Journal* and *Booklist*. Once I did, I was feeling like Mr. BigTime, so I sent the book—and those reviews—to *BOMC* and *QPB* (sister clubs under *bookspan*) and, within a month, got the thumbs-up.

I remember what the acquisitions editor said: "We just haven't seen any book quite like this on the market." Ponder that litmus test when you're contemplating your book's subject, title and cover design. Book clubs—and *anyone* for that matter—want unique, different, distinctive.

By the way, from a distributor standpoint, book club deals may vary. Obviously, in a royalty situation (where there's nothing for the distributor to do), all royalties would go to the publisher. If the book club is buying books from the publisher, the tune might change a bit. I know BookMasters doesn't take a piece just for being the distributor (except a charge for packing and shipping), but that may not be the prevailing standard. Ask the question.

Catalogs

Catalogs can be great places to sell books, especially if you have a niche book that might appeal to a select segment out there. Check out **www.cybercatalogs.com** or **www.catalogcentral.com** for hundreds of catalogs across the spectrum.

Selling to "Indies"

In this age of mega-bookstore chains that increasingly only stock the sure bets, independent bookstores can sometimes be a self-publisher's best friend. The "indies" are typically run by true book lovers, so they're more likely to give a voice (i.e., shelf space) to new talent when a chain store won't. And if they like a book, they're notoriously good about spreading the word. While the bigger chains have slowly squeezed out much of this bookselling segment, they're still a force to be reckoned with. And don't forget the *BookSense* program we discussed in Chapter Four—geared to the "indies."

> ### Excuse me, Mr. Distributor, could you tell me...."
>
> A few questions (though by no means all) to ask a prospective distributor:
>
> 1) In addition to handling warehousing, inventory, shipping, invoicing, collections, and returns processing, do you field a sales force to promote my book?
>
> 2) Do you put out a catalog that would feature my book? How many copies go out, how many times a year, and to whom?
>
> 3) What other sales/marketing programs do you offer?
>
> 4) Do you handle toll-free order processing and shipping, and/or "shipping only" for orders already processed through an author's personal web site?
>
> 5) How do you deal with book club sales if it's necessary to ship books? Are there any other charges besides normal fulfillment and shipping fees?

In truth, I haven't gone out of my way to woo the independent bookstores. It's a labor-intensive process, and as we're often talking about single-location entities, it's hard to do appreciable numbers. As long as you're listed in one or both of the wholesalers, the indies can get hold of your book.

I cover my bases by including a "Booksellers" link on my site that tells them a bit about my books, steers them to more information, lets them know they can get both books through Ingram, outlines the terms if they want to order directly from me (which occasionally they will, especially if the terms are better than Ingram's), and the four modes of contact they can use to order books. Most indies are used to getting roughly 45 to 47 percent discount. My terms are 50 percent discount, minimum of five copies, and they pay shipping. Because I have BookMasters handling all book shipments, my contact roads all lead to them, so again, I'm out of the loop.

NON-RETURNABLE BOOKS?

Something to ponder: the percentage discount offered to independents is often tied to returnability. Offer perhaps 55 percent off (the same terms that Ingram, B&T, and Amazon get anyway), or maybe even 60 percent, but make the books non-returnable. If they're paying shipping, then it becomes—if not necessarily a high-profit sale—a nice, clean, assured-profit, *final* sale.

Hire an Outside Salesperson?

If you don't want to mess with a distributor, you might want to explore an alternative I heard about from a friend recently. She came across a website (**www.rephunter.net**) for independent sales reps that another author was using to sell his books. You pay a fee of $300 to join the site, and $99 a month from then on (though once you get your rep, you can cancel).

Given that the site features reps for many different kinds of products, she had to dig through to find the ones who repped books. Specifically, she was looking for a rep who worked the college bookstore market. She finally signed with one of them on the following terms: bookstores buy for 50 percent off retail, non-returnable; minimum order 10 books; rep gets 7.5 percent of retail. Given that I would love to penetrate that market too, I asked my friend for the rep's contact details. We'll see how it goes.

Google Book Search (formerly Google Print)

Leave it to the most successful search engine in the world to come up with a powerful tool to help authors sell more books. It's called *Google Book Search*. I won't get into an exhaustive description of the program, since they do a great job of explaining it on their site (**http://books.google.com/intl/en/ googlebooks/about.html**), but here's a wildly simplistic "quick 'n dirty" of how it works.

You upload ebook versions of your title(s) to Google's server, and in a few weeks, they've loaded your book onto their site. Every time someone does a Google search in their "Book Search" area, using a keyword that matches your subject matter, a string of books (including yours, perhaps) shows up on screen. When they click on a particular book, they're taken to a page summarizing the book, and offering a chance to view selected pages (similar to Amazon's "Look Inside!" feature).

TOTAL WIN-WIN

If the visitor wants to buy the book, they'll then find a list of places where they can do so. The author determines what links go there, and in what order (in my case, I'd list my own web site first, then Amazon.com, then BN.com). The visitor then clicks through to that site, and Google takes nary a dime. What's in it for them? They get to place a few exceptionally unobtrusive ads at the bottom of the pages called up by a viewer's search. And if those ads get clicked, the author even makes money whether their book is purchased or not!

I've uploaded my books, but it's too early to tell if it'll turn into anything. More importantly, there's really no downside to this and plenty of upsides. It doesn't cost a dime, it increases exposure, offers direct click-thru access to the purchase venue(s) of your choice, and even offers passive income potential from the ads.

Some authors have expressed concern about the program from the standpoint that the ability of a visitor to view a small chunk of their book amounts to "free content being given away." How terribly short-sighted. That reader would see far more standing in a bookstore or taking it out of a library! All I see is more exposure, and that's great. It's simply another promotional avenue to pursue.

Large Print, Perhaps?

After signing up for the Google Book Search (GBS) program while at the BEA show, I visited the *Lightning Source* booth (Ingram's POD arm; **www.lightningsource.com**; 615-213-5815) to explore the possibility of having my books converted to large print POD editions for sale through them—one of the services they offer, and the only really good application of POD for a publisher like me (much more on POD in Chapter Twelve).

When I told them I'd just signed up for GBS, they said, "Ah, that makes things easier." Seems all Lightning Source Ingram (LSI) books can be included on GBS for free as well, and LSI even had a little flyer from GBS they included with their info package.

Now that we've explored a few of the main ways our books actually wind their way through the various distribution channels, let's look at one more venue that deserves a chapter of its own...

Chapter 7

I remember my first experience with **www.Amazon.com** as an author. I went to the site to figure out how to set up my book profile. Just on a lark, I did a search for my title and—Shazam!—like magic, there it was. Granted, it was a bare-bones profile, but, nonetheless, in the eyes of the (apparently) all-seeing, all-knowing Amazon gods, I existed. I was legit. How could this be? How did they know? What kind of infernal sorcery was this?

Well, while I never got the definitive scoop straight from the horse's mouth, I'm guessing that the actual explanation was a bit more prosaic than magic: Amazon was sufficiently wired into all the new book listing databases that when mine came up with an ISBN number assigned, the creation of the profile was automatic. Which nicely underscores a point I've been making in many ways throughout this book, and in my others: Make it easy for people to do business with you. Which, in turn, goes back to one of my core mantras: "audience." Understand your audience and tailor your message (substitute: offering, service, product, pitch) to that audience.

Making it Easy...

In the case of Amazon, they know if they want authors to do business with them, they need to make the process as simple as possible. As my initial experience demonstrated*, they kicked that off by essentially rolling out the red carpet and saying, *Welcome. We've been waiting for you.*

*If, in fact, your book profile isn't showing up automatically, then go through the steps of joining the Amazon Advantage program (**www.amazon.com/advantage**), and once registered, sign on with your login and password, and on the next screen you get to, click Add Titles at the top left of the page.

123

Using the Amazon Advantage program (**www.amazon.com/advantage**), it was then just a matter of going through the steps—adding author bio, book synopsis, cover artwork, and more. Now, of course, Amazon has added the wonderful "Look Inside!" functionality, which lets the prospective buyer read the back cover, the book's introduction, the first 10-15 pages, index, etc. The visitor has a virtual "holding-the-book-in-one's-hand" experience.

As discussed in the earlier section on *Google Book Search,* don't get all weird about how *They're giving away 10-15 pages of my book!* Yes, they are, and you should be thrilled that your prospective buyers have that opportunity. Again, far less than what they'd see in a bookstore (or taking it over to the café for an extended perusal before putting it back on the shelf).

Amazon is a wonderful outlet for authors, and the fact that, a few years back, they finally turned a profit for the first time in their history bodes well for their future, and is good news for authors everywhere. I'm not going to spend a lot of time discussing this great resource, when visiting their site will get you up to speed faster and in more detail than I could ever do here. And while these folks want to sell books, their communication and follow-through, as we'll discuss, are often their weakest links.

Cool Marketing Resources

Once you've set up an account, check out their *Marketing Resource Center* for more ideas about, and support in, marketing your book. Last time I checked, there were some pretty nifty marketing plans written by different authors, each using an actual book as an example. You'll learn a lot.

To participate in these programs, you need to send your book to a particular channel editor along with supporting information on the book (a press kit usually does nicely). Here's where we get into the few downsides of dealing with Amazon. While I applied twice to have my book accepted as a featured book in the writing channel, it never came to anything. I never heard from anyone, and my specific inquiries to that editor were never answered.

After that first application, I made a more general contact, and the best they could suggest was to reapply, which I did—with no more success the second time round than the first. Which underscores the most frustrating aspect of dealing with them: there's no way to contact anyone by phone.

No Calls, Please

All contacts must be by email, and it usually takes two to three days to get a reply. Then, be prepared for the likelihood that the reply will be nice, polite, and totally *not* answer your question (*Did you read my note at all?!?!* you'll bark at your computer screen). If you reply back, you can pretty much count on getting a response (after another 48 to 72 hours) from a different person—

who is blissfully unaware of the conversation trail to that point, making it even less likely that they'll give you a halfway useful answer to your original question.

The "New Edition" Glitch

One other area where Amazon reportedly stumbles is when authors come out with a new edition of their book. Because of some arcane technological quirk, their system doesn't recognize the new edition, and keeps referring to the old one. If that first edition is out of print (often the case, by definition), the author's out of luck. And, I'm told, weeks, even months, of increasingly frantic emails doesn't achieve a whole lot in terms of getting things ironed out.

Eventually, the problem gets resolved, but not without authors resorting to medication in the meantime. At press time, while Amazon has acknowledged the problem, they haven't yet solved it, and in an uncanny impersonation of a government agency, has even been heard to say their system is working the way it's supposed to. Whatever you say, guys.

But these are small complaints. Overwhelmingly, I've been more than pleased with my dealings with them. They'll sell a lot of books for you.

By the way, Amazon.com just launched their *Talent Acquisition Program*, which can put self-publishers in front of bigger name publishing houses who'll consider picking up their books. IF that's your goal (never was mine...). There's no cost (at press time) to participate. Direct any questions or requests for an application to **TAP@amazon.com**.

Monitor Your Reviews

I've been very fortunate (okay, writing a good book does help) to have received (at press time) roughly 100 customer reviews on Amazon for my first book, and about 30 for my second, with an average rating of close to five stars.

At around the 40-review mark for my first book, a one-star review appeared that was a real doozy. It was abusive, scathing, and screechy, and amazingly, never directly addressed anything in the book. Instead, this... gentleman... railed on and on about how it must all be so much B.S., because after all, why would anyone with such a lucrative secret (i.e., how to tap into a wealth of writing work that paid $60-100+/hour) share it with the world? He went on to speculate, with a great deal of certainty, that no one could really be successful doing this, and that he'd certainly never heard of anyone who had.

This isn't a valid review, I thought. If he'd taken issue with specific points or claims in the book, based on his own experiences, fine. Instead, his underlying premise was, "It's all a scam." Adding to the bad news was that, for some reason, it was a "Spotlight Review," making it one of the first a visitor would see. Not good. Call me a control freak, but I was P.O.'d and I thought, I'll be darned if I'm going to lose sales because some angry dude with an overactive imagination has chosen to rain down his paranoid worldview on my parade, *and* Amazon's gone and put him on a pedestal!

Protest Pays Off...

So I sent an email to Amazon protesting the review on those grounds, and requested its removal. Well, they wrote right back and said, in essence, "Thanks for bringing this to our attention. We have no idea how this review slipped by in the first place, given that it indeed fits our criteria of 'spurious and spiteful' (the standard by which they filter out the junk). It will be off the system within 2-3 days." And it was.

As an editorial aside, this practice of spotlighting several one- or two-star reviews in a sea of five-star ones—which has happened to me several times— is mystifying. If there were a bunch of them, sure, but to highlight the anomalies when you're supposedly in the business of selling books? Doesn't make any sense. Maybe it's the enlightened, Pacific Northwest, Starbucks-sipping, everyone's-opinion-has-value attitude, untainted by filthy lucre. Who knows? C'mon, this is a business, guys. You want to sell books, right? Then spotlight the five-stars. The one-stars are still there if anyone wants to scroll down and read 'em all, but to give them top billing? Please.

...Sometimes

But, lest you think that a polite, well-written complaint is all that's necessary to make an unfavorable review vanish, think again. Emboldened by my previous success, I tried one other time with another one-star review written by someone who clearly, obviously, unquestionably hadn't read my book. If he had, it would've been categorically impossible for him to write what he had. Alas, this time my articulate case fell on deaf ears. The review, according to their response, fell within their guidelines and, they went on to say, "we like to encourage a diversity of opinion." I see.

Unable to resist, I wrote back, all ornery, saying, *Um, so 'diversity of opinion' means including comments both from those who **have** read the book and those who **haven't**.* I got no reply. What the heck. It was worth a shot. You're going to get your head-scratchers. And actually, in a perverse sort of way, a single one-star review in a sea of five-star entries will actually lend more credence to a book, in essence, discrediting itself. Just thought I'd share the tale so you know that "review management" is occasionally a feasible exercise. Email **community-help@amazon.com** when you do come across a review that might fall into that "spurious and spiteful" category.

The Amazon Marketplace Program

I must confess, when I first saw used and nearly new copies of my book being sold by others through the *Amazon Marketplace Program*, with no profit accruing to me, I had mixed emotions. On the one hand, I was none too happy to be financially cut out of a transaction involving my masterpiece. On the other, I've purchased my share of used books from Amazon over the years, so for me to whine when the shoe was on the other foot was just a tad disingenuous. So, given that I'd have to live with this reality, I decided that if I couldn't beat 'em, I'd join 'em.

Now, what I'm *not* doing is selling pristine new books at cut-rate prices on Amazon. That would get my full-price book buyers understandably ticked. What I *am* doing is selling dinged books—some more dinged than others—at a lower price. In the book biz, it's inevitable you end up with some books that don't weather the vagaries of travel as well as others. In my case, it's both the ones that have traveled through bookstores and back to BookMasters (which they'll set aside and send to me) and ones BookMasters ship to me periodically for my own needs that have been handled a bit roughly en route.

Well-Traveled Books?

Most of the damage is minor, but I can't sell them as unblemished. Nonetheless, you want to try to undercut the price at which the competition is selling your books. To determine a logical price, go visit Amazon, visit your book profile, and click on the "Used & new from $____" link. In my case, the price usually hovers around $9 to $13, depending on the competition and the condition of the book.

To learn about the *Amazon Marketplace* program, go visit **www.amazon.com** and scan the top tool bars for *Sell Your Stuff.* You'll go through a series of screens that describe this program, which actually allows you to sell a lot of merchandise, including books. For books, they do nickel-and-dime you pretty ridiculously. After processing the customer's credit card, Amazon takes a $.99 transaction fee, plus $1.23 on books for something called a "closing fee" (WHATever…), *plus* 15 percent of your asking price.

But, this is cool: they reimburse you for shipping, because they're collecting that from the customer. You get (at press time) $3.49 for "standard" shipping, which will likely be more than what you'll pay for Media Mail shipping, and, of course, higher amounts for expedited or international options. Your listing lasts for 60 days, or until the item sells. Once it sells, you'll get a notifying email that provides shipping instructions, and another one later letting you know the money has been deposited in your checking account.

Once you've set up your account, bookmark your "Seller Account" page, then when a book sells, if you have others to take its place, relist the item by going to the "Seller Account" page and clicking "Relist this item." At that point, you can edit your listing to reflect a new price, or a book in better or worse condition. If you have multiple copies to sell in similar condition, when you list the item, enter the number you have and avoid having to relist the book after each sale.

Signed Books Earn More!

When you create your listing in the first place, do as I do and start your listing with these six words in caps: "PERSONALLY SIGNED TO BUYER BY AUTHOR!" You've got a bit of an unfair advantage here, so use it. Chances are, people would pay a bit more to get a signed copy, but again, the goal is to have the lowest price so your listing is up top. Speaking of price, if I notice I haven't had any activity for a while, I'll check my listing to see if I've been undercut again, and if so, I'll return the favor.

Bottom line, through the *Amazon Marketplace* program, on, say, a $12 book, with fees taken out and a typical net gain on shipping costs, I end up clearing around $9. What do I net on a normal Amazon sale (or one from the bookstores, for that matter)? $8.98 (55 percent discount on a $19.95 book). So, on a dinged book, I'm making about the same as I would on a new one, and each one I sell is one less "profitless" (for me) sale that goes to someone else. It all works out. Yes, you've got to mess with packing and shipping books, but once you have your shipping system in place (see Appendix D), it's no biggie.

As for the ones that others sell, for which I make nary a dime? C'est la vie. Since there are plenty of other reasons to return to my site (ebooks, CDs, paid mentoring, free ezine, etc.), and because my URL is prominently displayed on both covers, chances are excellent they'll eventually amble on over to my site, and probably buy something else.

I say this is a healthy way of viewing your books: not as an end in themselves, but simply as the initial hook (again, "the book as a base") that brings them into your "network." And once in, because you've continued to create new products and services, they continue to buy things. I promise, if you build up a good rapport with your readers, and give them good information, and good reasons to keep returning, you'll get plenty of notes that say, in essence, "whatever you write or create, I'll buy it." Sweet.

A "Dinged Books" Link?

Of course, you could just do what I did recently, and add your own "Dinged Books" link to your site and get rid of your scuffed beauties that way. This option has the added advantage that you can offer some free bonus, like free shipping or personal inscription, or anything else to sweeten the pot, and usually make a few extra bucks as well.

To the Next Level

Given that *Marketplace* buyers obviously like a deal, I came up with a "$4 BOOK-BUCKS OFF!" certificate, which I print out and include with all my Amazon dinged book shipments. In essence, I offer these buyers the chance to buy either of my books (personally signed, of course) for four dollars off the regular price when they buy it through my site, along with free shipping and a free ebook (which costs me nothing except the time it took to create it in the first place).

Even at a $4 discount, I'm still making more than a regular Amazon sale, and the customer is usually paying less than a typical *Marketplace* sale (which are *not* eligible for Amazon's "free-shipping-for-orders-over-$25" policy). Win-win.

The certificate states that it's only good for use by people who've bought one of my other books. In truth, there's little way to verify that, but they don't know that. You may be plodding along in a relative stone age, database-wise, but let them think you're wildly automated. More importantly, if someone who doesn't "qualify" goes ahead and uses one, so what? As a self-publisher, I'm still nicely profitable even with this discount, so if it means making a sale that I wouldn't have otherwise had, I'll take it.

How do you handle these discounted orders through your site? Simple. Just set up "mirror image" web pages, identical to your regular purchase pages, with all the same features, and adjust your price down $4. Put a line through your regular price, and put the cheaper price in red, complete with exclamation point. Then, have it accessible through a special "side-door" link—which they type in manually—unseen on your main site and unpublicized except through the certificates.

FLYERS FOR FULFILLMENT

By the way, discount certificates are great things to include in all the book packages you send out. If you're using a fulfillment company to handle your "onesie-twosie" buyers, for a small extra fee (usually 15 or 20 cents per shipment), you can provide a bunch of one-page flyers to them and they'll include one in every book package that goes out.

Follow-Up = More $

Given that you collect email addresses from all *Marketplace* orders (to which you should always send a thank-you email when they first buy a book), you have the opportunity to offer discount certificates electronically as well. In addition to including a certificate with the book when you send it out, it's not a bad idea to send them the "cert" again, by email, a month or so down the line.

www.bn.com

The other big online bookstore. I'm really not trying to give B&N's online entity short shrift here. It's just that I've focused most of my energies (and testimonial solicitation) on Amazon. But, the drill on both are similar, and you should get hooked up with both. Truth be known, I did virtually nothing on my bn.com online book profiles, and they simply took it upon themselves (as Amazon does) to set up a basic profile and sell my books. While you're at it, check out this link for a list of about 30 online bookstores. Perhaps you'll find a few more worth wooing: **www.allbookstores.com/stores/**.

Amazon & "Distribution"

Piggybacking on the distribution discussion in Chapter Six, if you end going with a distributor, they will handle your Amazon piece, and take a healthy slice, so know that upfront, and find out how much. If you end up going the fulfillment company route, they'll just handle the logistical shipping of books to the online retailer (plus invoicing and collections), and you'll make out a little better.

Are You a Rankings Watcher?

I've never been one. Oh sure, in the early days, as my first book rose to around 1,000 and perhaps even higher (who can watch it all the time?), it was fun to occasionally see where I stood. But, you're far better off just consistently getting the word out and letting the chips fall where they may. And from the few articles I've read over the years, the process by which Amazon arrives at their rankings is so complex and convoluted that the upshot is, at any given moment in time, it doesn't mean a whole heckuva lot anyway.

Of course that doesn't stop people from addictively monitoring their books, watching to see if any recent little marketing pushes here and there have caused any blips on the radar. Then there are the "How to Turn Your Book Into a #1 Best-Seller on Amazon!" articles, which chronicle the tortured process of funneling a huge chunk of your marketing into a one-day campaign for world dominance, sending out countless emails to friends, neighbors, Romans and countrymen, beseeching them all to buy your book on this one day, and during this one brief window, bribing them with all sorts of freebies to make that happen. Hey, if it gets your book to #1, even for just an hour, and gives you bragging rights, more power to you.

Manufactured Best-Sellers

Maybe I'm just lazy, but something bothers me about all that. A friend forwarded an article to me about a couple of guys who, huffing, puffing, and grunting, pushed their book—a shamelessly repackaged series of past articles of theirs—onto *The Wall Street Journal* business best-seller list. Apparently, they didn't care too much about making money; they just wanted to be able to claim they'd made the list. They inputed thousands of orders manually, one by one, selling their hardcover book for $14, and giving away two free copies for every one purchased. And yes, they made that list. Sigh.

Call me a shortsighted little brownie, but as I see it, manufactured rankings don't mean much—and that's what this was. The ranking they earned had ZERO to do with the quality or value of the book (and isn't that what people are concluding when they see "#1 Best Seller!"—that the book was worthy of its ranking?), or even, in their case, the actual number of copies truly sold. It had everything to do with "working the system." The content was just past articles. Is that worthy of "Best Seller" status? I think not.

And heck, offer three hardcover books for fourteen bucks, you'll have a lot of takers. Great. They hit their goal. But it's all smoke and mirrors. They got to say "#1" but it wasn't achieved honestly. Ditto in most cases with the "#1-on-Amazon!" strategies.

"Pseudonymous" Reviews

One last thought before I descend from my soapbox. Apparently, it's pretty standard these days for authors to enlist all their friends and family members to post gushing reviews on Amazon about said author's book—most of whom have never read said book. If that's what you've got planned, my little finger-waving here probably won't stop you, but if someone hasn't read the book, then it's a bogus review. Period.

As for the whole business of recruiting friends to post negative reviews for books that compete with yours (complete, of course, with the suggestion to check out *your* book for the "real deal"...) when they haven't read that competing book either? That's just downright pathetic. Three words: *The Golden Rule.*

Ask For Reviews

What I *will* do regarding reviews (and we touched on this earlier) is this: whenever someone writes to tell me he loved my book, I politely ask if he'd be willing to go on over to Amazon and write a review. Make it easy on yourself by making the request a "stationery" item in your email program. That way, when you get those nice notes, you simply do a *Reply With*, choosing that response (which then "populates" your screen), and you're done. Then make it easy on *them* by including the actual link to the book on Amazon. Mine looks like this:

BTW—if you're so inclined to run on over to Amazon and write a review, I'd be most grateful... Thanks much! Here's the link:

www.amazon.com/yourbooksimpossiblyindeciperablecode

Okay, now that we've got a feel for how to cut through the Amazon jungle, let's take a look at the game of publicity—media and otherwise...

Chapter 8

Persistent Reporters

In September 2002, I traveled to Alaska for eleven days—four days in Anchorage and a seven-day cruise (magnificent, by the way). Those eleven days were all vacation, but just to appease my inner slave-driver, I scheduled one of my all-day commercial writing seminars in Seattle at the end of the trip. I had one of my early enrollees, who was located in Seattle, helping me by handling emails/calls and enrollments while I was out of phone range (I just steered people to her on the seminar enrollment page of my web site).

Early in the cruise, I decided to check my email account, although I almost didn't spring for it, due to the truly usurious rates they were charging. But, I'm sooooo glad I did, because there were two emails from a reporter with *The Seattle Times*, responding to a press release I'd sent to the paper (not to him specifically, but you never know where they'll end up), and looking to do a small piece on my upcoming visit.

His second email said he really needed to talk with me soon or he would have to skip the story. He'd been trying to get hold of me for a few days, and was intrigued with the story I was telling with my book. Seattle had a high unemployment rate at the time, and given the connection I made between corporate downsizing and greater freelance opportunity, he saw a good angle.

An Author's Dream

All of which underscores an important point: the focus of any press release you write promoting your book should *never* be about the book, but about why the book is relevant to the publication's readers today. More on that later...

Anyway, this was an author's dream come true: a newspaper reporter making repeated attempts to get hold of you. Suffice it to say, if you're not a celebrity or have THE HOTTEST TOPIC OF THE DAY, it's a rare occurrence. Sure, you can get media attention; it's just that, typically, it's *your* persistence that makes the difference, not a reporter's. Which is why I've never pursued media coverage as the main vehicle for getting the word out. Given my niche topic, it's just too fickle and unreliable.

In any case, basking briefly in the all-too-rare position of being "sought after," I borrowed a friend's cell phone, climbed up to the top deck of the ship and tried to reach this persistent soul. Oh, the constant harassment from media and paparazzi...can't they give a man a moment's peace? (Hey, a guy can dream...).

He answered on the second ring, we did our 10-minute interview, and the story ran two days before my seminar, at which point I had eight enrollments. On seminar day, I had 16 smiling faces in seats (my goal was 15; the extra eight meant about $1500 in my pocket). And undoubtedly, that publicity sold me plenty of books. For every person who shows up at a signing or seminar, you have to figure there are 10 or more who don't, but go check out the web site and maybe buy a book.

I've felt the potent impact of one good media hit many times before and since, as well as the no-fun outcome of delivering a seminar to four people when I *couldn't* get anyone in the local media to pay attention. Which highlights the fact that I only pursued mainstream media coverage when I had a seminar and/or signing scheduled in a city. Trying to get the media's attention about my book in the absence of an actual visit is a borderline masochistic exercise—too much work for too little return.

Fickle MM Folks

Even though I didn't make mainstream media (MM) coverage a priority, you should certainly pursue some media coverage in addition to your Internet contacts. Just know that the media is exponentially more fickle than "targeted-audience" contacts.

Fact is, when I targeted my search to writers, at-home Moms and home-based business seekers, I was getting a 30 to 40 per cent positive response rate (*Yes, absolutely we'd love to review your book! And if you want to write an article or do an interview with us or perhaps even...*—you get the idea). It's no surprise. I'd picked groups that, by definition, would have an interest in my book. Mainstream media is just that—mainstream, not nearly as focused.

The Media as Fish

Picture the media world and its practitioners as a school of hungry fish. Of course, fish have very specific likes and dislikes. They dig worms, grubs, bugs, flies, etc. Translation: today's issues, events, stories, trends, fads, conventional wisdom—in short, a journalist's bread and butter. Obviously, that also includes books with mainstream appeal (i.e., health, dieting, exercise, romance, relationships, parenting, psychology, financial security, investing, religion, etc.).

Okay, now that's their preferred diet. However, when those tasty morsels are in short supply, they may go for lumps of bread, crackers, and the like. That'd be the second-tier issues and niche stories, perhaps related to books written by folks like me.

But, regardless of whether your topic is a potentially juicy worm (a mainstream topic) or some cracker crumbs (a "slow-day" topic), you have to package it so it looks like the real thing, and is just as ready-to-eat. You wouldn't go fishing with an unopened can of worms, bread wrapped in tin foil, or a sealed package of peanut butter crackers. You've got to give the fish *what* they want to eat and *how* they want to eat it. And as we'll discuss later, fish (media folks) like their food *au naturel*—minus the (editorial) "seasoning."

Here's the reality: unknown authors with niche topics face an uphill battle getting reasonably major-market newspapers to give them exposure. Doesn't mean you shouldn't try, but just a heads-up. If you do plan to go for it, DO NOT, as discussed earlier, just send out review copies en masse with no personal contact. If you do, you will almost certainly succumb to *The Dumpster Factor.*

Are You "Donating" Review Copies?

According to a friend who works at a major metropolitan daily paper, the newspaper gets approximately 125 unsolicited review copies daily, and more like 250 a day during the holiday season. I was told that they literally have a dumpster in the mail room, and most of them get tossed, unopened. OR they have internal book sales a few times a year as a charity benefit to clear out the stockpile. I'm totally serious. None of us mind making our occasional donations to worthy causes, but I'm not at all certain we'd want most of our review copies suffering such a fate. And they *will* if you're sending out a pile of them to book editors who aren't expecting them. Which brings me to the next point...

Unless you're a big name, a recognized local talent, or have a white-hot timely subject, forget sending a review copy to the book editor of a major daily paper. They don't care. Do however, contact those book editors with info on upcoming signings to go into their calendar, and try to get them to include your web address in the listing. How about your own small or mid-market-sized hometown paper? Given the "local-boy/girl-makes-good" angle, I like your chances. It's worked for me.

Have a Mainstream Topic?

I'll be the first to admit that I'm no guru on getting MM coverage. I have no doubt that if I'd pursued it more vigorously, boned up on all the "Write-Killer-Press-Releases" literature and taken a bunch of seminars, I could have done a lot better in this arena. But again, I had to pick my battles, and I simply won far more with my targeted Internet approach than I ever did with MM.

IF the subject of your book falls into a classic mainstream topic (sex, money, religion, dieting/health, relationships, etc.) and you've come up with a fresh, unique angle for the category, then, by all means, pursue MM for all it's worth. Check out media maven Marisa D'Vari's great book, *Building Buzz* (**www.deg.com**), for an excellent primer on getting the most from your MM campaign.

Press Release Basics

At the risk of getting way too basic (a la Vince Lombardi's classic "Day-One-of-Training-Camp" speech: "Gentlemen, *this* is a football…"), let's talk about the press release: the fundamental, all-purpose publicity tool for anyone trying to get media attention for anything. It's mandatory. Non-negotiable. The first, and often *only*, thing any media person (and most non-media reviewers as well) will want to see. And it needs to be pure, unvarnished information.

I'm not going to get into an exhaustive study of press releases here, given that there have been whole books written on the subject. A great one is Paul J. Krupin's *Trash-Proof News Releases*. Score a free ebook version at **www.imediafax.com/tpnr/** on his site. Krupin runs a targeted fax/email press release distribution service through his site (**www.imediafax.com**) for pretty reasonable prices.

Anyone embarking on a self-publishing campaign needs a one- or, at most, two-page press release (a.k.a. "news release" or just "release"). It's *very* important to get the format right, and fairly easy to run foul of the rules. Send out a release without all pertinent contact info right at the top, without the word "more" centered and bracketed by dashes at the bottom of the first page of a two-page release, or without three hash marks centered at the end of the release, and you'll invite a quick disposal.

In late 2003, I took John Kremer's (author of *1001 Ways to Market Your Books* and an all-round nice guy) excellent three-day weekend *Book Marketing Blastoff* seminar in Atlanta. It was there that I was unequivocally disabused of the notion that the release I'd been using was any good. The feedback I got from John and several other participants on my prevailing version was worth the price of admission alone.

BTW, check out John's great site (**www.bookmarket.com**), chockfull of great resources for independent publishers. Let him know (**info@bookmarket.com**) that you want to be notified of seminars in your area.

See Appendix B for a sample of a good press release (and my separate ebook (**e**) for *The Amazing Evolving Press Release*: four versions of a release, starting with gruesome and working up to a few decent serviceable ones).

For a Great PR Primer...

Check out **www.publicityinsider.com** from PR maestro Bill Stoller, a 20-year PR veteran with a list of credits as long as your arm. He puts out a monthly newsletter—*Free Publicity*—that'll run you about $100 annually.

For a great background on PR that underscores the things I've been saying, check out his link at **www.publicityinsider.com/freesecret.asp**. It takes you through the PR basics, how to think like a reporter, and provides an invaluable "real-world" example of a particular company showing how, using his fundamental strategies, they'd maximize their chance of getting publicity. Even if you never order his newsletter, this foundation is priceless, and will keep you from making the most common and costly PR mistakes.

Never written a release? Check out **www.publicityinsider.com/release.asp**. Using that "real-world" company introduced earlier, this section not only provides an accurate press release format, but takes you through the process of writing the release step-by-step, showing you how that company can come up with a compelling angle that can get a reporter calling them.

Press Release Distribution Services (+ a FREE one)

PR Newswire (**www.prnewswire.com**), the reigning leader in emailed press releases (and many other news/photo distribution services), can send your 400-word press release (approximately 1.5 pages, set at 1.5 line spacing) to thousands of media outlets across the country for $610 (at press time) or about $130-150 for one major metropolitan area. That said, PRN gears themselves more toward bigger, publicly traded companies (translation: ones with far juicier PR budgets than we have...).

Don't feel like paying (or don't have) the big bucks for pricey distribution of your release? Check out the budget marketer's best friend: *PRWeb™* (**www.prweb.com**), which touts itself as "The Free Wire Service." Despite offering a no-cost option (which is understandably bare-bones and low-priority), PRW's program is surprisingly sophisticated, full-featured, and user-friendly.

PRW operates through donations from their customers, and offers a menu of additional services for additional cost, rising to the $80 level, though even a modest $30 will juice up the distribution bells and whistles nicely and deliver an impressive bang for your buck. I spoke to customer service reps from both PRN and PRW, and walked away with this: while there's a huge differential between PRN and PRW pricing, the actual bottom line reach of both isn't that far apart. In fact, according to both, PRW actually uses some of PRN's transmission infrastructure!

I can't say I got tons of ripples from any of the release distributions I did (I also sprang for a service in the $300 ballpark, before I knew of PRW), but sometimes it's hard to tell. Sure, a lot of media contacts means it was worth it, but a lack of them doesn't necessarily mean you've thrown away your money. At *PRWeb* prices, you can afford to do regular (say, monthly) "trend-jumping" releases, or just experiment.

How Do I Send Them?

If I send out a review copy and press kit to someone, obviously, we're talking a hard copy press release. But if it's initial awareness-building I'm after, or more likely, advance work for an upcoming seminar appearance, I always just email my releases. That's becoming the accepted standard for many journalists, and given the instant click-thru to the related links that it offers, it's not hard to see why.

That said, it's also true that different journalists like to receive their releases in different ways. Some prefer snail mail, others fax, still others email. If you plan on sending a lot of releases to the same core group of media folks over time, then it definitely pays to find out what each prefers. Given that I haven't made the MM folks my focus, I just stick to email and leave it at that. In this day and age, if you had to pick one format to use across the board, email would be the way to go.

---

12 Tips to Writing Stronger Press Releases That Get Noticed!

The following list comes from both John Kremer and my own experience:

1) **One Page is Ideal**—Make every effort to keep your release to a single page. Single-spaced is okay. Hand-in-hand with this one...

2) **Focus on ONE Key Message**—NOT three or four. As John was quick to point out when reading mine, virtually every release of two or more pages tries to highlight three or more points and usually ends up rambling and unfocused. Which segues nicely into...

3) Include a "Background" Release 🄴—This piece, which could also be called a book info sheet, can cover all the supplemental info which, far too often, and inappropriately, ends up in the aforementioned scattered specimens. We're talking about any awards, book clubs, additional selling points, expert quotes, etc. In short, all the salient details that can give a reviewer/journalist more context on your book, and more content with which to craft their review, story or mention—without having to wade through what should be—but isn't—a "just-the-facts-Ma'am" release.

4) Include a Cover Letter—Like a background release, a cover letter (🄴) lets you do what you can't do in your release: get a little promotional, steering your readers to the overarching thoughts you want them to take away from your contact. It allows you to highlight a particular angle, and in general, add a friendlier, more personal tone to your correspondence.

I don't typically include cover letters with general "book-awareness-building" releases sent to media folks (and given my more targeted online strategy, don't send that many of them in the first place). I'm more inclined to include one (and send releases to the media in general) when I'm actually headed to a city to do a seminar or some other event.

TIP: Create files on your computer including, in order, your cover letter, press release, and background release (where necessary), so they're all ready to print out or cut 'n paste into an email screen, where you'll then tailor them slightly to your recipient. Make text-only versions of these files so that cutting and pasting yields clean correspondence on the recipient's end, free of all the techno-gobbledygook that so often results from sending formatted files across the Internet. *Never* attach files.

5) Avoid "Quote-itis" (as Kremer puts it)—This doesn't mean too many quotes from the author or other experts (that's fine), but rather putting certain words in quotes to draw attention to them. I had put quotes around the words "commercial" (to differentiate the kind of writing I was doing) and "guru" to identify Bob Bly, one of the big names in the freelance writing industry. In most cases, your audience will understand what you're saying without your punctuational prodding.

6) Start Strong—The average media person receives 200-300 releases every day and will trash 98+ per cent of them. Don't make that job any easier for them. In your lead paragraph, draw the reader in with a good story, strong statistic, or other attention-getting device. Contrary to popular belief, the lead doesn't necessarily have to provide the 5Ws—who, what, when, where, and why—like a regular news story should.

7) DON'T Talk About the Book—Refer to it only when identifying the author: "'Desserts aren't just for the dining room anymore,' commented Joe Blow, author of the best selling book, *Bedroom Jello*." Media people don't care that you've written a book. They want to know why their readers would be interested in reading it. Sure, if your release is geographically-targeted, touting an upcoming visit to the area, you should bring up that fact very early in the piece, which will necessitate being a bit more book-oriented. In a few pages, I'll tell you the *other* time you can focus more on your book in a release.

8) Avoid Promoting or Editorializing—Strike any flowery verbiage. Delete your opinions. No self-serving commentary. Do *not* gush on about how great your book is and "how the reader is left with a sense of joy and triumph as they close the book, sorry to see it end." Scary. It's just not the place for your personality to shine through. Yes, it needs to be catchy and attention-getting if you want it to be read, but it needs to follow the rules. Do any of the above, and hello, circular file.

9) Let Them Cut to the Chase—At the end of the release, include a paragraph linking them to the *Media Resources* section (discussed ahead in more detail) of your site, briefly noting some of the things they'll find there: author pix, cover artwork, sample chapters, cut 'n paste promo blurbs, etc.—all designed to make it as easy as possible to put together an article, mention, blurb, etc.

10) Tailor Your Releases—If the release is going to, say, a radio or TV station, or to a particular niche audience—and you have links on your site relevant to those audiences—highlight them in bold in that post-release paragraph and in the cover letter, if you've included one. On my site, I have radio/TV interview samples along with specific links for at-home Moms and the 55+ crowd. When sending releases to those folks, it just makes sense to draw their attention to what will speak to them. Don't make them hunt.

11) Think "Reader"—Put yourself into the head of your reader—a jaded, overworked, seen-it-all media type/reviewer. Put a lot of thought into your headline. Experiment with different ones. Switch them around for different audiences. And always be thinking *angle*, not book.

12) Skip the Book Editors—As discussed, unless you're a marquee talent, book editors won't be interested. Instead, figure out which editor would be best for your topic—food, jobs, career, business, features, computers, religion, real estate, etc. Bark up those trees instead. Poke around the paper's web site. Often, there's a staff contact section, listing the editors and their specialty, along with an email link. Click, cut 'n paste your pitch, and send.

The Angle, NOT the Book

Let's assume you've figured out the right subject editor and you want to boost your odds of getting their attention. Here's where you'll pitch *not the book, but an angle represented by the book* (also known as a "news peg"; see some examples of "news pegs" for my book at the *Media Resources* link on my site: **http://www.wellfedwriter.com/media.shtml**).

As we discussed earlier, an editor, journalist or reporter doesn't care about you, your book, or your web site; he or she just wants a story their readers will find interesting. That being the case, they need to know why the book is relevant now. Think *audience. Your* audience (newspaper editors and reporters) wants stories, not book release notices. Why? Because they know what question *their* audience is constantly asking, consciously or (usually) unconsciously: *What's in it for me?*

For a long time, I've pitched three angles for my books: 1) the tie-in with all the corporate downsizing and accompanying outsourcing of writing projects at high rates, 2) the idea of the book discussing a lucrative direction for all those aspiring writers out there just trying to figure out how to make a handsome living as a writer, and 3) the growing trend of people dropping out of the rat race, starting their own home-based business, and recapturing precious quality of life, and time for leisure, loved ones, etc. Again, not the book, but why the book matters today.

Lately, in the wake of several articles in *The New York Times* on the poor state of writing skills in Corporate America (believe me when I say it's not always easy to find "pegs" for my topic), I've experimented with some new approaches, like this headline/lead paragraph:

BAD WRITING: A BUSINESS'S NIGHTMARE, A FREELANCER'S DREAM.

Atlanta, GA—May 20, 2005—As reported recently in the New York Times*, American business is wrestling with the costs of the poor writing skills of many of their workers. Yet, one man says that's good news for freelance writers. Observes Peter Bowerman, author of **The Well-Fed Writer** *and* **TWFW: Back For Seconds***, "Writing skills amongst many American workers, are frankly, atrocious. Yet this opens up tremendous opportunities for capable freelancers to step in and pick up the slack."*

Then, in the background release, in addition to, of course, the book accolades and awards, I included the bibliographic detail on the actual *Times* articles (the asterisked references).

Remember: every web-based (or even print-based, to a certain extent) review, article, interview, mention, or blurb you can get out there that includes your web address becomes the fastest way to connect your prospective buyers to more information (including how to buy the book!) that's every existed. Literally. And all while you're off doing something else. Pretty powerful stuff.

When You CAN Talk About the Book

The preceding suggestions on crafting a solid press release apply to contacts with general media types, who, by definition, are terribly jaded, and have no patience for even a whiff of a promotional tone.

However, as part of your ongoing book marketing and promotion campaign, over time, you're naturally going to build a list of the 25, 50, 100+ best contacts for you, given your book and audience(s). In my case, that would include the founders of scads of writing, at-home Mom (AHM) and home-based business seeker (HBBS) web sites and web-based associations and newsletters. Plus editors of publications like *Writer's Digest, The Writer, HOMEBusinessJournal,* and a handful of other magazines.

For the writing-related folks, given the established relationship I have with them, if I were to come out with a new book, that fact *would* be the news. That's exactly the kind of information they'd want to know. In that release, I'd want to discuss the nature of the book, what was in it, how it was different from the first (depending on whether I was calling it a "follow-up" or a "revised edition"), etc.

Certainly for my secondary markets of AHMs and HBBSs, a press release that finessed the subject more, and discussed trends and tie-ins, would be more effective, but I could still discuss the book more prominently in the release than would be the case for the general media (remember the more book-centered release we looked at in Chapter Four that spoke to published authors?).

Weeklies Deliver More "Shelf-Life"

While getting your story told in a daily paper is golden and reaches the most number of people, remember: at the end of that day, your story is likely housebreaking puppies. Not the case with the weekly, alternative, and community papers. Because they're usually not quite as high-profile, not only might it be easier to catch their attention, but once your story is in there, it hangs around for a full seven days.

In early 2002, I did a seminar and a few signings in the Champaign/Bloomington area of Illinois, a deceptively robust area in terms of population, and with strong academic and commercial bases. In my pre-visit media hunt, I got nowhere with the Champaign daily, but a reporter at the local weekly, a very cool paper called *The Octopus,* liked the idea, interviewed me, and ran a very nice half-page story. About 90 percent of the folks in my seminar found their way to me via the informative tentacles of *The Octopus.*

Get Personal

Some years back, I was promoting my *Well-Fed Writer* seminar in Nashville, Tennessee. I contacted the executive producer of a TV station by email with a pitch to appear on their noon-day show. I'd heard nothing back, so the next week, I tried to reach him by phone and got voice mail. I checked the station's web site and found an "office" number listed for the show.

I called, and a woman answered. A secretary? Wrong. One of the hosts! She was very nice, we chatted, I pitched, she requested a review copy, and I said I'd get it out that day. As a parting shot, I suggested she visit my site. When I returned from UPS, I found an email: *Checked out your site. Looks great. I'm sold! Are you available on ____?* Convinced yet that you need a web site?

Whether you're promoting your book, seminar or both, try as much as possible to reach people personally. I'm certain that I'd have gotten nowhere with that TV station had I not connected with a real human being. Unless your book is so hot that the media is literally beating down your door, if you restrict yourself to impersonal shotgun press releases, it's liable to yield little fruit. It's always best to have an actual name. Obviously, few of us have the time to make hundreds of personal phone calls, but the more you can make, the more success you'll have.

Got this note from a fellow author who bought a dinged copy of one of my books on Amazon, after which he received a thank-you email from me. People notice. *Thanks for the nice note. You care about what you do and it shows. You and I are the only two writers I know offhand that send thank-you notes to people who buy our material. I find it gets me more orders than I would receive otherwise.*

When you're calling any media person for the first time, always ask the receptionist (unless you're dialing directly) for your contact's email address before they connect you. If you get voicemail, leave a message, briefly stating your business, and tell them you'll be emailing a press release. That way, instead of being just one more email in the pile, they'll be on the lookout for it.

Hire a Publicist?

Related to media coverage, of course, is publicity—an arena with a whole other industry attached to it. Once an abundance of solid reviews and good sales numbers had convinced me that I had a good book on my hands, I started pondering the question of formal publicity, and that means a publicist. Publicists are folks who can, through their vast network of contacts (if they're to be believed), connect you with the mainstream media that you dream of reaching, and launch your book into the next level of fame and fortune. Just a few placed calls and the world will be rushing the bookstores and clogging Amazon's servers. Okay, let's put out whatever it is we're smoking (though a bit of self-delusion *can* serve you very well…).

There are, without question, plenty of reputable and hard-working publicists in the business. And, by extension, there are plenty of others whose main talents include an unusually strong ability to promise you the moon *and* to significantly lighten your bank account, usually to the tune of $2500-5000+. Bottom line: *caveat emptor.*

Never take on a publicist at rates like those until you've done your homework. Ask to speak to their clients, ask industry people about their reputation, and find out exactly what they're promising for what fee. Even if you're hearing good things about a particular one, make sure that your book meshes well with their strategy and track record.

This is where being affiliated with good independent publishing associations (like PMA and SPAN) can come in mighty handy. They're quick to spread the word about good *and* unscrupulous operators of every description. By the way, publicity guru Joan Stewart (a.k.a. *The Publicity Hound*), founder of the popular (and free) ezine *The Publicity Hound's Tips of Week,* is the author of the ebook *How to Hire the Perfect Publicist.* Buy the book and sign up for her ezine at **www.PublicityHound.com**. Joan's ezine is always full of publicity resources and neat PR success anecdotes, and each issue gives you the opportunity to weigh in on a specific reader's PR challenge.

She offers up a few sites that are not only great independent publishing resources, but can help you begin sifting through the "publicist clutter:"

www.midwestbookreview.com/bookbiz/pub_mkt.htm—
Midwest Book Review

www.bookmarket.com/101pr.html—
John Kremer's *Book Marketing Update* site, which includes a list of book publicists and beaucoup other resources

I never did hire a publicist. My publishing consultant (*another* good idea, which I'll discuss later) saw what I was doing, and how well I was doing it, and told me I didn't need one. Sure, they might open doors I couldn't, but was it worth the cost? Especially given that I was pursuing a much more targeted marketing approach than simply trying to get the mainstream media interested.

A Plug...

Now, what I *did* do, as discussed in Chapter Four, was get involved with a company called KSB Promotions (**www.KSBPromotions.com**). Ostensibly, Kate and Doug Bandos are publicists, and good reputable ones, but three times a year, they publish something called *KSB Links,* a glossy catalog of sorts that only features about 30 to 35 books total. Each book gets the four-color treatment in a one-quarter to one-third of a page ad. At press time, the cost was $650 for the placement and a spot in the online edition for four months (additional months are $15 a month). *KSB Links* goes out to more than 8,000 media folks in the U.S. and Canada—of all stripes and in all venues: newspapers, newsletters, TV/radio show hosts, magazines, web sites, and a lot more.

Because they've been publishing *KSB Links* since 1989, they've established the value of the publication in the eyes of their audience, who anticipate its release. If people like what they see in your profile, they request a review copy directly from KSB, and that request is forwarded on to you. They say the average number of requests is 10-15, and if just a couple of those translate into a good review that spurs sales, you should easily recoup your initial investment. As it turned out, I've gotten roughly 80 requests to date, the lion's share off the first insertion, and a healthy number from small follow-up mentions in subsequent issues and on the web site. So, I can wholeheartedly endorse this promotional avenue.

Targeted Treatment

Incidentally, Kate and Doug also have contacts to tons of small pubs in many different subject areas and can turn you on to them quite economically, giving your story far more reach. As part of this, they can connect you with journalists working with, or freelancing for, many major pubs. Why are freelancers good bets? Well, if a freelancer likes the pitch, they know the appropriate pub to approach, given the topic, and their connections allow them to bend the ear of key editors far more easily and effectively than you ever could. If that editor knows, likes, and has good history with that writer…you get the idea.

ALWAYS Follow Up

Just as with review copies, or anything else you're sending out to someone, follow-up is crucial with press releases. Whether you're sending out general releases or doing some advance work for an appearance, following up by phone is always a good idea. It's just easier to ignore an email.

In fact, when seeking some pre-event publicity, I often start with a call, and then follow up with the release. Obviously, there's a good chance I'll get voice mail, but in most cases, I will have secured the journalist's email address prior to dialing.

I can then make my voice mail pitch briefer (always including the memorable moniker, *This is Peter Bowerman,* The Well-Fed Writer…), adding, *I've got your email address here, and I'm about to shoot you a press release and details on my appearance.* Then, I do just that, using "**The Well-Fed Writer following up on voice mail**…" as my subject line. That'll make the email stand out a bit more.

A few basic tips for contacting media people, including ideas for calling both before and after sending releases…

1) FIRST STOP: WEB SITE: When contacting media folks (especially news journalists), check out the paper's web site first (**www.newspapers.com**) and drill down to staff directories, where they usually provide email addresses and phone numbers. Often they'll get very specific as to that reporter's news focus, making it easier to pinpoint the right contact given your subject matter. Call first, and if you get voice mail, do as described above: tell them you'll be emailing a release with cover letter ([**e**]), and then do so.

2) NEVER ASK THIS: THE first rule of phone follow-up. *Never* call and ask a journalist: "Did you get my release?" They hate that. Assume they got it.

3) ALWAYS ASK THIS: Once you've identified yourself, ask them if they're on deadline. This shows a little sensitivity, that you have a clue about their world. If they say "Whatcha need?" or "What's up?" or "How can I help you?" (anything besides "Yes, I am. Not a good time to talk."), assume it's okay to proceed, and then...

4) TALK "ANGLES": Continue along the lines of, "I sent you a release about _____ last week" (again, the blank should be filled in with some *angle* that brings in your book, *not* the book itself). Then go into your pitch, giving your listener some good fodder for a story. You should have worked out your "talking points" on paper in advance. Don't try to make it up as you go.

5) HAVE "NEWS PEGS" HANDY: In addition to "talking points," have a list of "news pegs" ([**e**])—other angles to invoke if your initial one is falling on deaf ears. An example...

A few years back, I was headed to Cincinnati to do a seminar, and was in search of a bit of media attention. I hit the site for the major daily paper, scanned the staff directories, and found a gentleman who covered small business, home-based business, and entrepreneurship, penning a weekly column on the subject. Perfect.

I called, got voice mail, left a message, followed right up with a release, heard nothing, waited a few days and called again. This time I got him on the phone. He was very nice, but said, *Yeah, I got your stuff, but I just don't see how I can make it work.* With my list of "news pegs" in front of me, obviously using the ones that would resonate with him and his arena, I proceeded to try different ones out: *The cool thing about this topic is that it can really speak to a lot of different audiences. For instance...* And so on. Always answering the unasked question, "Why would my readers be interested in this?"

After a few minutes of this, he starts saying, *Okay, okay. I can see this. This is working for me.* Then we hashed out the specific points. What was I doing? I was helping this guy do his job, not making *him* try to figure out what the story was here. And helping him fill up some column inches, which is a challenge every journalist faces every day. And he appreciated it. He ran the column, it grabbed a lot of eyes, and I had a full seminar. No, it doesn't always end up like this, and more often that not, if yours is a niche subject, they're not interested. But you don't have to score on every call.

Media Resources Section

Don't make media folks hunt around for what they need to put a story together. Put it all in one place, and then tell them where it is in your emails and cover letters, what it includes (the high points, anyway), and that it's there to help them. Spell it out (see sidebar on the next page).

Media folks, being human beings like us, don't want to work any harder than they have to. They've usually got more than enough on their plates, so they truly appreciate it when you hand it to them on a silver platter. Got a note recently from a journalist in a small market who wrote: *Since you're smarter than most, and you know us reporters get squeezed for time, I'll probably use the info in your* Media Resources *area.*

Ready-to-Go Blurbs

In the past few years of writing for publications and sites, I've noticed a host of articles suggesting that given the rapidly shrinking available space in magazines, smaller "filler"-type pieces are often the best way to get in the door of a publication. Don't try to land 1000 words; shoot for 150. Cut 'n paste promo blurbs fall into that category, and are yet another way to move yourself closer to a little publicity.

A certain number of folks I contact for exposure just aren't going to spare the space to do a full review, interview, Q&A, etc., but short two or three line ready-to-go promo blurbs (or short 100-200 word articles) offer another, perhaps more feasible, option for getting the word out. Great. I'll take it. Given that it's often the higher-profile venues where space is at a premium, having one of those bigger sites or marquee publications slot in one of my blurbs could very well end up paying bigger dividends than a larger piece in a smaller pub or site. But it'll only happen if I offer them that option.

How Is Your Book Different?

Also, notice the letter to visiting media folks that appears on the main part of my *Attn: Media* page. It's here that I provide the critical "positioning" verbiage (also to be found on your press kit's "book promo sheet" that I discuss later). The first line? "What Sets *The Well-Fed Writer* and *TWFW: Back For Seconds* apart?" Here's where I tell a potential reviewer what differentiates my book in a marketplace full of other books on the subject. It's always one of the first questions on a reviewer's mind (especially in the mainstream media), and effectively separating your book from the herd is what can make your book and subject more newsworthy.

In the case of my first book, I was lucky in that there was only one other book on the market about commercial writing when mine came out. But because there were a million on "freelance writing" (often touting writing directions with far more dubious financial prospects), I had to make sure my reviewers knew they were dealing with a totally different animal.

A Reviewer's Dream

Here's what I include in my Media Resources section, linked from my "Attn: Media" link (**http://www.wellfedwriter.com/media.shtml**). It's a one-stop "Info Central" portal to make any journalist's (or reviewer's) job easy:

1) **Downloadable Cover Art** - High- and low-res images for both print and online placements, respectively

2) **Downloadable Author Pix** - Ditto

3) **Author Bio**

4) **Book Milestones** - Awards, accolades, book clubs, sales numbers, or any other recognition of note

5) **FAQs** - They also appear in their own "FAQs" link on the main site.

6) **Press Release** - See broader discussion in this chapter, and in Appendix B.

7) **"News Pegs"** - Don't just sit back and hope a journalist figures out the possible "angles" for a story; spell them out.

8) **Book Testimonials**

9) **Table of Contents**

10) **Sample Chapter**

11) **Sample Radio Interview** - See more details in Chapter Ten: Radio Shows.

12) **TV Interview Video Clip**

13) **Cut 'n Paste Promo Blurbs** - As discussed

14) **Online Publicity** - Online publicity is where it happened for me, as this impressive collection shows.

15) **Media Articles** - Only a few mainstream pieces, given my mainly Internet-based marketing approach

16) **Contact Info/Email** - Mandatory here; less so in other places on the site; see discussion ahead.

Poke through my links and see what they include. FYI, all the above are actually on one looooong continuous page and the navigation links in the box take you to the specific place on the page where you'll find that feature.

Creative Press Kits

Along with a book goes a press kit. When printing your books, have them print an extra 250-300 book covers (they should cost you no more than about 40 cents each, and are generally negotiable downward from there). A cover for a 6" x 9" book, folded in half and stapled at the bottom, will hold a sheaf of 10-12 folded pages nicely and, again, earn "clever" marks from your reviewers. Do *not* spend tons of money printing up fancy die-cut press kit folders. They're unnecessary, and I'd wager good money that most reviewers, media and otherwise, would agree—as they toss them in the trash.

Using book covers is a great idea when you're doing a follow-up book. I just used the book cover from my first book as a press kit folder when sending out review copies of my second. For those who reviewed my first, it was a reminder, and for those who didn't, it gave them a peek into what all the fuss was about (and spurred requests for review copies of the first as well…).

Press Kit Contents

Here's what I include in my press kits. Not the last word, but a good template:

1) Cover Letter—I always include a cover letter (ⓔ) in my press kits, but it doesn't have to be a formal customized version. Meaning, make multiple copies of the same letter, have "Dear" followed by nothing and just write in your recipient's name when you get ready to send one out. Also, I print my cover letters on bright goldenrod colored paper and put it up front of the press kit so they can't miss it.

In it, I reintroduce myself and my books, and steer them yet again to my *Media Resources* section. In fact the line they see right above the fold when they pull out the sheaf of papers is "One-Stop Media Center." Again, nothing is ensured in this game, but you gotta do what you can to improve your odds.

2) Press Release—Reporters are especially used to working from releases to put stories together; it's their preferred primary information source. I generally use the same "all-purpose" release with my review copy press kits, though obviously making adjustments in content and headline when announcing specific appearances like seminars and signings (or when approaching entities who are more interested in the book angle itself—yes, it sometimes happens). Whenever I'm printing out a release to accompany a review copy, I just change the date to one no earlier than a few weeks before the actual date I'm mailing the package. The release may have stayed the same for a year or more, but I keep adjusting the date.

3) Book Promo Sheet—Providing an 8½" x 11" quick-read info sheet (ⓔ) can offer up that critical "positioning" verbiage that tells a potential reviewer exactly what sets the book apart from other books in its category. It's one of the first questions any reviewer wants to know, especially if he or she knows that there are already plenty of titles that cover the subject.

Mine includes:

- Brief explanation of the book's premise and solution (the challenge the book addresses, and how)
- Book's selling points and afore-mentioned "positioning" copy (i.e., what sets it apart and makes it marketable). This copy (or similar) should also appear in the "Media" section of your web site.
- Key Testimonials
- Full Title Information—ISBN#, Publication date (called "pub. date"), trim size (6" x 9" in my case), number of pages, key distributor list (i.e., Ingram, Baker & Taylor, or actual distributor, etc.; no, Ingram and B&T aren't "distributors," per se, but in the context of physical "distribution," they can be considered under that umbrella), index, and appendices (for non-fiction titles, note whether your book has one or both; librarians take books with indices much more seriously).
- Full Publisher Contact Information—Publishing company name, contact name, snail mail, phone, fax, email, web site.

4) Key Reviews—In every press kit, I include the reviews I received from *Booklist, Library Journal, ForeWord* magazine, *Midwest Book Review* and several newspapers. (e) Because these items are usually printed in small type, and often jump between pages, do this: cut out your review, glue-stick it on a blank 8½" x 11" sheet and enlarge it until it fills about ½ of the page. Now, cut that out and glue-stick it to another 8½" x 11" sheet, leaving the top ½ of the page blank.

Cut out the magazine's banner, with issue date, off the front cover and paste it on the top of the page and then make your copies. Print or write "(OVER)" in the bottom right corner of the page and copy a second review, similarly constructed, on the other side.

Also, include the "mock review" (e) we discussed in Chapter Four, to help out those time-challenged reviewers out there.

5) Book Club Catalog Pages—When my book was picked up by *Writers Digest Book Club* and then *Book-of-the-Month Club/Quality Paperback Book Club* (sister clubs under the *bookspan* umbrella), they sent me the catalog issue in which the book appeared as a *Featured Selection* or *Featured Alternate Selection*. Again, cutting and pasting, I turned these into 8½" x 11" press kit inserts. In the case of *Writers Digest Book Club*, after a conversation I had with the editor letting me know how successful the book had been for them (second-best-selling *Featured Alternate* in more than two years), I had her write me a letter highlighting that fact, and I copied it on the backside of the catalog page. Together, these two were a nice little success chronicle.

6) News Articles—As a result of several road trips built around book signings and my seminars, I've been fortunate to get some nice—albeit limited—media coverage. When you do the same, copy those articles, cut and paste per the above-described process (after securing permissions from the papers to reprint, of course) and include them.

7) Author Bio—Always include a one-page bio (ⓔ) that establishes your credentials and gives the reviewer or reporter some good hooks to include in a review or story. Don't just tell your life story—sell yourself. If it's not relevant to establishing those credentials, leave it out. Provide the kind of information that will have a reviewer conclude that, indeed, you are an expert who's qualified to write such a book and speak on the subject. In my bio, I start with some chronological narrative and then go on to include a bulleted list of book "milestones." In my case, that means awards, book clubs, and number of copies sold to date (updated regularly).

8) Amazon Testimonials—Six months or so after my books came out, I pulled 10 to 12 of the best Amazon reviews I'd received and put them together on the front and back of an 8.5" x 11" sheet. I had actively solicited Amazon reviews from readers who had emailed me to tell me how much they enjoyed the book, ensuring that I'd get some good ones. At the top of the page I put this verbiage:

While industry reviews are essential to boosting sales of a book, the real measure of the quality, readability and relevance of a book comes from the actual readers. The following excerpted customer reviews speak for themselves. **The average customer review for this book was 5 stars (highest possible rating)**. *Visit Amazon.com for the full listing of customer reviews.*

●　　●　　●

Nuts 'n Bolts

A few more tips on the logistics involved in putting some of these pieces together. With online reviews, I print them from the web site, copying two to a page (front and back). If the review is further down on the page, I'll do as I discussed earlier: print out the review, print out the home page masthead, physically take a scissors to both, and put the review together with the masthead.

Once you have all these pieces assembled, make up a "Press Kit Originals" file with all these doctored-up pieces, and keep it in an easy-to-find place. Periodically (always on the lookout for office superstore copy specials), I'll print up 25 to 30 sets, and assemble a bunch of kits so that review copy requests are simple two-minute tasks.

Contests

One surefire way to get some buzz going for your book is to win a few awards—or even become a finalist. My first book won one award, was a finalist for a second, and received an honorable mention in a third, while my second book earned finalist status in three competitions. All were nice accolades to add to my promotional materials.

Given the steady growth of awards contests over the years, the cynical side of me takes flight. With entrance fees ranging from roughly $50-100 *per* title *per* category, and a mind-boggling array of possible categories (in some contests, you might be one of only four or five total entries in a category; gotta love those odds) one could be forgiven for concluding that many contests out there are little more than wonderful ways for the sponsoring organization to make boatloads of money. Especially when awards time comes around and, in some cases, all you receive is a mention of your name amongst many others (Note: you *do* get cool trophies with the *Ben Franklin Awards*).

But, I'm picking nits here. We all understand the *quid pro quo* at work here: I pay my money for the chance to be able to say, *Ben Franklin Award Winner* or *IPPY Award Winner*, or *ForeWord Magazine Book of the Year Finalist*. But even if the award you receive is from a smaller, lesser-known competition, the impact on a potential reader is arguably just as strong. After all, *we* may know the names of the premier competitions in our field, but do most readers?

The better-known contests out there for independent publishers (and the ones I enter all my books in) are:

The Benjamin Franklin Awards
Sponsor: PMA, The Independent Book Publishers Association
Web Site: **www.pma-online.org**

The IPPY Awards
Sponsor: Independent Publisher
Web site: **www.independentpublisher.com**

ForeWord Magazine's Book of the Year Awards
Sponsor: *ForeWord* magazine
Web site: **www.forewordmagazine.com**

Writer's Digest International Self-Published Book Awards
Sponsor: *Writer's Digest* magazine
Web site: **www.writersdigest.com**

For a larger list of competitions (including ones for conventionally published books), check out **www.writing-world.com/contests/index.shtml**.

A Novel Win-Win Publicity Scenario

The following account of a wonderfully creative use of press releases is reprinted with permission from Francine Silverman's November 23, 2005 edition of *Book Promotion Newsletter* (**http://www.bookpromotionnewsletter.com** to subscribe):

Travel author David Stanley has been using press releases to promote his travel guidebooks for more than two years. "*Most books only qualify as 'news' when a new edition appears, so I've switched to using other people's 'news' to promote my titles,*" he says.

"*Whenever I notice that a niche travel company has launched a new product in one of 'my' areas, I contact them to offer to write and distribute their online press release at no charge. All I ask is that they allow me to mention my guidebook and/or provide a link to my website somewhere near the bottom of the release.*

I've found that most companies are only too happy to cooperate in exchange for the free publicity, and many also add a link to my site from their own company website." David provides a few examples:

Fiji Hotel Chain Provides an Alternative to Packaged Tourism
http://www.prweb.com/releases/2005/2/prwebxml208450.php

Pacific Expeditions to Visit the Remote Pitcairn Islands
http://i-newswire.com/pr49662.html

North American Educators to Teach English in Cuba
http://www.prweb.com/releases/2005/9/prweb288560.htm

Find Your Island on Island-Search.com
http://www.prweb.com/releases/2005/7/prweb262187.php

David Stanley
http://www.southpacific.org
http://www.cuba-pictures.com

Get Creative

One of the best ways to stir up your creative juices for the big job of marketing, promoting, and publicizing your book is to stay plugged into all the many wonderful resources out there for the taking (or for a small fee). Publications like PMA's *Independent* and the *SPAN Connection* monthly newsletters, Marcia Yudkin's *Marketing Minute,* Joan Stewart's *Publicity Hound,* Francine Silverman's *Book Promotion Newsletter,* John Kremer's *Book Marketing Tip of the Week,* and so many others. You'll find contact info/sign up details for all these in Appendix A, Self-Publishing Resources.

And for more information on building a solid marketing strategy for getting through to media folks, including radio show hosts/producers, check out Marisa D'Vari's *Building Buzz* (Career Press; 2004), and Jessica Hatchigan's *How to Be Your Own Publicist* (McGraw-Hill; 2002)

Okay, now that we're a bit more media-savvy, let's explore a promotional avenue I personally think is one of the most promising, enough so that it deserves its own chapter...

Chapter 9

I got off the phone with the editor of *Writer's Digest* magazine with my marching orders: two articles, one about 250 words, the other about 800. Because the subject was my book, and entailed a few edited excerpts, they took me almost no time at all to put together. The smaller one went out in their ezine, the second in the magazine. Both generated nice traffic to my site *and* they paid me a total of about $450. Can't beat that.

There are lots of ways to let the world know about your book(s), but one of the best draws on your natural writing skills as the author. Best of all? It's free, *and* you might even get paid. (Note: while the following ideas can work for any book, many are best suited to non-fiction titles.)

Information is hot. Everyone wants to learn how to do something: make more money, get out of debt, find a mate (or have a stronger relationship with the one they have), explore new roasting techniques, hone their parenting skills, research an upcoming vacation, and a million other things. Those who can reach people with good, relevant, well-written information that feeds this insatiable hunger for information will be rewarded with their readers' eyeballs, and, potentially, their dollars.

Editors Want You

Editors of all publications, hard copy and electronic, have an ongoing need for well-written content relevant to their audience—the kind of content that keeps subscribers happy, informed, and renewing. Which raises the first point: make sure your story idea is a fit for their demographic. No *faux pas* is more common and irksome to an editor than the mismatched submission.

Free Publicity—the "Write" Way!

155

Read a few issues of the hard copy edition (at *least* flip through one issue on the newsstand) or visit the web site—whatever it takes to ensure you're making an appropriate pitch. Web sites and ezines are generally more receptive to story ideas and more casual about submission rules than hard copy pubs, but even with the latter, if you're a published author who's chosen your pubs well, the guidelines often loosen up.

Reviews: Just the Beginning

We all need reviews to drive sales, but a review coupled with a meaty article in the same issue (or close enough to deliver the crucial "multiple impressions" thing) packs significantly more punch than it would by itself. Furthermore, most editors will be more receptive to a request for a review or interview if you're offering a good article in return. After all, you've just made their life easier.

In the process, you'll get some of the best kind of advertising out there: you get to tell your compelling story *your* way, providing the exact information, persuasively crafted, that you've decided they need to know about your subject—info which will (hopefully) pique their interest enough to delve a little deeper.

Speaking of interviews, you *have* put together an extensive, clearly marked, and easy-to-find FAQs section on your web site, right? By directing an editor to your site, or better yet, emailing them the FAQs, you've made their life easier—always your #1 job. I've had editors use my FAQs as is, or pick a half dozen Q&As in addition to coming up with a few of their own. Editors like (and ergo, will be more receptive to the requests of) people who simplify their lives.

An article could take several forms: 1) a straight excerpt from the book (note it if that's the case); 2) an adapted excerpt with intro and outro verbiage to provide context for the uninitiated reader; or, 3) original work based on points raised in the book.

Deliver Quality and Value

There's plenty of bad, boring, worthless, and poorly written content out there. Don't add to it. Presumably, since you've written a book good enough to pursue commercially, the actual wordsmithing of the piece shouldn't be an issue. But that's just one component of an effective article. Is it a compelling piece? Does it draw the reader in? Does it deliver valuable information that the reader can put to work right away to enhance the quality of some important sphere of his life, regardless of whether he buys the book? Does it scream "advertorial"? A good rule of thumb: don't even mention your book at all in any article, except of course, in the "attribution" paragraph at the end. Let's take these one at a time...

Make It Compelling

A great way to get the piece off to a strong start is by sharing a good, funny, dramatic, or poignant story or anecdote. Ponder the last few articles you read through to the end. I'd wager they drew you in quickly and effectively (*and* you had a personal interest in the subject). Well-written investigative, travel, or lifestyle features in your daily or Sunday paper should provide some good examples. As for writing style, what do you notice about this book? Hopefully, it sounds conversational, chatty—as if I'm sitting down talking with you. As we discussed in the list of writing tips at the end of Chapter Two, a great way to improve your writing 100 percent almost immediately is to *write like you talk*.

Pick a Piece, Tell a Story

So, what are you going to write about? Well, what's the premise of the book? What are the reasons why this book would speak to someone? What makes it different from others in its genre? What are the key components—probably defined by chapters—that contribute to, and build, the overall premise? A self-help book will likely have a handful of core philosophies and/or strategies, any one of which might work for a good article. A cookbook may feature different courses or categories of food, around any one of which you could build a feature. A child-rearing book may address a whole host of specific parenting challenges, each of which could be turned into a juicy, anecdote-laden narrative. You get the idea.

No Advertising Accepted

An editor can smell a promo piece disguised as real content a mile away. Understand the *quid pro quo* at work here: you provide well crafted, informative content which doesn't specifically refer to your book or services, in return for an "attribution" paragraph at the end that does. But you get even more: in addition to perhaps getting paid, with every article written, you get the opportunity to build your reputation by establishing yourself as an expert in your field.

As mentioned, one good strategy for approaching the writing—both philosophically *and* actually—is to start with one of your book's chapters, and then edit it down for space, or adapt it. Not only is it easier to edit than compose from scratch, it will ensure that you steer clear of thin, overly sales-y content and tone. Don't be stingy. Give the readers some substance, and more often that not, they'll pay the toll to get all of it.

Creating Article "Toolkits"

Interested in a strategy to turn yourself into a marketing machine—without stripping your gears in the process? The secret is having a lot of articles at your fingertips, and that means creating an article "toolkit." Come up with, say, four different article topics based on different chapters, core philosophies, key strategies, or other clearly delineated points discussed in your book.

Write a long version of each one—about 1500+ words. These may be ideal for web sites, where space restrictions and tight word count are less crucial. Then, for each of the four articles, create three or four shorter versions of the same piece: perhaps 1000, 750, 500 and even 250 words. Just take the 1500-word piece and edit it down over and over, doing a *Save As* at each word count milestone.

Now, you've got 20 or so pieces, one of which will undoubtedly be perfect for any relevant publication of any size. Not to mention that, with different topics, you can deliver distinct content to similar sites that wouldn't want to run the same piece as the competition. And you can deliver it instantly, or perhaps after just minor modifications. Yes, this takes some time to put together, but once you've done it, you're set for a while.

Given such a resource at your fingertips, think you might start getting a bit more aggressive about finding those "platforms" for your message? Remember also, you just might make a few bucks in the process. Hard-copy pubs often pay fees into the hundreds, while with online venues, you're more likely to earn nothing, or perhaps $10-25. But of course, we're all about the exposure, not the money.

Go visit the "Attn: 55+" link at **www.wellfedwriter.com**, then click on *Article Archive* for a slight variation on this, but still a good example of what I'm talking about: eight articles ranging in size from 150 words to over 2000.

Your "Article-Rich" Book

Have you noticed that this book is chockfull of lists of points on various subjects (e.g., tips for conducting successful seminars, or book signings, or radio shows; the links you should include on your web site; tips for writing a good press release, etc.)? This was intentional. Sure, it's a logical way to present information—and one that makes for easy reading. But, the "easy reading" point has larger ramifications...

Any of these lists lend themselves nicely—with perhaps slight modifications— to being re-packaged as an article for publication. By writing the book this way, I've kept an eye toward making it easy to pull virtually ready-to-go excerpts to use in my ongoing promotion efforts. By making it easy to come up with articles, I make it more likely that I'll actually get those articles out there.

Publications Seeking Articles

A few ideas for zeroing in on the right pubs for your writing gems. Check your library for the *Oxbridge Directory of Newsletters*, the *National Directory of Magazines* and others. Of course, Writer's Market is the source for periodicals – in hard copy and at **www.writersmarket.com** ($4/month or $30/year). Other magazine/newspaper links:

http://magazine-directory.com
http://dir.yahoo.com/News_and_Media/Magazines
http://newsdirectory.com (also for newspapers).
www.newspapers.com
www.onlinenewspapers.com

Interested in ezines? For detailed lists of electronic publications broken down by every possible category, here's a clearinghouse link that bills itself as, "The pick of the best eZine Directories on the Net today": **http://ezines. nettop20.com**. In addition, here are a few of the more prominent ezine directory sites we discussed back in Chapter Four:

www.new-list.com
www.go-ezines.com
http://bestezines.com/
http://zinos.com/
www.worldabooks.com/search-it/ezine
www.jogena.com/ezine/ezinedata.htm

Sites Seeking Content

While the info above steers you to actual publications—online or print—that might be open to your pieces, the list below is "content sites": article clearinghouses where you can submit articles on a variety of subjects, which are then offered free of charge to anyone looking for content for their publications. It just opens you up for more exposure, and perhaps to some publications you hadn't thought of:

www.IdeaMarketers.com
www.EzineArticles.com
www.GoArticles.com
www.ArticleCentral.com
www.ArticleCity.com

Automating the Process

I recently came across a link to some promising software called *Article Announcer*, put out by Internet marketing pro Jason Potash, whose program promises boosted traffic and sales, "without becoming a search engine expert, master marketer, or paying for advertising." I liked the sound of that. In essence, the program automates the process of sending articles out to bunches of directories. But it also does much more than that.

Check out **www.articleannouncer.com**, and scroll down a half page or so to view a most compelling video presentation of how the software works. It'll blow your mind. I went ahead and paid the toll, got the package, and am working my way through it. In the main 100-page info manual (a transcribed interview), there's a ton of really good information. A lot of it focuses on writing articles the right way for maximum impact.

Bottom line, there's a ton of really lousy, disorganized, ludicrously promotional, keyword-stuffed content floating around out there. If you can craft your articles with an eye toward providing good, relevant information in an organized, coherent, engaging, compelling, low-hype fashion, you'll stand out from the crowd.

Tips From a Pro

I got permission from Jason to share a few excellent points from the material about the whole article writing and placement process. Obviously, you're paying for the software, but rest assured, there's a whole lot more good stuff in there.

Five Tips For Maximizing Your Article-Writing Strategy

1) **"Useful, but Incomplete"**—A brief description of both how you should write an article, and what you want your reader to be left with. You want a reader to feel that there's a lot of good information in your article, but it doesn't tell them everything, so it spurs them to click through to your site and learn more.

2) **Create a CTA Resource Box**—Your final attribution paragraph shouldn't be just a static mini-resume (e.g., "Peter Bowerman is the author of..."), but rather, as Jason puts it, a CTA (call-to-action) Resource Box. Which isn't how I'd been doing it for a long time (in case you find articles of mine out there on the Web with the resumé-style box). In my case, the new and improved version might read something like:

Love to write, but hate to starve? For a free report ("Why Commercial Writing?") on building your own high-income writing career with enviable freedom and flexibility, visit **www.wellfedwriter.com**, *home of the award-winning* **Well-Fed Writer** *books by Peter Bowerman, one of America's leading experts on the lucrative field of commercial freelancing.*

3) **URL, not Email Address**—In your Resource Box described above, only include your URL, not an email address. Including the latter invites beaucoup spam as a result of all the email "harvester" programs out there. Plus, if your piece does get picked up by multiple publications, you want the full impact from drawing them to your site, not just the distraction of an email inquiry.

4) Only Your URL—For similar reasons, only include your *own* URL in an article, not others. Listing, say, five other addresses in the piece again diffuses the impact of that article. In the eyes of the search engines, your URL then becomes just one of many.

5) NO "Content Mirroring"—This was one of those head-scratchers, but pay heed. If you have a bunch of articles circulating out there on a bunch of sites, and they contain URLs pointing back to your site, do *not* put all those same articles in a data bank on your site. That's called "content mirroring", and apparently, it's considered to be a strategy to trick the search engines, which means if you do it, you'll lose search engine rankings points (or even be totally excommunicated) as a result. Don't ask why. I'm not sure I understand it either, but just don't do it.

Now that we've explored the potential of articles as powerful marketing tools, let's warm up our voices, smile big, and get ready for radio…

Chapter 10

Interesting story about—and a roundabout plug for—*Radio-TV Interview Report*, arguably the best known and most popular publication venue for landing radio and TV interviews. They endeared themselves to me a few years back when I contacted them to explore the possibility of placing an ad in their thrice-monthly magazine going out to 4000+ radio/TV producers and hosts.

When I described my book, its subject, and audiences, I was fully expecting a heartily optimistic (and hype-y) response: "Oh sure, your book will do really well! Would you like to place ads in two issues or three?" Instead, I was pleasantly surprised by their candor. The person I spoke with listened carefully, and then advised me against it. He felt like the topic—starting a commercial writing business—just wasn't mainstream enough to appeal to a broad spectrum of radio shows. Kudos for his honesty.

Sure, I've done a decent number of radio interviews (and a few on TV), but for the "niche" reason, radio hasn't been a key promotional direction for me. Hence, this is one of those chapters where I can't claim expert status. But, I'll give you some basics, and a few resources to explore it further on your own.

Landing the Gig

Write a good book—one with healthy mainstream appeal—and radio interviews can't be far behind. There are two issues to tackle when you're considering this direction: how to get booked, and the logistics of doing those interviews. Let's start with bookings.

Does your book potentially speak to a broad swath of readers/listeners out there? Think about the subjects you've heard being discussed on radio:

1) *Current Events (politics, international relations, race relations, etc.)*

2) *Health and Nutrition (exercise, diet, medicine, alternative medicine, etc.)*

3) *Sports (any questions?)*

4) *Financial Issues (investing, financial planning, real estate, etc.)*

4) *Relationships (dating, romance, sex, psychology, etc.)*

5) *Home-related issues (household fix-it, cars, gardening, etc.)*

6) *Religious topics (many of the above topics from the religious angle)*

Certainly, there are others, but these cover the biggies. Meaning that if your subject falls into one of the above categories, it's probably a good radio show candidate and, hence, an easier sale to a radio host.

What a Host Wants...

Well, what do you think they want? They want guests who are smart, engaging, knowledgeable, articulate, and will "deliver the goods" to their listeners. Translation: a guest who offers, *not* a 15-, 30-, or 45-minute plug for their book, but good solid information for the listeners. Further translation: information that those listeners can act on to their benefit, whether or not they ever buy your book. In my humble opinion, a smart author and radio interview guest will go out of their way to give away as many goodies as possible. Be generous, and it'll be obvious to the listeners and the host. You'll sell more books. *And* get invited back. So, how do you get to these folks?

Radio-TV Interview Report

As discussed, RTIR (**www.rtir.com**) is the big kid on the block in this arena, publishing three times a month and going out to 4000+ radio/TV producers and hosts. They've been in business for 15 years (at press time), building up a good reputation along the way. When they steered me away, not surprisingly, I was disappointed they didn't think my book would do well on radio, but at the same time, I wasn't too broken up about not having to drop a pretty hefty chunk of change on a big "maybe."

Speaking of which, they don't post their rates on their web site, but registering on their site for a free info kit gets you immediate access to those numbers. At press time, a half-page ad (the smallest size possible) for one insertion was just under $900, but that dropped to under $600 if you went with three insertions (just under $1800). They strongly recommend you don't even bother doing just one insertion, and I'd agree. You need the power of multiple impressions to make it worthwhile.

Take the time to read over the info kit. Lots of cool stories (but remember, everyone's different), and even some good ideas for promo letters to attract the attention of show hosts and producers. Yes, this is a sizable investment, but if you can land a bunch of appearances, it could return far more than the initial cost.

CAVEAT EMPTOR

FYI, depending on your topic, RTIR can be a very worthwhile medium. That said, in conversations with industry folks during the research on this book, while praising the integrity of the people who run it, I heard some rumblings that RTIR may have become, for many, an overpriced avenue that promises more than it delivers. Do your own due diligence. Ask for references, and *know* that they'll be sending you the best ones. Think hard about your book, and whether it's a fit.

In my case, I went to Plan B: buying a list of radio show producers and hosts I could contact myself—for a fraction of the cost of Plan A.

www.SabahRadioShows.com

I ended up going with Joe Sabah (**www.SabahRadioShows.com**, **www.JoeSabah.com**; 800-945-2488), a Denver-based entrepreneur who's sold a ton of his books through radio—$357,000 worth, according to his web site. His book is "How You Can Get On Radio Talk Shows All Across America Without Leaving Your Home Or Office." His pitch is pretty promotional, but it's a good product.

His marquee product is the "Radio Talk Show System," and the centerpiece of that is his radio station database (currently over 900 listings), which comes with his book and an accompanying audiotape. The book's full of good information (though it feels a bit dated), but in my mind, the main reason you drop the $198 (he often runs half-price specials for $99, so be sure to check it out) for all three is the database. This comes on CD, has full station info and contact details, and is importable into any program with an "import" feature (like Excel). Obviously, compared to *Radio/TV Interview Report*, this is a do-it-yourself program. You have to make all the contacts, but it may be a better bet if you have that niche subject.

On top of it all, Joe's a really nice guy who usually answers his own phone and likes talking to people. If you do order it, ask him for his BOGO ("Buy One, Get One Free") offer: order the package and sometime down the road, when you want an updated database, he'll send it to you free of charge.

Bottom line, I've used his list with good success (relatively speaking, given the small numbers of interviews I've done). He keeps it current, delivers it in a very user-friendly fashion, offers a fresh updated version one more time of your choosing, and is great to deal with. Check him out.

Ten Tips to More Profitable and Enjoyable Radio Shows

1) Call, Don't Email—When making your initial contacts with radio show producers or hosts (often the same person), use the phone. Even though chances are good you'll still get voicemail (always ask for their email address from the receptionist before they connect you or get it from their web site), it's important for the producer/host to actually hear how you sound. Make no mistake, in many ways this is an "audition." Don't treat it as just another voicemail message, just leaving your name and phone number and little else. You've got to give them a reason to want to contact you. Write out your pitch and deliver it clearly, confidently, and naturally, without sounding like you're reading it.

In my phone pitch (**e**), I include all the basics—name, title of book, premise, accolades, web site, phone number, and, most importantly, the angle the book represents. Remember, just like news reporters, radio folks also don't care about your book, only the angle represented by the book. I started adding the little joke about the oxymoron ("Well-Fed Writer") after getting a laugh from many media folks when I shared the title of my book. They often reply, *Oh, what kind of book is it? Fantasy? Science fiction?*

You can boost your chances of actually catching your target "live" by calling just after their show ends; a good database will generally list the show's time slot. Once you chat with the producer/host or leave your voicemail message, follow up with an email, confirming what you just shared with them on the phone, and linking them to your site for more information. Ideally, you'll include a strong email "pitch letter" (**e**) with a catchy headline and compelling copy to pique their interest.

2) Put Interview Samples on Your Website—If you can score a tape/CD of your interview, that's ideal. When you're setting up the appearance date, just ask if they can give you a dub. They may charge you a few bucks for this, but it's worth it. Load up the interview—or at least five minutes of it—to your web site. I have a friend who's in the audio/video production business and, playing the role of radio host, he taped a "sample" radio interview with me in his studio, then converted it to an audio computer file which my web guy loaded up to my site. Check it out at the "Attn: Media" link at **www.wellfedwriter.com**.

Then, with audio clips in place, you can link right to them in your verbal and email communications. In that email follow-up pitch letter **e**, bold the phrase that says "sample audio clip," and then cut and paste the actual link to the clip on your site.

3) Keep "Talking Points" Handy—Whenever you're talking with your radio show host/producer, whether in the initial call or during the actual guest interview, always keep a list of "talking points" nearby. In my case, I use the FAQs that are on my site as my "cheat sheet."

After making up your list, read it over several times until the answers become familiar, and easily "verbally retrievable" in your mind. Think of yourself as an actor learning your lines. Until you do, you're going to sound a little wooden in your responses. Once you've got them down, you can put more effort into your "performance"—being smooth, enthusiastic and knowledgeable—all those things that make hosts and listeners happy.

Without a doubt, much of that fluid delivery will come as a result of being very familiar with your subject matter. But take the time to get all the key points of an answer down in writing, so your responses are even and thorough. Going through this exercise will end up paying big dividends, not only during radio shows, but any time you're talking about your book and subject (i.e., signings, seminars, talks, book fairs, etc.).

4) Move When You Talk—Every time I do a radio interview, I move around. I stroll around my house with my wireless headset on, allowing me to fully get into the "body-English" of the whole thing—gesturing, waving my arms around, stabbing the air with my finger, etc. I promise, it makes a big difference. You'll come across as more animated and dynamic than if you were seated, and it'll help you think better as well (maybe that's where "thinking on your feet" comes from...).

5) Send a Thank-You Card to Your Host—Before the interview, start writing out a quick thank-you note to your host. Have the envelope addressed and stamped, and once the interview is done, finish the note, perhaps including a specific reference to something in the interview, if appropriate. I promise, hosts don't get many thank-you cards. You'll stand out, and leave a nice impression for the next time you call.

6) Promote, Promote, Promote—As mentioned earlier, your goal during the interview should be to provide as much good solid value to the listeners as possible, whether or not they buy the book. But let's not be too altruistic. After all, the point is to promote your book. So, to that end, make sure you pepper your interview with frequent mentions of both your book title *and* your web address. Your host expects you to do it: it's the *quid pro quo* of the interview; you provide listeners with good, interesting (or "actionable") content, and you get to promote your book and your web site.

Remember that people are tuning into a show at different times, so make sure that 'late-comers,' no matter when they join the broadcast, don't have to wait too long to hear that title and URL. Just work it in naturally: in response to a question from the host, you might say, *That's a great question, Jack, and in my book* The Well-Fed Writer, *web site: www.wellfedwriter.com, I have a whole section about that...,* and then answer the question. At the end, a good host will give you another opportunity to share your "call letters," or they'll do it themselves.

7) Get Testimonials—Now, I must confess, I was very delinquent and didn't actually do this one (and I'm kicking myself as a result), so this is a "do as I say, not as I do" thing. Get into the habit right from the start of calling up the host right after the show, and if you felt it went well, asking for a nice one- or two-sentence testimonial. Offer to email your request, both to remind them and to make it easy for them to respond. And why not let them know, during the initial booking phone call, that you'll be asking for one when the interview's over. That not only makes the subsequent request an anticipated one, but also sends the message that you plan to deliver a show worthy of some glowing kudos.

If they balk at your post-show request, or reply with an unconvincing, "I'll try to get to it," why not suggest *you* write one up and send it to them for their OK? If they're fine with that (and you'll be surprised at how many will be, given how busy they are), start right then by asking something like, "To make sure I put something together that reflects your true sentiments, can I ask you what you liked about my talk? My personality? Knowledge level? Delivery?" Then use their answers to craft "their" quote.

Eight to ten nice testimonials from radio hosts about what an entertaining, thorough, prepared, knowledgeable guest you were, someone who delivered valuable content to their listeners, are worth their weight in gold. It becomes yet another compelling web link to which you can steer prospective hosts/producers.

8) Make a Special "Time-Sensitive" Offer—If your 800 # sales line can accommodate special offers, then make one during the show. For example: "And Jack, if your listeners call the 800-247-6553 number today to order the book, and ask for the "Fellow Writers Discount," I'll take $4 off the price." I sell books both online and through a toll-free line. It's important to offer both, so you don't lose those folks who are still a bit wary of buying online. Given how online ordering parameters are, by definition, more rigid than those on a toll-free line, it makes sense to channel your special offer through the toll-free line (unless you have a "promotion code" box on your site). And, don't forget to notify the people manning your toll-free line about the special offer.

Incidentally, when setting up my toll-free number with my fulfillment company BookMasters, I made it easy. Instead of giving them some long list of promotions and discounts, I gave them one very simple instruction: *if someone mentions ANY discount of $4 or less for a book, give it to them.* The way I figure it, it's highly unlikely that anyone will mention a discount unless they heard about it somewhere. Which, again, underscores the importance of steering people to your web site and toll-free number, given the higher profit margins on those purchases compared to sales through bookstores and Amazon.

9) Give Away a Free Book—Your host/producer may bring this up before you do, but if he or she doesn't, suggest it when they book you for the show. It'll be very well received, and will add some anticipation and excitement to the festivities. Plus, it gives them something to use as a promotional hook before and during the show.

10) Smile When You Talk—You've probably heard this one before in manuals on successful phone skills. Since this is a phone conversation, apply it here as well. It's a simple thing that makes a powerful difference in how you come across to an audience. When you smile, it shines through in your voice and just makes you sound more positive, confident, and friendly. People like friendly. And, of course, don't forget this tip if you're doing the occasional (and fun!) in-studio interview.

Podcasts

Just a word about the hot new trend of "podcasting" – which could be seen as do-it-yourself audio content creation. Of course, its name comes from Apple's iPod,, so it refers to media created as mp3 files that can be downloaded onto any mp3 player (or simply listened to on your computer). Do a google search for "podcasting software" to find simple kits for putting together your own programming on a shoestring. Written info is still top on of the heap, but audio allows for much more richness and texture, and more importantly, allows people to listen when and where it's convenient and in a format that's hot and growing. You can do interviews, mini-seminars, and more, turn them into downloadable files, and perhaps create yet another income stream.

Okay, that's the basic drill on radio. Now, let's go sign some books!

Chapter 11

I had a bizarre book signing experience a few years back. I had two signings scheduled in a Northwest U.S. city, on a Wednesday and Thursday. I didn't double-confirm the first one, and when I showed up at 6:30 p.m. for a 7:00 p.m. start on Wednesday, I discovered that for some mysterious reason, the manager (off for the night and unreachable) had suddenly decided that the signing was Thursday, despite emails back and forth that very week discussing and confirming the Wednesday date.

He hadn't checked with me before making the change, but his store signage had all been changed to Thursday, and one sign even had a bright yellow note pasted over the top announcing, "The date in the newsletter is wrong!"

The manager on duty had no clue why the change had been made. Of course, I had another signing across town the following night, and given the embryonic stage of cloning technology, we had a problem. What partially salvaged the situation was that the strange voices in the manager's head (I have no other possible explanation) that inexplicably compelled him to change the date had only piped up the day before, meaning that most people weren't aware of the change and showed up anyway, giving us a nice crowd of close to 20. We'll never know how many were turned away when they called, or showed up, the next night. C'est la vie.

Reality Check

Unless you're a big-name celebrity, don't expect book signings to sell a ton of books for you; look at them as building brand awareness in that market area. As for going on a book signing road show, want my opinion? By and large, they're a waste of time (again, unless you're a big name). If you're just a regular Joe/Josephine, I say there's no way you're going to make a book signing tour, by itself, a cost-effective exercise.

Assuming a $15 retail book, given the 55 percent discount you'll be giving to Ingram, plus production costs, shipping, etc., as a self-publisher, you'll likely gross roughly $4-6, depending on lots of things we've already discussed. If you have a niche topic, count on selling less than 10 books at a typical signing. If you've got a hotter, more mainstream subject, and you've gotten the word out far and wide, you'll probably do better.

Remember: just because 20 people show up at a book signing doesn't mean you're going to sell 20 copies. You've got the curiosity-seekers and tire-kickers, and the people who've already bought the book and just want you to sign it. And of course, that old standby favorite (I can already see the authors' heads nodding…): the guy who sits and listens raptly, asks a zillion questions, thanks you profusely for so generously sharing your expertise, and exits the store, book-less. Often the ones who buy books will surprise you, so be careful about investing too much attention on the mirages.

So, all that considered, let's be generous and assume you'll sell 10 books at each signing and make $6 a book. $60. Woo-hoo. Even if someone was putting you up and feeding you at every stop, it's still peanuts. Suffice it to say, your time is *infinitely* better spent staying at home and pursuing other marketing options.

Collateral Exposure

Yes, playing devil's advocate on the side of doing author "road shows," the true power of a book signing *is* in its promotion—the word you're able to get out about your book in both the bookstore and into the larger community. Many more people will read about your book (and often buy it) than will come to your signing. You've probably done it yourself many times. So, any media coverage you get will help you sell more books.

You can boost those collateral sales by making every effort to get your web address listed in any coverage. You definitely can't count on newspapers to get it done, but one thing is certain: it won't happen if you don't ask or don't provide it. As newspaper people will be happy to explain, their job is *not* to promote your book; it's to provide interesting stories to their readers. If they can end up doing both (though rarely by design), great, but they don't make it a high priority. But, even with those "hidden" sales, I still assert that the time you could spend on marketing efforts in one day will earn you more money in the long run than you could make doing signings on the road.

Part of a Bigger Plan

My books have done well for niche books, but my personal best at any one book signing is 20 copies (and that was with my own active media promotion efforts as well as the store's). The average is a lot less than that. Why did I bother? Well, all my out-of-town book signings were scheduled around all-day seminars, which were the focus of my visits (and which we'll discuss more in Chapter Thirteen). All my promotional efforts and any push for media coverage emphasized the seminar first and foremost, and the book signings as secondary events.

So for me, signings became an opportunity to promote my seminars. In probably 50-60 percent of cases, I picked up one or more enrollments for my seminars at the signings. So in that sense, it was always worth it. Needless to say, book signings in your local area are a different story. With none of the typical travel costs associated with an out-of-town book signing tour, there's no reason not to do as many as you can.

A "Weekly" Payoff

As we discussed earlier, if you're shooting to get a newspaper to write an article about you, make as much effort to woo the smaller weekly papers as you do for the big dailies. Yes, the big daily papers have huge circulations, but chances are good that you'll have a hard time getting more than a mention out of them. Even if they do write a story, you're a one-day wonder. Tomorrow, you're lining birdcages. The weeklies, of course, as mentioned previously, have that seven-day shelf life.

Eleven Tips for More Successful, Fun, and Worry-Free Signings

1) **Do Advance Planning** Visit **www.ersys.com** for some travel planning. Plug in any major metro area and it'll provide links to their Chamber of Commerce, Visitor's Bureau, and all kinds of media links (click *Local Media* off to the left) serving that area. For more detailed media lists, check the *Gale's* directory or *Bacon's Newspaper Directory* in your library (they do have an online presence, but it can be hard to figure out how to get at the info); in most cases, both will include actual names of key personnel and editors, often with phone numbers and email addresses. Of course, info can be outdated, so make a quick call to the media outlet to confirm before sending releases. Don't forget **www.newspapers.com** and **www.onlinenewspapers.com**.

2) **Mass Email Releases** As discussed in Chapter Eight, contact *PRWeb* ™ (**www.prweb.com**), the budget conscious marketer's best ally for emailing press releases to hit lots of media outlets with a single release. You can choose

to distribute your release in a specific metropolitan area or nationwide, for anywhere from $0 to $80, depending on the transmission bells and whistles you select.

3) Book Early Generally speaking, most bookstores—both the big chains and the independents—book their author signings at least 75-90+ days in advance. Don't think you're going to call B&N or Borders on a month's notice and snag an open date.

4) Identify Busy Nights When calling to schedule a signing, ask for the store manager, or in the case of B&N, the CRM (Community Relations Manager), or simply "the person who books authors for signings." But, before you get connected to that decision-maker, I suggest asking the store employee who answered the phone which nights are busiest in the store. The busy nights for a downtown store might be very different than for a suburban location. I found that out the hard way when I sat in a very quiet store on a Wednesday night, only to find out that Friday would've been far busier. Of course, every employee knew it, and would have been happy to share it with me, if only I'd asked.

5) Schedule Later in the Month If you have the flexibility, try to schedule your signings later in the month. This way, a signing scheduled for, say, the 25th of the month gets nearly a month of promo time in the store newsletter *and* any monthly publications in which you've gotten it listed.

6) Send Postcards If you've made up four-color postcards with your book cover and details, put together a list of any friends, colleagues, and other contacts in the area who might be interested in coming. Even if they don't come, you've let them know you've got a book out, and that could lead to referrals.

7) Confirm in Advance Always call the store a few days in advance to confirm the signing. You'd think a manager of a big chain bookstore would be on top of things when it comes to a calendar of signings. But, as the chapter's opening story demonstrates, it ain't necessarily so. So, call before. You dig?

8) Be Proactive on "Positioning" When it comes to setting up the signing, be gently assertive with store personnel about location. They'll often go with your suggestion. If they stick you in the back of the store, there's less chance of people finding you. The ideal spot would be near the front (and close to the café), so you'll pick up walk-by traffic. Though I've experienced the exception, as a rule, don't expect store managers to be savvy about all the marketing strategy of signings. They're typically nice, earnest people, but they're not going to get a bonus if they sell a few more of your books. Your signing is just another event for them, not an income opportunity. *You* have to be the proactive one.

9) Create Eye-Catching Signage I discovered a trés cool (and trés cheap) strategy to get some pretty slick signage for your book signings—not to mention any other public appearance. Using the graphic files of my book cover artwork, I had FedExKinko's™ print out some 11" x 17" sheets, laminate them, mount them on foam core board and attach a cardboard easel at the bottom. Ta-dah! Attention-getting visuals that can be seen from at least 100 paces. I also made up another one, listing the book accolade highlights: book clubs, awards, etc. These great visual aids will set you back less than $20 each (at press time).

10) Do Discussion/Signings If you have a non-fiction or how-to book, definitely do a discussion/signing: talk for 30 minutes or so, open it up for Q&A, then sign books. If it's fiction, do a reading, then a Q&A. Tell people you'll stay around as long as they want to talk. Figure on 90 minutes for a typical event, from start to finish. Chat with people while they're waiting for you to start. Introduce yourself, shake hands, ask their names, what brought them there, etc. Don't cop the typical "Author Attitude." Friendly authors sell more books, and earn brownie points with readers (who talk to friends).

11) Collect Testimonials After the signing, get some comments from store managers about the signing/discussion and load them up to your web site, so it's easier to sell other managers on what a great author you are to deal with. This is obviously more important if it's a discussion type signing, but good feedback on any appearance is a positive.

●　　●　　●

Your "Inner Alpha Dog"

Point #8 on "positioning" underscores how you need to be politely assertive about where they place you in the store. This assertiveness also extends to meeting your guests, and the small talk before and after. I realize many authors consider themselves introverts, but work on ratcheting up your gregarious, in-charge persona. I know, not necessarily easy for many, but remember what we spoke about in Chapter Two about what's required to be successful as a public speaker: *know your subject intimately, and be passionate about sharing it with others.*

Chances are, that *will* be the case if you write a book, so don't worry about it. A few months back, I went to hear Malcolm Gladwell (author of *The Tipping Point* and *Blink*) do a talk and signing for his second book. Malcolm definitely comes across as bookish and somewhat shy, yet his enthusiasm for his subject came through like trumpets, and he ended up being a fascinating and engaging speaker. You can, too.

Other Signing Opps

So where else besides bookstores can you do signings? Look no further than your friendly local library. Check out the web-based *American Library Association* program called *Authors @ your library:* **http://www.ala.org/publicprograms/ authors@yourlibrary**. The program connects libraries with authors and publishers looking to promote their books. The site provides all the info you need to arrange an event at a library—location, venue size, event lead times, how books are sold, possible honorariums (yes, you might get paid, though usually not), and more. Register on the database, and librarians looking for speakers can find you as well.

A word of caution: don't rely on your local library to handle all the marketing and publicity efforts. Like bookstore folks, librarians are uniformly nice, helpful people, but their goal is simply to provide some decent programs for their patrons. No bumps in their paychecks for nice turnouts, either. If you're doing an event for free through a library, then by definition, the only way you're going to make money is if you sell books. And that means a lot of "butts in seats."

If that means contacting a few local media outlets and pitching them on your appearance, then do it. Again, *not* the event per se, but the *angle* represented by the event: why their readers should care, why the event addresses some need or desire on the part of a potential attendee, etc. Remember, you've got the imprimatur of "The Library" bestowing a glossy layer of credibility on you (i.e., in much the same way that bookstore signings boost your seminar creds), so they're already more inclined to pay attention. I promise you, the library won't mind. They'll likely be impressed, be eager to invite you back and, heck, they might even learn a thing or two.

Keep Talking

Bookstores and libraries are just two possible speaking venues. If you're an expert on a particular topic (whether the subject of your non-fiction book, or writing in general because of your fiction work), there are always groups who'd love to have a "real author" come speak. Sometimes you'll get an honorarium, sometimes not, but there's always the chance to sell books. Also, check **www.allconferences.com** for possible speaking opportunities at conferences spanning the gamut of industries and subjects.

As an author of books on making more money as a writer, I've been asked to speak before any number of local writing groups—bookstore-based and independent, business and technical writing associations, marketing groups, etc. The smaller the group, the less likely it is you'll get paid, but book sales can often net you $100-150. Remember, when you're self-publishing, direct sales are usually about 80-85+ percent profit. $100-150 isn't a windfall, but doing two or three talks a month can make for some decent walking-around money. If it's all local, you've got little overhead. Besides, they're fun.

Road Shows

Speaking of which, while the limited financial potential of talks like these don't make them a good bet for out-of-town gigs, if you know you're going to be headed somewhere on vacation, why not try to slot in a talk or two somewhere, and in the process, spread the word a bit more, make a few bucks, meet a few of the locals, and perhaps give yourself some possible write-offs come tax time?

To land some of these events, do a search of larger national organizations related to your subject (you probably already know most of them)—ones with lots of local chapters. Look into local business organizations, whether Kiwanis (**www.Kiwanis.org**), Rotary (**www.Rotary.org**), Jaycees (**www.usjaycees.org**), or one-off local groups. Women should check out local "ladies' clubs", Junior League (**www.ajli.org**), and others. All represent potential speaking opportunities.

Check out local historical societies. Home for Christmas last year, I was talking with my Mom about our local small town historical society that brings in speakers (usually authors) for their monthly meetings, typically paying $150 honorariums. Definitely explore this direction if you have a historical subject (whether related to the local area or not), but even a broader, topical subject could work for these entities. Listening to her, it was an ongoing challenge for them to find engaging, interesting speakers.

When milling around with attendees after your talks, especially local ones, ask them if they know of other groups that might appreciate hearing you speak. If your talk was well received, don't be surprised if you get approached before you even have a chance to ask.

Speak and Grow Rich

The May 25, 2005 edition of Francine Silverman's excellent *Book Promotion Newsletter* (**www.bookpromotionnewsletter.com**; she's also the author of *Book Marketing from A-Z; Infinity Publishing.com; 2005*—a great book) featured the piece below, giving us a pretty heady taste of where speaking can go.

In particular, this story underscores the idea we've already discussed (and will touch on again in Chapter Thirteen) about looking at your book as a *base* upon which to build—a base that offers greater income potential from the spinoff activities than from the book itself. Hasn't been the case with my books, which have done very well in their own right. But just know, even if your books don't sell a scillion, just the fact that you wrote one opens up many potentially profitable doors along the way:

Canadian author Katherine Gibson has "made more money speaking to organizations" than she has from royalties and would like to share her secret:

"When 'Unclutter Your Life: Transforming Your Physical, Mental and Emotional Space' (Beyond Words Publishing, 2004) came out, I had the biggest independent bookstore in my city advertise that I would do a presentation, not just a book signing. We had 250 show up! A couple of people who heard me asked me to speak to their groups, which I did for free with the understanding I could sell my books. From those events, I not only sold books, but received more speaking engagements as well, which I did for small fees until I felt I had enough confidence to move to the next level. I now charge $1500—$2500 per keynote (and still sell books). I have done more than 20 presentations since the book came out May 2004, and have not spent a single cent advertising myself as a speaker. It is all word of mouth.

"This coming January, I will be hosting a cruise to Mexico where I have teamed with another author. We will provide seminars during the days at sea, have a great time, and earn a good fee. So your book can spawn new opportunities and promote itself while you earn royalties plus additional fees." http://www.clutterbook.com

Two words. Wow-wuh.

Multi-Author Events

Another great idea, mentioned above, is to partner with other authors—either of related books or not—and do a richer, more broad-based event. Sure, if it was all writing-based, it'd be a "Writers Conference" or "Writers Boot Camp," but it could also just be a single afternoon or evening event. Events like these—with more to offer to a broader audience—are obviously easier to promote than solo appearances and can be a lot of fun. In the same issue of *Book Promotion Newsletter* mentioned above was this:

Michelle Ailene True (author of TRUE RELECTIONS; PublishAmerica 2004; http://www.michelleailenetrue.com) finds teaming up with other authors among her best promotional gigs:

"I found out firsthand that participating in multi-author receptions and book signing events brings bigger crowds, which means more exposure for all participants. I participated in a multi-author event last night at the Vernon Area Public Library in Vernon Hills, Illinois. There were 11 authors, representing a wide variety of genres as well as writing experience. The event drew over 50 attendees—not bad for a rainy Tuesday night in the north suburbs of Chicago!"

Back to School

Another avenue worth checking out is speaking opportunities with the K-12 arena. Schools regularly bring in speakers, and often have the budgets to pay presenters up to $500 per appearance (money often coming from *Title I* funding and *Arts in Education* grants). A good source to land these gigs is **www.schoolbookings.com**.

Although currently a news journalist, Kymberli Brady is the self-published author of the award-winning children's book, *The Sleepy Little Star* (which she sells both alone and "bundled" with a *Sleepy* nightlight or hand puppet; **www.kymzinn.com**). Kymberli has made school talks a regular fixture of her book promotion campaign, often landing fees of $400+ per talk. In addition to talking to elementary school students, she's done author visits and career day appearances with middle and high school kids, and landed dates at national and international writers conferences.

Sometimes, I can't believe I get paid to talk to kids, she says. *There's nothing more gratifying and motivating than being surrounded by hundreds of children who are unconditional in their appreciation and adoration of an author. It's like being a rock star!*

While pay varies, Kymberli says that elementary schools typically pay $300-500, plus expenses, *and* her revenues from juicy, high-profit book sales.

Here are some tips Kymberli offers (in her own words) to help you maximize the potential of this direction:

UNDERSTAND THE $CHOOL'S INTERE$T

For every $15 book "we" sell, a school makes $4.50 to $6.00 (perhaps less if I've agreed to a lower speaking fee), plus profits on the nightlights and hand puppets. The more they sell, the more we both make. Ka-ching!

BE FLEXIBLE ON FEES IF...

If I can piggyback on school fairs and festivals (which can attract thousands), I may speak for less or even for free—especially if, a) the event is close to home, b) I can sell books, and c) the school is willing to cut their commission on book sales. Sometimes, I'll cut my fee in half if they can successfully refer me to another school for a same-day appearance. Your willingness to reduce your fees—I do it because I'm passionate about the kids—will help the school live within budget constraints, while earning you far more than you gave up in positive publicity.

SEND ORDER FORMS IN ADVANCE

Send the school a black and white order form for advance sales (ready to copy and insert in students' weekly envelopes). Explain that by autographing them ahead of time, you will have more time for the kids.

START LOCAL AND LET IT BUILD

Always start local. Become a neighborhood celebrity first, then branch out from there, like the ripple effect from a stone falling into a pond.

MAKE IT MEMORABLE

Relax, have fun, and engage your audience. Break the ice by starting with the book upside down, and then talk backwards until they correct you (kids live for these moments). Stop periodically to ask questions. Point suddenly to an unsuspecting student or take a show of hands. If they weren't paying attention, they'll be on high alert from then on. After all, bragging rights are at stake and you have a captive audience.

MAKE IT EASY TO SAY "YES!"

The biggest obstacle between you and a 'YES' is money. I like to improve my odds by providing schools with a fun list of fundraising ideas that not only provide the capital to pay me, but most often result in bonus community-building activities for the school.

•   •   •

www.schoolbookings.com is a subsidiary of www.authorsandexperts.com, a clearinghouse for those in media, radio, and TV to find authors and experts on topics across the spectrum: $149 a year to join, at press time.

Bookstores are Terrible Places to Sell Books

Came across a great article with the above title a few years back by Fern Reiss, the author of several great books on publishing (www.PublishingGame.com). This excerpt underscores the necessity to get creative about thinking of other more potentially profitable outlets for your book:

[In bookstores], the margins are low—you gross less than $4.50 on every $10 book. You get crummy display space—just the spine of your book shows. And let's face it—the competition is awful. But you can sell thousands of books each year to non-bookstore outlets. Here's how:

Think audience and think niche. Whatever the topic of your book, the audience hangs out in places other than bookstores. So think about that audience, and think about where they're hanging out. If you have a golf book, think golf courses and golf pro shops. If you have a golden retriever book, think pet stores and dog shows. Any venue that isn't a bookstore is a great place to sell books—because you can display your books as you like, get a larger cut of the retail price, and best of all, you're often the only book!

So take your book to the sci-fi convention...the firemen's ball...the ski shop...the writing convention. Bring it anywhere there might be an audience for it. And see how well it will sell in markets that aren't bookstores.

Think about building reality into your book (especially with novels, which can be particularly difficult to market.) Put in real place names, real restaurants, real hotels, real associations, real websites and organizations. And then market your book to those venues. If your book mentions the local neighborhood Italian restaurant, try asking the owner if she'd like to sell copies at the register. If it mentions a real association, find out if they'd want to consider a quantity purchase for their members. If it mentions a corporation, find out if they'd like you to give a talk—and then sell your books at the back of the room. All possibilities, and all pay better than bookstores.

My Publishing Game series were all written at my local Seattle's Best Coffee. Because they were so nice to me while I was writing the books, I mentioned the Seattle's Best Coffee staff in my dedication. When the books were published, I brought them in as a thank you, and to show the staff. The books were left sitting behind the counter for a few days, and the next time I came in the manager asked me if they could sell the books in Seattle's. "So many people have come in asking to buy them," she noted.

At the local bookstore, they only stock one or two of each of my books. They shelve them spine out. They pay me 45%. At Seattle's, they stock ten copies of each of three books. They shelve them attractively on bookstands and in carefully arranged stacks; they're the only books in the store, so they stand out next to the coffee paraphernalia. And they pay me 75%. Guess where I'd rather be selling my books?

So, you starting to see that bookstores are just the beginning as far as places to speak and sell books go? Now, let's turn to an area where confusion, misconception, and excess hype often rule the day, and see if we can't shine a little light on things...

Chapter 12

In a recent year, *Xlibris*, the #3 company in Print-on-Demand (POD), published more than 7,000 titles and sold over 300,000 books. That same year, I remember reading about a much-heralded celebration they had after paying out their one-millionth dollar in royalties. Let's do the math. One million dollars over 7000 titles comes out to an average royalty of $149 each (and I'm being generous here by letting them count that $1 million for just that year, despite it likely being a *cumulative* figure for several years). I promise you, they charged each author far more than that to "publish" their book.

How do you separate the POD truth from the hype? Well, let's do a reality check first. As I see it, POD is great for two scenarios (and we'll discuss a third shortly):

1) If your goal is simply to get in print, be able to say "I'm an author," and have the book available for friends and family; OR...

2) If you're a publisher with out-of-print titles into which you'd like to breathe some new life. Related to that would be a publisher with a book whose sales have tapered down to a trickle, and POD becomes an attractive, cost-effective alternative to doing another multi-thousand unit printing.

A Technology, NOT a "Revolution"

Print-on-Demand is a very simple concept. You submit your book to a POD publisher in electronic format (usually an MS Word file). The company typesets the book (lays out the interior), designs the book cover, and loads it onto their system. No physical books are printed until someone actually orders the book (i.e., you or a bookstore, driven by a customer request). Given the capabilities of digital printing technology, it's actually cost-effective to print books one at a time. Though, in many cases, the quality of POD books is demonstrably inferior to those printed conventionally; ask to see samples.

If you're looking to be profitable with your publishing, don't count on POD to get you there. If you're looking at POD realistically, have read all the fine print, know all the many limitations of the model, and, bottom line, are going in with your eyes open, fine. Go for it. Understand that the real value of POD is in the technology. And that's the key. It's just a *technology*, not a program, or a "groundbreaking marketing strategy," or some kind of miracle. Just a technology. POD allows for the relatively inexpensive typesetting, design and printing of a small number of copies of your book. Arguably, an inexpensive short run printer with typeset and design capabilities.

The "Upsell"

That being the case, when they start pushing the marketing, promotion, and other after-production services, accompanied by tantalizing images of "successfully breaking through the traditional barriers to publishing success," you need to hold on to your wallet.

They'll pitch you on their aggressive plan to market your title—with a host of extra costs, of course. Don't put too much stock in it. For the most part, it'll be an impressive sounding menu of window-dressing. They'll promise to send a press release to thousands of potentially interested parties. The release will likely be a standard cookie cutter job, mass-mailed to people who get far too many releases every day anyway.

More importantly, unless you provide the release yourself (the only circumstances under which you should even consider this avenue, in which case you're paying for the distribution of that release, and is *that* worth the toll, given inexpensive services like **www.PRWeb.com**?), I'd wager that the one they send will focus on the book, not the *angle* represented by the book, making it even less useful to these people than it already is. And when that potential reviewer sees the POD publisher's name on the release, chances are its next and final stop will be the circular file. We'll discuss why shortly.

More importantly, successful marketing and promotion of a book has to be an ongoing, consistent, and multi-faceted proposition. What you'd pay a POD publisher to "handle it," so to speak, would be both too little and too much.

Far too little to even begin to do the job right, yet way too much for what you'll get.

Reality Check

Realistically, you just can't outsource the marketing of your book unless you literally have tens of thousands of dollars to burn, and even then, it'd be extraordinarily easy to get extraordinarily ripped off. Hopefully, by this point in the book, you've got a more realistic idea of what it's going to take to market your book effectively. And the idea that sending out one or two off-the-rack press releases constitutes a "comprehensive marketing campaign" is a joke.

As one wise insider observed, "Self-publishing is not about writing. It's about business." The fact is, most new authors are naïve, aren't business-savvy, don't do their homework, and don't understand the realities of the book publishing world. They go in with stars in their eyes, hear what they want to hear, and because of the nature of the POD business model, in essence, get sold a bill of goods on what POD can do for them. Heck, they're creative types; what do they know about business? What do they even *want* to know about business?

Raining on Parades

I have a number of friends who've been working on books over the past few years, and we've kept in touch with each other. During that time, most of them have been hunting for a publisher. In several cases, I've gotten an email sharing their excitement in having found one. Eager to join in the celebration, I've asked who they ended up with, only to hear the name of a POD publisher.

Now, as mentioned earlier, if they fully understand the POD deal and have modest expectations, great. But most of these folks really believe they've landed a publisher on a par with a real publishing house, and that these folks are going to make them wildly successful. Wrong, and wrong.

Publishing (Un)Success

The typical POD publisher charges upfront fees ranging from, according to the industry's top players, roughly $700 to $1500. Know that those upfront fees include the POD publisher's profit margin. They know that roughly 98-plus percent of the books on their system won't be successful. Why? Three reasons:

1) They're all self-published! There's essentially no quality control—*anyone* with a book idea and a relatively small financial investment can "get in print."

2) Overwhelmingly, mass-produced book covers will mark the book as an amateur work, further stacking the deck against it. And finally...

3) Precious few POD authors, being the marketing novices they are, have given any thought at all to who'd be interested (besides friends and family) in that book, and how to reach those audiences.

THIS'LL BLOW YOUR MIND

Check this out. Guess how many books the average POD author sells? About 100-200 (according to the top three players). Of that 100-200 books sold, guess who the biggest buyer is? You sitting down? Straight from the horse's mouth (i.e., Xlibris): *64% of books sold on Xlibris are purchased by the authors themselves!* It's even higher for children's books. And likely the numbers are similar for the other players.

The POD Business Model

Which brings us to the POD business model. I'm going to actually defend POD for a moment. Because they've got economies of scale down, for that $700-1500 you get typesetting and cover design, which is actually pretty cheap. If you were to hire people to do that, you could easily pay $3-5K for the two. However, for those higher rates, you'd be getting *exactly what you wanted* (though, all that said, take note of point #3 on p. 190...).

With POD, you don't have nearly as much control over the final product, which, of course, as hinted at earlier, is why POD's cheaper. You have to stick to some pretty generic choices for both, and that's understandable; it's the only way they can make it financially feasible for everyone. And, sorry to say, that means you'll likely end up with a lame, amateurish book cover that's simply part and parcel of any assembly line publishing operation.

But once a POD publisher has those economies in place, and can turn a profit offering a fixed menu of choices for its basic packages, and because it costs virtually nothing to put another book on their system, that company has every incentive to sign up *anyone*, regardless of the quality of the book. And, because of that aforementioned 98+ percent failure rate, once the starry-eyed author is signed up, the POD squad has virtually no incentive to promote those books (unless the author's picking up the tab). Heck, they've made their money! Why invest more effort when the returns will likely be minimal?

Never forget: for most POD publishers, their business is signing up authors and collecting upfront fees (a sure road to profitability), *not* helping to make those authors successful (a financial crapshoot, at best...).

Straight Talk on POD

Don't buy the line that POD is some "revolutionary printing model that's providing the keys to the serious publishing kingdom for all those authors heretofore locked out of the game." It's not. In essence, it's simply a more technologically advanced form of "vanity publishing." What's that? Little more than a system in which you pay to "publish" your book and "market" it to wholesalers, retailers, and potential reviewers who, frankly, aren't that interested.

Why? Well, the major bookstore chains and key reviewers don't consider POD books serious works. Bookstores shy away from POD works because they're often of inferior quality, and because the POD model dictates higher unit printing costs, and hence higher retail prices, it makes those books harder to sell. Add a bookstore-unfriendly return policy (i.e., usually not permitted) and you can see why the big chains (not to mention distributors) wouldn't exactly be falling all over themselves to carry these books. Though, in reality, returnability isn't much of an issue for most POD authors...

AuthorHouse, the #1 POD company, in a nod to the crucial importance of returnability to the overall distribution equation, offers their authors the option of making their books returnable. It's an option apparently chosen by a "great number of people" (quote from a podcast discussed a few pages ahead), according to *AH*'s CEO, Bryan Smith. Cost for returnability (at press time): $700.

But...would an *AH* author drop that kind of cash if he knew he'd only sell, on average, 100-200 books (and *he'd* be buying nearly two-thirds of them!), essentially making returnability a moot point? It's like turbo-charging a car that has a top speed of 50 mph. Kind of pointless. Nonetheless, these companies play on author hope and naiveté, and capture that additional $700, despite the fact that, overwhelmingly, they'll never have to invoke that returnability feature. I'm in the wrong business.

The Pecking Order

POD books aren't taken seriously by the trade for the same reason "vanity press" books aren't. It comes down to a perception of POD as being relatively "barrier-free" publishing. Let's examine the perceived pecking order here.

At the top, in the eyes of the industry, is a book that's been conventionally published. Obviously, a book with any reputable publishing house's imprimatur has jumped through many hoops before finally making the grade. Given that a traditional publisher makes no money until *after* making a hefty financial investment *and* selling lots of books, a publishing house can't make those financial decisions cavalierly if it wants to last more than a season or two.

The next grade down is a book like mine that's self-published using the approach set out in this book. In this scenario, because the decision to publish resides solely with the author, by definition it skips any rigorous screening of the sort employed by a conventional publisher. Which explains why so many self-published books are mediocre.

But, on the plus side of this second scenario is the fact that a self-publishing author has to totally finance his or her own venture, which in itself can be a pretty powerful screening process. Presumably, that implies at least a marginal grip on reality when it comes to the perceived quality of one's own work. Few people are going to drop $10-14K on a lark (what it could cost to bring 5000 copies of a book's first printing to market) unless they really believe in what they've written, have done the research, and know there's a market for their book.

Then, at the bottom of the totem pole, there's POD publishing (and ebook publishing for that matter) which offers the worst of all worlds: a publishing decision left completely to the author (i.e., no real screening except for pornographic or other highly offensive content) *and* a relatively minimal investment on the part of that author.

So, very legitimately, key reviewers and bookstore chains ask: *What's stopping any Tom, Dick, or Harriet from getting "published"?* Not much, anymore. Which, of course, is the spin being made by POD publishers to attract authors: your *desire* to be "published" is all that's required, *not* your talent or even much of your money. Not surprisingly, desire alone is not exactly the stuff from which springs real respect. Low barrier = low respect.

POD = "Self-Publishing"?

A few years back, I read an article in my local daily paper on "self-publishing" ("Self-publishing allows writers to print, market own books," by Don O'Briant; *The Atlanta Journal-Constitution*, October 7, 2004) and in it, they cluelessly—in my humble opinion—talked about POD as "self-publishing." Ditto with a much more substantive piece in a more high-profile venue ("How to Be Your Own Publisher," by Sarah Glazer; *The New York Times*, April 23, 2005).

Both these pieces grated on me a bit. OK, more than a bit. Yes, technically, it's self-publishing in the sense that you, your*self* are deciding to *publish* and are no longer at the mercy of the hoity-toity publishing houses. But that's where the similarity ends.

And it's not just reporters for major daily papers who are confused. You know it's bad when, arguably, THE rag for the publishing industry, *Publishers Weekly*, which absolutely should know better, gets it wrong, too. Check out these comments from PMA Executive Director Jan Nathan, writing in the October 2005 issue of *Independent*, the monthly newsletter of PMA. Note her reference to POD as a "printing process." Again, clarifying that it's just a technology, not the keys to the city:

I [was] incensed by a column in **PW Daily** *(the daily email newsletter from industry giant* **Publishers Weekly***) that referred to a print-on-demand printer as a self-publisher, and I had called some people at* **PW** *to voice my complaint* *about the use of these terms. I wondered how a publication that's supposed to be a voice of the book-publishing community could possibly equate a printer with a self-publisher. If* **PW** *doesn't know the difference, how will everyone else realize that print-on-demand is a printing process?*

Squeaky Wheels...

Incidentally, why is it that the mainstream media repeatedly positions POD as "self-publishing," while essentially ignoring the vast universe of SP'ers like yours truly, doing it the ...old-fashioned way? My theory? It's the POD publishers who are regularly and consistently getting their press releases into the hands of the media and driving home that association. Meanwhile, the true self-publishers are too busy busting their humps to get the word out. So, when media people hear "self-publishing," pretty much all they know about the term is what they hear from the POD crowd. Sigh.

Basic Differences

From a purist's (translation: someone who's invested truckloads of blood, sweat, tears, time, and cash into his own self-publishing venture in order to turn a tidy profit) point of view, no, POD is not self-publishing. Especially when you consider that most everything else about the POD scenario is *very* different from self-publishing as I did it. A few key distinctions:

1) ROYALTIES VS. EXPENSES/PROFITS: With POD, you pay less for the production (though you're forced to operate within *their* parameters), but most fee-based POD publishers will have you sign a contract that pays you royalties. And those royalties are often based on *net* proceeds (after discounts to wholesalers, etc.), *not* retail price, reducing them even further. These royalty arrangements can be extremely complicated and confusing, no doubt designed—he said cynically—to lighten the wallets of unsuspecting authors.

In my scenario, after footing the bill for all production, marketing, and promotion expenses, all proceeds were mine.

2) PROCESS CONTROL: With POD, you relinquish a huge amount of control over production, again, having to work within pretty rigid guidelines. As mentioned, you'll likely end up with a cheesy book cover that screams, "SELF-PUBLISHED!" And we all *know* how important covers are, right? In addition, you probably won't own your ISBNs. With none of the three top POD players—*AuthorHouse, iUniverse or Xlibris*—do you own your own ISBNs, meaning that in all the databases out there, those entities, not you, will be noted as the "publisher-of-record."

With true self-publishing, you maintain total control over the production process: cover and interior book design, trim size, paper quality, timetable, etc. And since you bought your own ISBNs, there's no question as to ownership and "publisher-of-record."

3) RIGHTS: With POD, you may be required to turn over the rights to your creation—at least for a certain period of time. POD's Big Three, *AH, Xlibris,* and *iUniverse,* all own your "produced" files. Meaning, if you choose one of them, and they go ahead and lay out your book, and design your cover, should you decide that you want to leave them at some point, what you'll take with you are only the original text files you showed up with; they'll hang on to the enhanced version. You still retain the rights to your work, but they retain the rights to the produced files.

With true self-publishing, since you're simply hiring service providers to execute various production tasks related to your books (design, editing, typesetting, printing, indexing), you retain all rights to your work, in any form.

4) COST OF BOOKS: With POD, if you want copies of your own book, you'll pay rates that hover close to 40-50+ percent of the retail cost (another way they make the model financially viable—for themselves). Not to mention that many POD publishers require their authors to purchase a certain number of copies of their own books at those same inflated rates (compared to typical offset printing rates).

IF you want commercial success with your book, this is one of single biggest reasons not to go POD. With true self-publishing, yes, printing can take a big financial bite, but once it's paid for, you own those books. Commercial success means a LOT of book marketing and promotion, and that means sending out LOTS of review copies. Purchasing books from your POD "publisher" means that, even generously assuming a cost of only 40 percent of retail, a $20 book runs $8, which with packaging, press kit, and postage, puts you way over $10 per package. You could go broke in a hurry. At my cost of under $2.50 a book (delivered), I'm below $5 for a package—far more do-able.

Trunk Sales

Let's not forget personal sales of books at events, seminars, and of course, out of the trunk of your car. I always carry books in my car, and have sold a steady trickle of them over the years. At that $2.50 cost (retail $20), I can afford to be generous, sell them at a 25-50 percent discount, and still make a healthy profit. And when you can discount like that, Econ 101 dictates you'll just sell more. With POD, you can kiss that possibility goodbye. *WARNING: not having a cheap and steady supply of your own books will absolutely hobble your ongoing marketing efforts on many levels, while effectively eliminating many incremental income streams as well.*

POD Rationale #3

In addition to the two main applications for POD discussed earlier, I've come to realize there's a third—one that's made me temper my somewhat strident anti-POD stance. Thanks to fellow writer and author Susan Stephenson for helping me see a bit of light here. I met Susan after a talk and book signing at the gorgeous new library in Columbus, Georgia one warm Saturday in March 2005.

Susan sagely offered up POD as an avenue for authors who are taking the long view, and trying to build up their name in the business—book by book (and don't have the time, money, or inclination to self-publish as I have). If an author simply can't get a publisher to take them on, but knows that he has a voice that needs to be heard out there, POD does offer an outlet to have his work see the light of day.

Yes, for the most part, POD allows an author to get virtually anything into print, even junk—on only their say-so—and as such, drives the lack of respect that follows POD around like a black cloud.

LONG-TERM "BRAND BUILDING"

However, that author trying to build a strong "brand" for themselves, a book at a time, could choose to approach the crafting of his book (i.e., content, editing, design, title, etc.) with the same rigor and exacting standards we've discussed throughout this book, with an eye toward a creating a book indistinguishable from a conventionally published work.

Take this commitment to quality into your conversations with your POD publisher, and do all you can to ensure that *your* final product comes as close as possible to being that high-quality "industry grade" product. The groundwork in excellence laid today can yield dividends down the line, as one can then refer to an existing body of quality work. In that sense, POD can be a great tool for authors who view the process as a much longer journey, and don't expect to make much money in the short term.

Just remember that the POD model usually charges extra—and often a *lot* extra—for *any* deviations from the standard templates—even if you provide, say, your *own* cover artwork. But, given the importance of a cover, it might be worth it.

The Cost/Price Problem

A final point about one of the key flaws of the POD model. As *Xlibris's* VP, Dave Maturo admits, while POD technology is wonderfully flexible in that you can print any quantity, even one book, reasonably cost-effectively, the flip side of that coin is that, because quantities are almost always far smaller compared to offset printing (traditional printing press technology, typically used for large print runs), the per-unit cost for POD-printed books is significantly higher than for offset. Which can create a problem when POD books go head-to-head with competitive titles printed offset.

> ### Listen & Learn
>
> Check out a handful of enlightening interviews with top brass from *AuthorHouse* (formerly *1stBooks*), *iUniverse*, and *Xlibris* (the #1, #2, and #3 POD players in the business, respectively, at press time) – all via podcasts with Ron Pramschufer, founder of the great sites **www.publishingbasics.com** and **www.selfpublishing.com** (For all the POD podcasts on POD, visit Ron's related site, **www.wbjbradio.com/archives.php?aid**).
>
> Listen as Bryan Smith, CEO of *AuthorHouse* (*AH*), stumbles through his interview, Dave Maturo, VP of *Xlibris*, does better, but with several "deer-in-the-headlights" moments, and Susan Driscoll, CEO of *iUniverse*, comes off the best—comfortable, knowledgeable, and down-to-earth. And visit **http://blog.selfpublishing.com/?p=103**, one of Ron's most-visited links, for an unvarnished take-no-prisoners snapshot of the whole POD milieu, plus some great response posts from listeners, several pointing the crucial distinction between "POD printers" and "POD publishers." Bottom line, there are a lot of potential minefields in POD. So, *caveat emptor*, BIG time.

As Ron pointed out in his podcast with Maturo, a 256-page book (the average length of all books, incidentally) printed via POD ends up retailing for roughly $22, about 50 percent higher than an offset printed book of similar length, which comes in at about $15. And the ratios are far worse for full-color children's books, as color POD technology lags even further behind black and white.

BAD ECONOMICS

So, we end up with this semi-surreal moment in the podcast with *Xlibris's* Maturo, *summa cum laude* in economics, where he has to concede Ron's point, and furthermore, that the POD model, in order to be financially viable, *for the company*, requires POD pricing to be based on actual production costs, *not* what the market will bear. And *that* most economically unsound business model, until fine-tuned, will, by definition, significantly impact a POD book's ability to compete.

You'll pay $3.49 for a loaf of small-batch ciabatta bread at your local fru-fru bakery rather than $1.49 for supermarket white bread, but you do it because you're getting far more for your money. But would you pay 50 percent more for basically the same white loaf, but just a different brand name? Not likely. Same thing here.

Of course, all this is somewhat self-evident, if you take the 30,000 foot view. A "onesie-twosie" operation simply can't compete, price-wise, with books printed offset, in quantities of many thousands. Unless you're talking about distinct content that's in high demand, and whose value is set by a buyer who simply must have it. But, if you're talking about a book comparable to many others, it's a whole other ballgame. Look to POD to simply "get you into print," in a fashion, but don't quit your day job.

"Platform-Building"

Remember "POD Good Reason #3" mentioned earlier, for authors taking the long view? Indeed, I heard this very "platform-building" point made with a different spin on Ron's podcast with *iUniverse's* CEO Susan Driscoll.

Driscoll pointed out that, "We are trying to position iUniverse as a farm team for traditional publishers. If you're good at marketing and have a quality product, you are much more apt to get a traditional publisher's attention once you have some sort of a track record, and we can help you do that."

The emphasis, says Driscoll, is on educating authors as to the ins and outs of publishing in general, and the POD model in particular. Which is good to hear, since, as Driscoll readily admits, "Authors are very naïve. They have big dreams, a lot of hope, and great expectations." Might part of that author education process be to get them to *not* expect to make a lot of money with POD?

If You Must Go POD...

While, obviously, I'm not a huge fan of POD, if you're leaning in that direction, and your circumstances are a match for it, as I've described above, from all I've heard, *iUniverse* would be a good choice. They seem to be more upfront about acknowledging the limitations of the POD model, while highlighting where the technology can make a difference for an author.

Interestingly enough, *iUniverse* is also more discriminating in terms of the quality of manuscripts they'll accept than *Xlibris* and *AH*. Dave Maturo of *Xlibris* actually conceded this point, adding that both his company and *AH* will essentially accept anything (except, as mentioned earlier, literary sewage).

Another plus for *iUniverse*: Susan Driscoll, CEO of *iUniverse*, had 25 years of publishing industry experience before taking over the helm at *iU*. Meanwhile, Smith and Maturo, while both boasting impressive business resumés, had none. Nada. I'd say that counts for something. The one minus as noted earlier: *iUniverse*, not you, owns your ISBN.

By the way, I've also been hearing more and more about a relative POD newcomer, **Lulu™ (www.lulu.com)**. Their web site claims: "No set-up fees. No minimum order. No catch. You keep control of the rights, the design, the price, and 80% of the profits. Really." That's different. Plus, **Lulu** apparently offers the interesting twist of allowing authors to rapidly update and/or customize book covers for their target audience at no additional cost. Might be worth a look. As always, *caveat emptor*.

Summing Up

When it comes to marketing and promoting your book, my feeling, right or wrong, is this: You should either do it, and really jump in with both feet, or not bother at all. I say this because it takes a pretty massive amount of work to market a book effectively. It's a *critical mass* thing. A half-assed effort will yield results *far* closer to *no* effort than to a major one. If you decide you're not going to bother—perfectly honorable decision, incidentally, and far better than a toe-in-the-pool approach—POD is a decent way to go. Problem is, people think—and are sold on the idea—that POD is actually like "jumping in," when it's not.

Remember, 100-200 books on average, and the lion's share bought by authors themselves. But, should that really be surprising? After all, the companies accept inferior manuscripts. They design and typeset them, *not* with an eye toward ultimate marketability, but with strict financial considerations in mind. Ditto the price—again determined by the financial realities of the POD model, not what the market will bear. Finally, far and away the most important part of the success equation—the marketing—is reduced to generic one-size-fits-all efforts. That's a pretty lethal quadruple whammy.

Contacts and Lowdown

The big names in POD publishing are AuthorHouse (**www.authorhouse.com**), *iUniverse* (**www.iuniverse.com**, 50% owned by Barnes & Noble, for all you trivia buffs…), *Xlibris* (**www.xlibris.com**), Trafford (**www.trafford.com**), and *PublishAmerica* (http://www.publishamerica.com). If you're considering *PublishAmerica*, you *must* check out this podcast (**www.wbjbradio.com/ viewshow.php?id=42&aid**) with Ron Pramschufer. We're talking some pretty damning stuff.

For a good look at the potential minefield of fine print, check out this article by Clea Saal on the *booksandtales* site: **www.booksandtales.com/ pod/rword.htm**. And on the same site, you'll find head-to-head comparisons of POD publishers and tons of interesting articles: **www.booksandtales.com/ pod/podpublish.htm**.

A great straight-shooting article (along with some good links) on the whole POD thing is at **www.sfwa.org/beware/printondemand.html**.

Another promising resource is attorney Mark Levine's book *"The Fine Print: What Print-on-demand and Ebook Publishing Contracts Really Say"* (more info and purchase details at **www.book-publishers-compared.com/ AuthorHouse.html**). And check out Mark's podcast with Ron Pramschufer at **www.wbjbradio.com/archives.php?aid**.

Hopefully, you've got a bit straighter scoop on POD than you had before we started. Now let's turn to a *most* important discussion—the one that gets into how, indeed, you turn one book into a full-time living. It's all about "spinoffs"…

Chapter 13

The situation had gotten pretty desperate. On a light day, I was spending probably two to three hours answering email. My productivity was vanishing under a tidal wave of seemingly endless keystrokes. Don't get me wrong. I love hearing from my readers, and relish hearing their warm accounts of how my books made a difference for them. And you will too. It's one of the most gratifying parts of being an author.

Given the genre of my book (non-fiction how-to), I naturally get a lot more "mechanics-of-the-business" questions than a fiction (or even creative non-fiction) writer would. And when someone has just heaped on the praise for a paragraph or two, you feel like the least you can do is return the favor by answering their questions (it's never just one...). In fact, I'm pretty sure that readers will often deliberately gush on and on, in order to feel that they have, in a sense, paid the toll for a little free advice. Yeah. I'm wise to your game... ☺

That said, the joy of "being there for my readers" was devouring increasingly larger chunks of my day. Something had to give. So, I launched my paid one-on-one mentoring service to start making money from something I'd given away for free for a very long time. Since that launch, I've had quite a few takers for the service—not tens of thousands of dollars worth, but certainly enough to pay for a few nice vacations a year. And that's with minimal promotion. No reason you couldn't make it a bigger income stream with a little focused marketing.

Books: Just the Beginning

This story underscores an important point: a spinoff business might come out of necessity, as in the case of my mentoring service. Or it might just be a natural evolution. Whatever the reason, spinning off different income streams is one of the best ways to indeed turn one book into a full-time living. That said, while I've earned income from a lot of directions, which I'll discuss in this chapter, for me, book sales are still tops. Though I don't think I've even come close yet to maximizing revenues from other directions. Which makes the future even brighter.

Put your best first efforts into book promotion, because it's the credibility that springs from your new-found notoriety that builds the momentum into other related businesses. Adding a few (or more) thousand dollars to your bottom line from each of four, five, six or more offshoot ventures will not only build your bank account, reputation, and resumé, but it'll make life that much more fun and interesting.

A Book as a Springboard

The great thing about writing a book is that even if you don't sell a lot of books, it truly *can* be that base that leads you into far more lucrative avenues, because of your growing credibility as a "published author." Arielle Ford, who's been called "America's #1 Book Publicist," says this very thing in the direct sales letter promoting her comprehensive book publicity program (**www.everythingyoushouldknow.com**):

The book is your ticket into the lucrative speaking and workshop game, and this is where the REAL money is. This is where your income can really take off. And if you're smart, you'll harness the expertise and credibility that being a book author gives you, and profit from these lucrative opportunities. It's criminal how under-exploited this strategy really is. But it is not surprising, given only a handful of publishers and authors really understand how to make it work.

While I couldn't agree more, your success in accomplishing what she talks about will depend, to a large extent, on your subject. If it's a mainstream subject, sure, the sky's the limit. If it's a more niche subject, there will be, by definition, fewer windfall opportunities. Yet, regardless of your subject, I want to help you figure out how to maximize that potential.

Same Person, Different Person

Write a book, and an interesting and amusing thing happens. The world suddenly views you differently. You're still the same person, but in the eyes of your fellow man, you take on the "Author Aura." I see it in the shocked emails I get from readers, amazed that I'd actually taken a few precious moments out of my day—chock-full of doing all sorts of "author-ly" things, no doubt—to respond to l'il ole them. Not my take, mind you, but theirs. I see it in the hesitant way in which people approach me at events. It's pretty funny actually.

By the way, you'll reap this benefit whether or not your book is commercially successful. Indeed, writing a book is a great strategy for any businessperson who wants to boost their name and image in their particular industry, not to mention being a great springboard to other offshoot businesses. And those businesses will be taken that much more seriously, because, after all, you're an author. That means you're an "expert" on your subject, whether or not you consider yourself to be. Sometimes we're the last to be convinced that we've done something pretty cool and amazing. If that's what you're hearing from those around you, just go with it. Remember: "Your own mind is a dangerous neighborhood. Don't go there alone."

The Five-Year NO-Plan

For the record, when I self-published my first book in 2000, I had no visions of building a budding little empire here. Yet, as I write this, I'm looking at two books (and this one makes three), a slipcased set of two, ten ebooks, seminars, teleseminars, four CD programs (including three from teleseminars), a critically acclaimed monthly ezine (now in its fifth year), fee-based one-on-one coaching, and of course, my commercial writing business itself (the subject of my earlier books). That's in just six years. Who knows where it'll be in another five? And every one of those avenues—directly or indirectly—makes me money.

While many of you might end up writing one book and leaving it at that, others may be taking a longer view. Fact is, while I truly had no grand five-year growth strategy at the outset, over the course of the past five years, I was slowly building a *platform*. "Platform" is a popular buzzword in many circles these days, especially book publishing, and for good reason. Many conventional publishers now expect authors they're considering taking on to have some sort of platform. For us SP'ers, a platform is a surefire way to enhance the viability of any publishing venture.

Building a "Platform"

What's a platform? I guess you could say it's *enhanced standing, higher visibility, and greater credibility (i.e. "expert" status) within a specific community, by virtue of years of tangible, successful contributions—books, ezines, speaking, media coverage—to a particular subject or "conversation" with that community.*

If you've thought that your subject potentially lends itself to the creation of a platform, then your first book will be the *base* of the platform. It's often the first thing that brings you and your ideas into the public's awareness—though not necessarily. Think of a columnist who eventually writes a book, making the book even more successful because of the platform he or she has built through their column. Which is another way to approach this game: build your name through other means *before* you write the book.

While it may certainly be possible (and no doubt tempting) to plan out every additional platform-building product, service, or enhancement in advance, my own experience reflects a less premeditated, more intuitive process. Simply put, I let things evolve naturally—as the timing felt right. It's worked out well.

Keeps On Giving...

Regardless of how you do it, just know that I'm living proof that taking the long view with an eye toward building something more substantial and far-reaching is a wonderful way to create multiple streams of income—many of them with that wonderful, magical prefix: *passive*. It's a great feeling to put a structure in place over several years, and have that structure regularly deliver money to your mailbox, PayPal account, and bank account, unrelated to any specific recent actions. Get a taste of that and I promise you, you'll start getting very creative about thinking of ways to keep that gravy train going—*and* growing.

So, what possible side businesses could you spin off from your book (or column) on your way to creating a platform of your own? Let me share a few of mine. Given that my book is in the genre of non-fiction how-to, I had some avenues open to me that might be tougher for fiction or creative non-fiction authors.

Seminars

This was my first offshoot business. Obviously, a how-to subject lends itself nicely to the seminar route, though a published author of any book can certainly give seminars on the art and practice of writing itself. Fact is, many unpublished writers teach writing classes, so certainly, dems dat done it should have little problem.

Between late 2000 and early 2004, I did close to 30 seminars across the country. Not exactly a blistering pace, but most happened in the first two years. The early ones were all-day Saturday affairs—from 9-5 with about two hours for lunch and breaks—and generally in a hotel meeting room.

Wouldn't It Be Nice...

Typical attendance was 12-20 folks, as I'd made the decision to deliver a more personal experience. Much more than 20 and it became difficult to cover all the material, address everyone's questions and still get done by 5:00 p.m. Okay, okay. I'm lying. I would have loved to have packed 100 people in the room and charge $200-300 a head for a weekend seminar—who wouldn't?— but given my marketing strategy and the fact that I had a fairly "niche" topic, I just wasn't attracting hundreds of takers. Smaller groups *do* make for a richer and more intimate experience, and allow you to cover more material. As such, people walk away feeling like they've gotten far more than their money's worth. Probably wouldn't be the same with a "cattle-call" version.

After a few years of the Saturday programs, I switched to an evening weeknight format, 7:00-9:30 p.m. All day Saturday events are exhausting for both parties, and because of the full day, weekend slot, and higher price, they were harder for prospects to commit to. Evening programs are easier to sell, easier to deliver, and easier to sit through.

I briefly explored the possibility of contracting a seminar marketing/promotion firm to handle the job (check *Literary Marketplace* in your library for a list of these companies), but the few firms I spoke with felt, again, that the subject matter was too narrow in scope. If your subject has broader appeal, perhaps that might be a more viable avenue. Let's look at a bunch of strategies I've used to maximize the seminar spinoff direction.

Eleven Tips for Delivering More Profitable and Enjoyable Seminars

1) Do Signings as "Feeders" Whenever I had a seminar planned for some city, I tried to schedule one or two book signings during the few days prior. In addition to creating a buzz and selling more books (both during the signings and in general, simply as a result of the additional promotion and media exposure), most signings were good for one or more seminar enrollments. If you're doing a seminar in your own city, do as I did: schedule five, six, or more signings during a two to three week period, culminating in the seminar a week or so later. That should definitely stir things up.

Also, it's definitely easier to land some media coverage for your seminar if you've got signings scheduled. If a B&N/Borders/prominent independent bookstore is willing to book you, it's like a calling card to the media that says, "This guy/gal is alright."

2) Partner with Others For most of the seminars I did, I wore every hat—advance man, promoter, marketer, seminar leader, bookseller, etc. I wrote all the promo materials, contacted all the local media, radio and TV stations, and sent countless emails to writers groups and other promising-sounding organizations that might be even remotely interested in my humble offering. I made all my arrangements, rented the meeting room, set up any book signings in advance, showed up early, arranged lunch, set up the room, delivered the goods, handled book sales, etc. Suffice it to say, it can be a grueling process, with no guarantees whatsoever.

For a much less stressful experience, try teaming up with a local organization with a similar mission. You'll split the profits, but also share the burden of getting the word out. The actual split of profits—I've done 50/50, and 60/40 (me/them)—depends on how you split up the work. If you're doing most of it, and they're mainly lending their organization's name and local credibility, that might only be worth 25 or 30 percent (which they'd likely be happy with). In one case, since I already had a merchant account, I handled the registration process, while their local number was a logical contact point for questions, which were usually then steered to my web site for answers and signup.

I've done it three times so far, with good results. You'll usually find, as I did, someone in the organization who, in exchange for free tuition, volunteers to be your "Girl/Guy Friday," handling product sales, handing out course materials, turning the thermostat up and down as needed—all those little things that free you up to focus on your job. Well worth it.

THE LEARNING ANNEX

I've also done one seminar through *The Learning Annex* (TLA) (**www.LearningAnnex.com**)—the North American chain offering a full and eclectic catalog of inexpensive adult-ed classes. You don't do TLA for the money. As a rule, they pay presenters 10 percent of proceeds (though that's occasionally negotiated up a bit if they really want you), and with courses typically $40-50 or less, you're not going to get rich even if you get a high turnout (30 to 40, by their standards).

You do it because you get listed in their catalog, often for several consecutive issues, which goes out to many tens of thousands of people in that area, as well as often getting promoted in email blasts. That spells fabulous exposure that would cost you a tidy bundle if you had to spring for it yourself. *And* you do it because you get to sell your products.

My experience with TLA is limited, but mixed. I actually had two scheduled (NYC and Toronto), but only ended up doing one (the latter). While TLA generally has a good reputation, apparently, the individual centers vary widely in their efficiency, as I found out.

I'll spare you the gory details, but suffice it to say, the NYC center totally dropped the ball. After supposedly locking everything in (contracts signed and faxed with their Frisco office), 100 days before show time, my course completely fell through the cracks, never made it into their catalog or onto their web site, and with just *one* enrollment a week before showtime, I dropped back and punted. We're talking multiple screw-ups here. I shake my head at the memory. If you're planning on doing one there, stay on top of them.

Toronto couldn't have been more different or more positive. The center manager, Paul Keetch, worked his tail off promoting me (*and* put my URL in the catalog; the NYC folks said they wouldn't; Canadians really *are* nicer), got me in touch with local media, and we had 60+ butts in seats at the appointed hour. They handled all product sales (close to $1000 worth—*and* in the local wampum), taking just 15 percent for their trouble.

While the media coverage Paul sourced didn't happen before the event—heck, we didn't need it—a reporter did contact me, and a week after the seminar, a story appeared in the weekly city tabloid, nicely extending the buzz, and resulting in a bunch more sales. Way cool. So. I know TLA can be a good experience. Just not always. Sadly, Paul has moved on, but I'm certain the good work continues at the Toronto center.

3) Sell Through Your Site While I'm assuming you'd promote any scheduled seminars on your web site, make sure you provide everything a prospect might need to make an enrollment decision. I include:

a) *Seminar Premise*: a full-page description of the "why" of the seminar along with the goals, actual hours, and scheduled breaks

b) *Testimonials* from past participants

c) *Complete Proposed Course Outline* with section timeslots noted (subject to change)

d) *"Current Dates/To Enroll"* page, with time, date, tuition fee, and what that buys them (i.e., course materials, copy of the book, lunch, etc.). Include location details along with directions (include the actual street address of the meeting location and a link to MapQuest.com), together with any special room rates that you've negotiated with the hotel. There are always a few out-of-town attendees.

e) *Multiple Payment Options.* I discovered that securing a merchant account to take credit cards, while easy for tangible, immediately deliverable products like books or CDs, is much tougher for "future deliverables" like seminars. Given how many shysters are lurking about, collecting hefty fees for seminars in the future, only to vanish under cover of darkness, credit card companies are understandably leery. So you may have to jump through a few hoops; every company has different policies.

My merchant account provider *does* allow seminar charges now, but I only asked them to consider it after logging over a year of unblemished track record—no complaints, virtually no returns, etc. Maybe that helped their decision. Of course, in addition to allowing registrants (and buyers of *any* of my products for that matter) to pay by credit card through my site, I give them the PayPal (**www.paypal.com**) option, as well as snail mailed checks (which, for seminars, must arrive at least a week before the event).

4) Tier Your Pricing Offer graduated pricing tied to time of enrollment. Offer one price as an "Early Bird discount" rate for enrollments up until, say, two or three weeks before the seminar date, a price roughly 20 percent more up until the day before the seminar, and a higher price at the door.

This graduated system allows you to offer enrollment incentives to "fence-sitters"—perhaps someone who's called or emailed you with questions but hasn't committed yet: *If you sign up, I'll give you the Early Bird price, even though we're past the deadline.* Or *Show up tomorrow with the check, and even though it's 'at the door,' I'll extend the regular price.* In many cases, it was the prospect who asked for the discount. And if they're asking, then they're sold. Bird in the hand and all that...

Leave all your prices on the site, even after deadlines have passed, so they can see what they missed, and to give context to a special offer. I say anyone who's *really* interested won't be dissuaded by a higher rate, so you're probably OK leaving it all in *and* giving yourself some possible leverage to prod the indecisive.

I also offer discounts to students (with valid ID) and members of local organizations (especially groups I've partnered with) that are willing to get the word out to their communities. In the latter case, I'll provide ready-to-use blurbs to send out to their members (making it easy), offering, say, 10 percent off tuition, and instructing them to sign up under the "Student" option on the web site, as opposed to the regular price. Organizations love it, of course, since they get to be the hero ("A 10 percent discount off seminar tuition: yet another benefit of membership.").

5) List in Free Directories Go to **www.shawguides.com** (working in conjunction with *Writer's Digest* magazine; **www.writersdigest.com**), and for no charge, you can list your seminar in their database, which covers a wide variety of categories.

Also, *The Writer* magazine (**www.writermag.com**) allows you to submit conference listings to their online calendar (click *Contact Us*, and scroll down). *Craig's List* (**www.craigslist.com**) allows free listings as well, *and* is a pretty juicy site on many levels.

6) Send Pre- & Post-Seminar Notes (e) The morning before the seminar, I send out an email to all registered attendees with final instructions, directions, and what to bring (pens, though I'll have some on hand, a sweater for room temperature changes, extra paper, etc.). I tell them to arrive at least 15 minutes before the scheduled start time, but even then, there are always a few stragglers, so work enough time into your seminar timetable to allow for starting, say, 10 minutes after the published start time.

The notes are a nice professional touch I got into the habit of doing after experiencing construction delays on one of the major highways around Nashville the day before my seminar there. I wanted to get the word out so people could scope out alternate routes. Seemed like a good idea in general, so I stuck with it. After the seminar, send another one, thanking them for their attendance and participation.

7) Make It Interactive No one enjoys listening to someone lecture non-stop for hours on end. Sure, any how-to topic will entail a certain amount of front-of-the-room time, but mix it up. Add exercises, both paired and whole group, and don't miss opportunities to teach through questions. Don't just recite information: ask them to guess the answer. Your attendees will have a much more dynamic and memorable experience.

8) Serve Lunch (All-day Seminars) Busy restaurant lunch hours, 18 separate checks, disappearing waitresses, etc. Who needs it? Often, the hotel can provide a lunch for $10-12 a head. Or, ask them about nice local sandwich shops that deliver. Have them fax you a menu and take orders during your morning break, or even have your attendees provide their order as part of the enrollment process.

Unless you're charging $500—in which case, the sandwich/chips/cookie/drink brown bag probably ain't gonna cut it—I promise you most people aren't going to be too picky about lunch. If you insist on going out, at least try to find a pre-paid scenario like a sandwich shop or buffet. Be careful with the latter though: buffets invite overeating, and that can lead to near siesta-like conditions for the afternoon session. Trust me, you'll feel a kinship with camp counselors trying to keep a bunch of bored 10-year-olds amused.

9) Provide "Note-Taking" Outlines I create a "note-taking" outline—the main section headings and subheads, with large blanks between each one. Check out mine to see the level of detail I provide (**www.wellfedwriter.com**, then *Seminars/Events*). They provide meaningful "content-in-context" for participants to refer back to easily (and share with others).

The outlines I give attendees have times included for each section (e.g., Introduction—7:15-7:30 p.m.). Ask for a volunteer to keep you on track (give them some product gift at the end). Make up two big yellow cards with "5 MIN." and "TIME" written in big letters. Ask your volunteer to keep an eye on both the clock and the outline, and to hold up the cards, five minutes before that section is scheduled to end, and when it's up. You may still be a little behind, but I promise, you'll stay a *lot* closer to the schedule.

10) Discount Your Books This one is strictly optional, but I've made a tradition of selling my books at my seminars for 25 percent off ($15). I used to provide a free book to attendees, since many come to my seminar not having read the book, but once I stopped doing that and sold about $600 worth of stuff at the back of the room, I realized my early strategy might have been shortsighted. Your call. If you're getting a juicy price for your seminar tuition, you might want to include a book. That way, something that only costs you a few bucks can be billed as "a $20 retail value!"

11) Provide "Participant Directory" One of the biggest by-product benefits for seminar participants is the chance to network with kindred spirits.

After spending an evening, whole day, or weekend with a like-minded group, they might just want to stay in touch with each other (especially if the seminar has been some business-building opportunity). At the tail end of the event, (and after getting everyone's OK), I pass around a sheet for them to fill out their name and email address.

As a nifty memory aid, I number the list, then create a mock seating chart that mirrors the one we had in the room, inserting the numbers on the chart to match the person's seat location. Just looking at a list of names, someone might not remember who each person was, but if they know where they were sitting, they're much more likely to remember them. A quick trip to the hotel's front desk for copies and you're in business.

Ezines

I started my ezine, THE WELL-FED E-PUB (named by my readers), in May 2002. It's probably been the single best move I've made since writing my first book. It's raised my profile and built my platform more than anything else I've done except my books.

Why such an impact? Because it's regular and ongoing. Every month, it shows up in the inboxes of roughly 5,000 subscribers (at press time), providing information and inspiration with my name on it. As an added bonus, I regularly hear from my readers about how it's helped create a nice sense of community.

Of course, a crucial benefit of my ezine is that monthly reminder about all my products and services (every first of the month sees a reliable jump in sales). And that's the thing: an ezine allows you to capture an as-yet non-buyer, bring them into the fold, and with their permission, court them into becoming a buyer through your regular contacts.

Of course, it was never quite that premeditated. I focused first and foremost on providing good information through my ezine, but the upshot is that that content and those regular contacts have indeed created new buyers.

Nine Tips for the Care and Feeding of Your Ezine

1) **Focus on Content/Don't Oversell** Understand the *quid pro quo* here: consistently providing good, substantial content—relevant to your audience—earns you the right to softly "pitch" your readers on your wares. For several years before I started my ezine, I was subscribed to a handful of others, and got to see firsthand how *not* to do one. Many of these ezine editors were obviously thinking: "How can I make a bunch of money with this thing?" Big mistake. The reader gets beaten up with a pile of ads on the front and back ends, and much of the content in between is fluff. A few issues and I was gone. Where's the value? Where's that *quid pro quo*?

With those bad examples fresh in mind, I set out with the primary goal of offering up solid, worthwhile information every month. I honestly didn't even think about making money right away. I figured that if the newsletter established its value every month in the minds of my readers, everything else would fall into place, and it has.

I've read in any number of places that you should limit any real promotion (for products and services) to 20-25 percent of your ezine. About what I do. A few offers up front (ones they'll catch if they're skimming quickly), and then a larger chunk at the end. And lots of good promo-free content in between.

2) Don't Oversend Outside of my monthly ezine, I send as few additional emails to my subscriber base as possible—probably one to two per month on average, max. Even that, believe it or not, elicits cries of "Spam!" from a handful of...um... overly sensitive souls (who I generally just quietly unsubscribe, whether or not they've asked to be; life's too short).

The fewer you send, the more seriously the ones you do send will be taken. I save those extra transmissions for reminders of upcoming events or, more commonly, to focus on a particular product promotion I'm running. As I learned a long time ago, not every subscriber reads my newsletter right away or even at all. Shocking! Seriously, that's reality we can all relate to (see the section on ebooks to discover what I do to capitalize on that fact, to my financial advantage).

As a result, if I send out a separate email with a subject line promoting a specific product, I get a far higher sales boost than if that product promo is just buried deep in the newsletter. Logical. A few years back, I extended a holiday promo on my new 6-CD seminar set for two weeks. I mentioned the extension in the ezine and sold one set. I sent out a separate email dedicated to the promo, and sold 17 sets. There you have it. But, you've got to walk that fine line. Too much, and you lose subscribers (translation: lost access). Too little, and you'll lose income.

A sidebar about my philosophy. I know I'm not as aggressive as many in my field when it comes to regularly "hitting up" my database with heavy promo. I'm sure I leave money on the table as a result. As time goes on, I may step things up a bit, perhaps automate the marketing process more, but I'll never turn into a carnival barker. And the countless emails I've gotten from subscribers letting me know how much they appreciate my softer approach (with an emphasis on solid, meaty content) is a nice vote of confidence. Doesn't make me a better person; it's more of a personal preference.

3) Be Creative Have fun with your ezine. I milk the "Well-Fed" theme exhaustively in my ezine, setting up the content like a menu, with the different sections of each issue as individual courses. The *Appetizer* starts things off, and is the only piece I actually write myself. The rest are contributions from subscribers (see "Solicit Content" below). That's followed by *Crisp From the Field Greens, the Main Course, Dessert (Sweet Success Stories and Tips)*, and finally, *Coffee, Mint, and Toothpicks*, where I promote my different products and services, and ask for submissions.

Campy, yes. But it works. Take a look at a few archived issues at the *Free Ezine Signup* link at **www.wellfedwriter.com** (scroll down). If your book is a fun, creative topic, maybe you can do the same. What's clever is memorable.

4) Be Consistent I've talked to a number of industry colleagues over the years who tell me they also put out ezines, but then sheepishly add, "Well, truth be known, I don't always manage to get it out every month." My response? Better not to do it at all than to do it sporadically. In this case, some is *not* better than none.

Look at it this way. Say you've written a book, perhaps added a few other products (but no ezine as yet), and have a good reputation on the street. So far, so good. But add an ezine, and only get it out every two or three months (while claiming it's a monthly), and you risk tainting that reputation and replacing it with one for, well, flakiness. Not good.

Unless you can commit to doing it like clockwork every week, two weeks, month, quarter, whatever, don't bother. But get it to the point where people can set their watch by it, and you'll see your good name take on an even rosier glow. I get regular emails from subscribers along the lines of, "I so look forward to your newsletter, and every first of the month, I know I'll open my email and it'll be there."

HOW FREQUENTLY?

Joan Stewart, editor of the great ezine *The Publicity Hound* (**www.publicityhound.com**) and Marcia Yudkin, editor of the equally fab *Marketing Minute* (**www.yudkin.com**) do theirs weekly. Marcia's is a quick read (hence the name), and while Joan's is a lot longer, it's easily skimmable and always interesting. They claim that monthly, as I do it, is too infrequent. That people will forget you. Well, I'm not convinced, but mainly because I'm not ready to put it out more often! Every two weeks sounds about right, but monthly has worked for me. We'll see where it goes.

5) Less is More Regardless of frequency—but certainly in the case of weekly—shorter and sweeter, as Marcia does, is always better. It's easier to put together, and easier to get through. That spells more actual readers, and that, of course, is the point. As discussed, get creative about format. Marcia's *Marketing Minute* is a fabulous idea. Easily remembered and easily appreciated, precisely because it does, in fact, take about a minute to get through.

6) Solicit Content As mentioned earlier, I only write the first section of my ezine, and tap my subscribers for the rest. Every single issue puts out a call in the final *Coffee, Mints and Toothpicks* section for content, along with a listing of the sections where I need input and the word count ranges for each.

Obviously, given my how-to subject matter geared toward practicing commercial writers, it's easier to attract a steady stream of "from-the-trenches" accounts. Speaking of that, I describe my ezine as a mix of *information and inspiration*. Obviously, readers want good solid how-to info they can quickly put into practice to make more money as commercial writers. But what they *love* are the success stories—someone making it happen, landing the big one, turning a chance encounter into a juicy job, overcoming obstacles and prevailing, etc., and sharing how it all unfolded.

While getting readers to submit their stories obviously makes your writing job far easier, you still have the job of editing content. Though, at this point, I've got this thing down to a science, and assembling a six-page issue takes me about three or four hours, max.

Don't be afraid to tap your readers when you're stuck for creative ideas. As mentioned, I did just that to come up with the name, THE WELL-FED E-PUB, conjuring up the image of an actual pub where people came to "fill their plate" with information. Ditto with title ideas for my second book, as well as cover graphic ideas for this book (putting some money and free books on the table in both cases to sweeten the pot). People *love* these little creative exercises—anything to divert them from what they should be doing. Loyal readers who know you and your books are great resources, and they'll blow you away with the great ideas they come up with.

7) Text is Best I send out my ezine as plain text. Which, by the way, is also what both Joan and Marcia do, and strongly recommend to others. With a veritable minefield of transmission challenges lurking out there just waiting to trip up anyone sending regular emails across a spectrum of platforms and email programs, it just makes sense to keep things as simple as possible.

My ezine is compiled from various contributions, cut 'n pasted from email text windows and Word documents. After it's assembled and edited, the last thing I do before sending it out is to drop it into an MS Notepad screen, to cleanse it of all formatting, then drop it from there into my email text window (as "Unformatted Text"). If I want to emphasize something, I just put it in caps (don't overdo it), not bold or italic. I also remove all ellipses—for some reason, they cause trouble. Knock on wood, I've received few complaints since the rocky early days of experimentation.

8) Make it Easy to Subscribe Something else I learned from Marcia and Joan: Put subscribe boxes on every page of your web site. NOT subscribe *links* that take you to another screen to subscribe; I already had that. We're talking boxes, on every page, where they can enter their email address directly. You *will* boost your subscriber volume.

Ideally, you do a "double opt-in" process, which we're all familiar with: you sign up initially, and then you're sent an email, which you reply to in order to double-confirm your intentions. I actually don't do that, but it's a common feature of the email management programs I discuss below.

9) Use a Third-Party to Send Don't send your ezine out through your regular email account unless you have, like, 14 subscribers or something. Get up into larger numbers and you could easily run afoul of your ISP's anti-spam policies, which, understandably, get more draconian daily. Just not worth it.

My web guy has a homegrown email program, which he lets me use to send out my newsletter for free. People automatically subscribe/unsubscribe through my web site (I can manually add/delete addresses as well).

There are a bunch of fee-based email management programs, like *Constant Contact*, for example (**www.constantcontact.com**), that will also provide this functionality. Plus, they'll allow you to create graphically snappy communication with a variety of cool templates that lock down your content to avoid those same formatting-based transmission issues we discussed earlier. They generally charge by the number of subscribers, starting from around $10 monthly for 250 subscribers and rising from there. If you're bound and determined not to send out safe, text-only missives, this might be a way to go.

Bonus Functionality

Programs like *Constant Contact,* and others that are similar, also typically provide tracking information on your mailings—very important. They can tell you how often different links in the body of the email have been clicked, so you can learn what interests your audience and what causes them to take action. Useful information.

Here are a few of these email marketing programs:

- Constant Contact: **www.constantcontact.com**
- Cooler Email™: **www.cooleremail.com**
- Vertical Response™: **www.verticalresponse.com**
- IMN™ (formerly iMakeNews): **www.imakenews.com**
- Ezine Director(sm): **www.ezinedirector.com**
- Topica: **www.topica.com**

Visit **www.wilsonWeb.com/wct5/listserver_intro.htm** (available at press time) for an article providing brief, independent reviews of a bunch of these programs.

Also, see Appendix A for additional resources for the budding ezine editor.

Should You Charge?

I'm still wrestling with this one. The day you begin charging for your newsletter, you'll lose probably 80+ percent of your subscribers, and with it, that crucial access. For now, I've decided that I'd prefer to keep building the subscriber base and preserve my connection. But I'd be lying if I said I didn't turn the math over in my head a LOT (if just 10 percent stay with me and pay $50 a year, that's $25K annually...hmmmmm).

Fact is, there are plenty of newsletters (especially in the investing arena) out there providing very specialized information for which people are willing to shell out hundreds or thousands of dollars annually. Not likely numbers for our arena, but hone your offering over several years, build the value into something which seriously enhances people's lives in some specific, measurable ways, and who knows?

Ebooks

Ebooks are the closest thing to "found" money out there. No books, no inventory, no shipping costs. Just ephemeral electrons hurtling across cyberspace, but resulting in cold, hard, decidedly un-ephemeral cash. It's a beautiful thing.

Two Categories

There are two types of ebooks you'll likely be creating: 1) ebook versions of your hard-copy books, and, 2) standalone ebooks consisting of related content you've decided isn't worth the expense of printing in hard-copy form. Let's explore the first category...

Offering ebook versions of your hard-copy editions is a no-brainer. The logistics are a snap (and you're talking to a technical moron here). Once your typesetter has laid out your book and you've got your cover artwork done, have them stick your cover artwork at the front of the finished file and convert the whole thing to a PDF, using Adobe Acrobat®. Voila! Instant ebook.

Make sure that, for this purpose, the document is locked down, with your security settings on the PDF document pretty tight, not allowing any copying, content extraction, editing or other tampering with the content. Once it's created, you should sell it a few ways: on your own site and through resellers.

Being an e-commerce novice at the start, I actually didn't sell my first book as an ebook on my own site, but just went through resellers. When my second book came out, I put both books up for sale on my site, while continuing to use the resellers as well.

Resellers Extend Your Reach

Resellers are web-based entities who will promote your ebook on their site in return for a piece of the action—usually 40-50 percent, depending on the company. I just send it to them, they handle the setup and sales, collect the money, and periodically send me a check (or *PayPal* me). Again, found money.

I got the ebook version of my first book on writersweekly.com (part of booklocker.com), and it ended up the #3 best-selling ebook in the fourth quarter of 2000.

There are several key benefits of publishing an ebook in addition to printed books. Ebook sales will naturally drive hard copy sales. If someone likes your book—and especially if it's a how-to or reference that they'll want to keep handy and mark up—chances are excellent they'll want their own "hold-in-their-hand" copy.

Also, if you do a good job of marketing, promoting and publicizing your book, as I feel I have, the word will spread across the globe. For many readers in remote locales around the world—or at least remote from cost-effective delivery from Amazon—an ebook is by far the quickest, easiest, and least expensive way of getting their hands on the book. I have ebook buyers in Singapore, China, India, New Zealand, Romania, Sweden, Hong Kong, Russia, and many other places. In these cases, ebooks remove the barriers to connecting with your readers—and profiting off those connections—wherever they might be.

Create "Reseller Marketing Kits"

Yet again: make it easy for people to do business with you (especially people who can make you a lot of money). With ebooks, that means creating marketing kits to send to your resellers so they can handle the job of getting the product up on their site quickly and easily, and everyone can start making money faster.

Remember where I mentioned about getting multiple versions of your book cover artwork from your graphic designer when he or she creates it? Here's one application. This is what I include in my marketing kit for my ebooks—in separate files:

1) Copy of the ebook in PDF format

2) Three different sizes of the cover artwork (1.75" and 3" high and a 6" x 9" version). They won't need them all, but give them a choice.

3) The Table of Contents in its own file as a teaser

4) Promo copy file

Tailored Promo Copy

For the promo copy (e), I include most of the copy that appears on my web site, but adapted slightly, as if the reseller is talking about the product, not me. On my own site, since they're already there, they know about my first book and I can just talk about the new product. On another site, you'll need to remember that they may not know who you are and what you've done, so a bit more explanation may be necessary. Remember "audience"!

Know who they are, understand what they know, and more importantly, what they *don't* know about you and your offerings, and speak to them in those contexts. The best part? You get to present the product the way YOU want. You highlight the points you feel are important, meaning you're not at the mercy of their efforts and whatever they may come up with, which may not do your masterpiece justice.

Pricing Your Ebook

While ebooks typically sell for 50-75 percent less than the hard-copy version (or what a hard-copy equivalent *would* cost if you don't have one), I was able to get away with pricing the ebook versions of my hard-copy books at $12.95 (vs. $19.95 for the print version). I used the same rationale I applied to successfully pricing a 300-page hard-copy non-fiction title at $19.95 (one that "realistically" should have sold for $14.95 to $16.95): I wasn't just selling a 300-page non-fiction book; I was selling a complete blueprint for a new career. Maybe I'd have sold more if I'd priced them less expensively, and I'll likely experiment as time goes on.

Focus, Focus, Focus

Right after my first book came out, I went with a writing-related ebook marketer (Angela Adair-Hoy of **www.writersweekly.com** and **www.booklocker.com**) to market the ebook version. Angela was very aggressive about promoting it, and it did extremely well on her site, earning each of us (given the 50/50 split) probably $8000+ over a few years. Amazing when your only investment is a computer disk with your book on it.

Based on that very positive experience, I've listed it with a few others, with mixed results. A few other writing-related resellers have delivered to this day with steady—if not massive—checks. Others have done nothing. What I've learned is pretty logical: picking an ebook marketer who specializes in your niche as opposed to being a general ebook store will yield better results. Duh.

The other benefit of going with a niche reseller? They'll be more likely to charge you little or nothing to load your book onto their system. If they consider your book good and salable, they'll see the financial potential. By contrast, a general ebook publisher/reseller is far closer to a POD publisher in profile. Their strategy is clear: *the overwhelming bulk of ebooks won't make any money* (for reasons we'll discuss soon), *so we'll get our money up front. If it does do well, then we'll both profit.* Win/Win for them. Lose/Maybe-Win-a-Little for you. Hence, a somewhat ironic conclusion about both POD and ebook publishing: the greater the upfront investment, the less the likely return on the back end.

Like POD publishers, ebook publishers will also try to "upsell" you on their marketing packages, but again, be very careful. Unless it's a white-hot topic, the key media influencers (to whom they'll be sending releases as part of their packages) just don't take ebooks seriously.

Only Ebooks?

Given the simplicity and truly negligible expense of creating an ebook, there's an understandable temptation to say, heck, I'll just bag the whole hard-book route and just sell ebooks. Nice thought. Bad idea. Unless you do a totally mind-blowing amount of marketing, I don't give *standalone* ebooks (with no hard-copy "anchor" book) much of a chance of financial success. Here's why.

For starters, an ebook isn't nearly as visible as a physical book, and certainly not in the main traditional outlets: bookstores and libraries. Without those two, say goodbye to any real buzz. And all that wonderful, targeted, Internet-based promotion I talked about way back when? Well, all that is predicated on getting large numbers of *real* review copies into many sets of hands. Try contacting all these folks, on whom you're counting to spread the word to their communities, and tell them you just have ebook review copies, and *can I email it to you?* You'll hear them laugh from the other side of the world. It ain't gonna happen.

AN UPHILL BATTLE

Finally, most ebooks aren't successful because the lion's share of readers aren't really sold on the technology. Who likes to read books on their computer? While "reader" technology (paperback book-sized electronic gizmos onto which you can download multiple books) is improving, it still hasn't caught on in a big way (though downloading books onto Palm Pilots is heating up). Despite the grand early proclamations of the ebook mavens, the imminent demise of the hard copy book has been greatly exaggerated. People still like to curl up with a book, and that's not likely to change any time soon.

The One Caveat

Arguably, the only way a standalone ebook strategy will work is if you're a writer in a very specific niche—perhaps an esoteric business arena or highly specific technical subject—that attracts a targeted audience with a constant hunger for new information.

Given that many ebooks are considerably shorter than print versions (40-50 pages is common), if you want to focus on writing, and can crank out multiple short books on various aspects of a subject of real interest to an existing audience willing to pay for that information (or that *needs* it to do their job), theoretically, you could make a tidy sum. If that *is* your scenario, or if you're simply bound and determined not to have a hard copy book, at the very least, digitally print some galleys for review copy purposes.

Related "Standalones"

As mentioned, the second category of ebooks you'll likely be putting together are stand-alone ebooks related to your main hard copy books, but which make more financial sense as an ebook.

First, the most obvious example. In Appendix B of this book, I've included several key examples of marketing materials I created in the course of putting this book together. I've also put together an ebook, with dozens more of those written marketing tools—in fact, virtually every piece of marketing copy I crafted throughout this whole adventure. In my humble opinion, for the newbie self-publisher, that's a pretty happenin' resource, and as such, it's worth something. So, I'm selling it separately as a related standalone. One example.

Earlier, I alluded to my reluctant acceptance of the fact that my ezine subscribers, despite their best intentions, might not always get around to reading my monthly ezine right away—or even at all. But I can turn that negative into a positive by making it easy for them to catch up on past issues, while making a few bucks in the process. Not a completely original idea, but still a good one.

REPACKAGING THE PAST

About four months after putting out the 13th issue of my ezine in 2003, I decided to repackage that first baker's dozen into, as the promo copy read, a *Compiled-Categorized-Easy-To-Use-Amazingly-Handy-All-In-One-Place Reference Tool*, and called it *The Banquet*. After originally pricing it at $9.95, I reduced it to $6.95 to boost sales. Try different prices until you get the right one. Because it was now a "book," as opposed to just a bunch of back issues of the newsletter, it was easier for people to focus on and digest, making it an attractive product (view the format at **www.wellfedwriter.com**, then *Ebooks*, then *The Banquet*, then *The Banquet Menu*).

Four months after the 26th issue, I created *The Banquet II* (issues 14-26, also $6.95), and *The BIG Banquet* (Issues 1-26; $12.95). Ditto after issue 39.

MAKE 'EM PAY

It's absolutely standard procedure for most of the higher profile ezines—and most major online daily newspapers—to provide content (articles, reports, case studies, etc.) on a "free access" basis for a short window, and then begin charging for it. Newspapers typically give you a week of access (before hitting you up for $2-5 per article), while ezines might offer two or three weeks. Compared to them, I'm Mr. Generous, offering free access for at least 13 months. Then the content is packaged and available to view only if they pay the toll, which at seven bucks, is a freakin' bargain. I'm so easy. But, if I priced it much higher, it likely wouldn't sell as well.

BETTER AS BONUSES

An even stronger application for these standalone, related-content ebooks— at least in my case—is as a purchase bonus. Sure, I've made some nice bucks from selling my *Banquet* series as standalones. But, when I released my second book, I decided to make purchasing the book off my site a sweeter proposition, offering them free shipping and their choice of one of two free ebook bonuses (*The Banquet* and another I'll discuss shortly) for buying it there, as opposed to Amazon or the bookstores.

One reason for this was to beat Amazon at its own game. Now don't get me wrong. I love Amazon dearly; they've sold lots of books for me. But, I gross about $9 a book on Amazon (and bookstore) sales vs. roughly $15 for a book sold off my site. Given that you're the "manufacturer," you'll always make more money by selling to your customers directly than you will going through the wholesale/retail chain and giving up a chunk to them, so try to maximize those juicy "direct" sales. But, back to the Amazon thing…

Undercut By Amazon

As discussed in the introduction, I released my second book in September 2004 for sale solely on my own site. While Amazon didn't have books to sell yet, after posting my listing for the new book on their site, I soon noticed that they were taking pre-orders for the book at 30 percent off retail—$13.97 vs. my retail price of $19.95! And at press time, it's still at that low price.

If I wanted to compete with that, I had to make it worthwhile for a buyer to order through my site. Hence, the free shipping and free ebook bonus strategy. On orders of $25 and over, Amazon offers free shipping as well, but below that, it's $3.95, which made my offer even better.

While I processed my online orders through my merchant account, I had BookMasters handle the physical fulfillment of books (for online orders, as well as those direct purchases through PayPal and checks), for which they charge me roughly $1.40 plus "Media Mail" postage (about $3.25 total).

Have Books Wherever People Shop

Regardless of how good a deal I offered, X number of people would still end up buying my book through Amazon, which was fine. I had publicity running on a bunch of writing-related web sites with "Buy" buttons linking directly to Amazon (where they'd make a bit of "affiliate" income). And some people want to buy in bookstores as well, making it important that you have your book in all the above places (remember, we don't approach bookstores until we know we've built the demand and can make that case in a proposal).

But, I wanted to grab as many high-profit online sales as possible, so I used my ezine, where I could pitch a huge chunk of my most loyal readers/buyers directly. And, as discussed at the beginning of the book, I logged $11K in sales in the first two months—just in online sales—about 80+ percent of which was pure profit.

The OTHER Ebook

Once I'd decided on the free ebook bonus route, I came up with another idea for an ebook which, if your genre is also non-fiction how-to, might just resonate with you. My books, if I do say so myself, are full of a lot of pretty useful info, a healthy chunk of which I could envision readers wishing they had in electronic form. Things like sales letters, contracts, cold-calling scripts, lists of web resources that in digital format would quickly become a list of click-thru links, etc.

I compiled 45 pages of resources from both books, turned it into an ebook, and called it *The Well-Fed Tool Box* (check it out at **www.wellfedwriter.com/ toolbox.shtml**; link at end of second paragraph). I created two versions: the "read-only", with locked-down content for viewing purposes only, and the actual downloadable version, that had the "content extraction" feature enabled, so it was all easily cut 'n pasteable.

Well, apparently, it was a pretty good idea. Given the choice of *The Banquet* and *The Well-Fed Tool Box*, my buyers have chosen the latter by a margin of roughly 10 to 1. And, of course, I've done the same thing with this book, packaging my promo kit separately.

Other Applications

I didn't stop at offering these ebooks just for book purchases. I've tacked one or more onto my 6-CD set, my single teleseminar CDs, and even my mentoring services. Once created, they're just electrons. They cost nothing to store, nothing to send. When purchased as standalones, they yield pure profit. When tacked on to a tangible product, they absolutely will bring in sales you wouldn't have otherwise landed, and at zero incremental cost to you.

Just as importantly, ebooks can make a nice "thank-you" or "sorry-we-screwed-up-let-us-make-it-up-to-you" gift. They can have any number of uses, and so will always represent infinitely more value than the money you make from straight sales.

Think about how you can package any related—and potentially valuable and salable—content for additional profits. I've only just begun to tap the potential here. Dan Poynter, the SP guru, does a bang-up job of packaging and reselling tons of reports on his site (**www.parapub.com**), undoubtedly ensuring a pretty steady income stream. He da man.

Adobe or Not to Be?

A few years back, I bit the bullet and anted up the $300 to buy Adobe Acrobat (Standard Edition; no need to go to the $450 upper-end Acrobat reaches). It's a good investment if you think you're going to be getting into creating ebooks to any appreciable extent. Even if you don't have a spate of ebooks planned, I promise you'll find all sorts of applications for this nifty program. Any time you need to create any document you want to appear the same to everyone, regardless of what email program it's received in or what browser it's viewed in, Acrobat gets it done. I've started emailing invoices to clients, which cuts down my payment period by a few days.

Only have a few documents you want to PDF-ize? In the short term, check out **www.PrimoPDF.com** for a free, shareware type program that gives you all the important features of Acrobat. Can't beat the price.

Ebook ISBNs

If you have a set of 10 ISBNs, and you've only used one or two, it's not a bad idea to assign ISBNs to your ebooks. Though if you're only going to have limited distribution (i.e., only through your own site and/or a small group of resellers), it's not essential, and you can always do it later if need be.

Teleseminars

While, at press time, I've only done three teleseminars, I get more excited every day about the potential of this medium. Yes, I spent several pages talking about in-person seminars, and if you have a how-to topic, chances are good you'll end up doing some of those, especially on a local level, where overhead is far less.

Some months back, I listened in on a teleseminar about teleseminars (is that like two mirrors facing each other?). Steve Harrison of *Radio-TV Interview Report* (**www.rtir.com**) was interviewing info marketing king Alex Mandossian (**www.alexmandossian.com**). It was a free program, meaning, of course, that they were building up to a bigger sale—in this case, Alex's $1800 course on teleseminars (**www.makemoneywithteleseminars.com**). Listen in on one of these intro programs sometime, and see if it isn't oh-so-tantalizing. And he's talking to the general public in his intros, which means mostly folks *without* books. If you've got one or more, and they're how-to titles to boot, it's going to sound even juicier.

For starters, they drive home the point that it's far easier for your market to participate in teleseminars. And for you, they're far less hassle and far less expensive than doing in-person seminars, bookstore signings, etc. No travel, hotel, meeting room, or materials expenses. Yes, you'll charge less (which makes it a more attractive proposition to your market, and there's no limit on seating), but given the negligible set-up costs, they're potentially far more profitable. And we're talking phones here—no strange new technology to learn. Just a short learning curve for the teleconference system, but nothing beyond anyone with an IQ above plant life.

Bottom line, you can do this from your home, or *anywhere* in the world for that matter. Alex talked about being at the hospital when his kid was being born, and doing a teleseminar from his cell phone in a broom closet…and making over $12K on one call. Okay, come down from the ceiling for a moment, and realize that nothing's that easy out of the gate. The guy's been at it awhile. But, I'm guessing you'd be happy with 10 percent of that in the early days.

The Teleseminar "How-To"

It's an easy drill. You pick from one of the many teleconference services out there, which even include FREE ones such as **www.freeconference.com**. This one actually has a pretty darn good reputation; one regular teleseminar leader told me she had fewer problems with it than with a fee-based service she was using! It's free because they have other more fancy services they do charge for, but their complimentary one is plenty good enough for our needs.

Yes, that's anecdotal, and fee-based services (still reasonable) are recommended by the pros (i.e., **www.eagleconf.com**; **www.conferencecall.com**; or **www.buyerzone.com** to review several different services; scroll down to Telecom Services). Also, while you're at it, check out **www.netmeeting.com**, **www.webex.com**, or **www.livemeeting.com** (from Microsoft), which all get into the arena of "webinars": using online course materials viewable by all participants to enhance the teleseminar experience.

Okay, you and your participants call in to a particular number (typically a toll call) at the designated time, with the leader and guests (if any) punching in slightly different codes than attendees, so they'll be heard. Participants are muted so that background noise doesn't swamp the proceedings. In your Q&A session at the end (highly recommended), questioners can "un-mute" themselves by punching a few keys on their phones.

One of the most important things they stressed is something I've alluded to several times: look at your book as the base—as simply the starting point. It's the thing that builds your initial credibility, but then it's the springboard to far more lucrative ventures. By pursuing the teleseminar route, you can make far more money than you'd make just selling books.

I haven't even begun to really tap this avenue, but with two books on commercial writing and this one on self-publishing, I'd like to think that the possibilities are endless. They draw the even more stark contrast between an author who has his $20 retail book conventionally published, for which he may be making $1 per copy, and that same author packaging some of his content into teleseminars and making many times that amount per listener, creating an ongoing income stream in the process. Obviously, we self-publishers will be making a lot more than $1 a book, but the point is still well taken.

Teleseminar CDs

Audio tape your teleseminar (one of the services offered by teleconference providers), something you'll find is surprisingly inexpensive (usually $50-100). With CD in hand, find a good professional transcriber and have it transcribed (for a good transcriber, roughly $75-125 for each hour of recorded program), which gives you something to sweeten your offer with: *you'll not only get a CD jam-packed with information, but an accompanying 35-page word-for-word downloadable e-transcript of the program!* Of course, you could also charge one price for the CD alone, and a bit more for the e-transcript as an add-on. See the next section (CD Sets) for a bit more detail on the CD direction.

Pricing Your Teleseminar/CDs

Price your teleseminar so that it's essentially an impulse buy. In the program I listened to, they talked about keeping it in the roughly $20-35 range. If you're at the upper end of that range, you might consider including a CD and e-transcript with it, perhaps one or the other at a lower price. Given that your fixed expenses for putting one of these things together (bridge line, recording, transcription, duplication, etc.) are fairly low, you shouldn't get out of hand on your pricing. Remember: *think long term.*

Over time, assuming you're actively promoting your teleseminar CDs, you'll make good money. As such, don't freak out if your attendance on the actual call ends up being low. Sure, you'd rather have 50 folks paying $30 to participate than 10, but regardless of how many people are on the call, you'll still end up with a product to sell when you're done.

Instant Testimonials

Ask for testimonials right away—good advice for *any* event. You have an email list of attendees, so email them with something like: *If you enjoyed the call and got a lot out of it, could you do me a favor and reply back to this email with comments to that effect?* Ensure those comments are more compelling by requesting that they include their city and state, what they got out of the call, something they liked about you as the speaker, and a bit about themselves to give some context to their comments. Anything to avoid the unfortunately all-too-commonplace testimonial that reads: *I really enjoyed the teleseminar. Thanks a lot!* Why not include a sample of what you're looking for:

As a budding widget-maker, I'm always looking for good information on how to proceed. I found this call with Joe Blow (who's been there!) to be just what I was looking for. He generously shared so much good information; I'm itching to get going. I especially liked his insights on the widget marketing process.

Sure, you can't always determine what people will say, but why not try to steer them in the direction in which you want them to go? People are typically good about giving you what you ask for, especially when you ask nicely.

CD Sets

This is a bit more labor-intensive than producing teleseminar CDs, but could make sense if you feel there'll be an ongoing demand for such a program. A few years back, as mentioned in Chapter Five, I audiotaped one of my all-day *Well-Fed Writer* seminars and turned it into a 6-CD set, complete with professional artwork. Make sure that what you create is consistent with the high quality of the other products you sell.

I created a 40-page "Course Materials" guide, which included a note-taking outline (all the key points discussed, in order, and with space between them for note-taking), along with certain additional pages I'd used as teaching aids in the live seminar. The basic building blocks were:

1) ½" wide white three-ring binders with clear plastic sleeves on front and back, and flaps on inside back and front covers (from my local office superstore)

2) Three-hole punched plastic CD sleeves that held two CDs each, i.e. three of them for my 6-CD set (**www.polylinecorp.com**; 800-701-7689)

3) Four-color professionally designed course materials cover and 9" x 12" sheets inserted in front and back cover sleeves of binder

4) Thank you letter (ⓔ), personalized to buyer on store brand parchment

SELLING IT

It was an OK seller ($89-119, depending on promotions), but it was pretty capital-intensive on the front end, labor-intensive on the back end, and sales slowed to a trickle over time, so I just can't justify making it a long-term product. Plus, the information—close to five years old at press time—would likely be considered dated.

If you have a how-to topic with subject matter that's more "evergreen"—just as valid in, say, 10-15 years as it is now—multi-CD sets could be one avenue. What I *will* probably create soon is a multi-part teleseminar program on the craft of commercial writing, and sell the program in a similar CDs/course materials format.

One-on-One Mentoring/Coaching

If you have a how-to book, and you've developed a healthy knowledge base about your subject material—knowledge that people would be willing to pay for—mentoring can be another potentially juicy income stream. I charge (at press time) $125 an hour ($225 for two and $300 for three, all prepaid) for my services. In the professional coaching realm, that's actually quite reasonable, if not low, for what I deliver. To get a few ideas on setting up your own program, check out my *Mentoring* link to see how I structure mine.

Five Steps to More Successful One-on-One Coaching Programs

1) **Be Generous.** I offer people a free 15-minute "set-up" call on the front end to determine what they want to accomplish and how they think I can best be of service, given my expertise. So, an hour actually ends up being 75 minutes. Most folks just tack the setup call onto the front end of their first session. I have people suggest several date/time slots, and once we've agreed on one, they call me at the appointed hour.

Within reason, don't be a strict clock-watcher. If a session goes over a few minutes, I'll let it slide. If it hits five minutes over, then I'll start keeping track. People notice and appreciate that. It shows you're interested in their success, not just your billing. That said...

2) **Track Non-Phone Time.** Given the nature of my areas of expertise, clients often request a review of their marketing materials and/or web site links prior to our phone conversation—all of which counts against their total time. All we have is our time, so make sure you're getting paid for yours.

3) **Set Parameters.** I let my clients take all their time in one session, or break it up into 30-minute blocks. You don't want to get in the habit of letting people call you for five minutes here and there. For the most part, people stick to it. But I've also gotten lazy about putting my foot down, and often let people email me with a quick question, after which I'll subtract my time spent. But that can chip away at your day if you let it. I've even considered going to a more expensive option that allows people to use their time in small dribs and drabs whenever they need to.

4) Deliver Superior Value. I take coaching very seriously. I try to surpass my clients' expectations by being completely prepared for the call, offering suggestions that would never have occurred to them, providing helpful, relevant web links, a connection to a person with a similar situation who's further along the path, or anything else that can leave them feeling that the fee paid was, at the very least, money well spent, and ideally, a bargain. Given the feedback I've received in the *Testimonials* section of the link, I think I've succeeded. Speaking of testimonials...

5) Ask for (and Post) Testimonials. If I've just done a full hour with someone, and I know they truly felt they got a lot of value from it, I'll strike while the iron is hot and send them an email right after the call. Something along the lines of:

Have a little favor to ask. If you feel our time together was valuable to you, and I'm guessing you do, could I ask you to perhaps offer up a short paragraph as a testimonial that I could use on my web site? If you'd prefer to wait till you have a chance to implement some of the things we discussed, that's fine. And if so, may I remind you later? Thanks much and I enjoyed working with you.

Note the request for permission to follow up on your request down the line if they're not ready to offer it up right then. And then do just that. People are almost always willing and eager to offer up a gushing report, but it's just not the first thing on their mind. So, it falls to you to make it happen. Don't do it after the first session of a larger time commitment. But it's definitely fair to ask once you've finished whatever block of time they've paid for. And keep adding the new ones to the growing list on your web site.

Conferences

Every year, the April issue of *The Writer* magazine (**www.writermag.com**) provides a comprehensive listing of writers conferences (about 250 in any given year) across the country (by state), in Canada, and beyond. Listings include a brief description, contact email, web address, and more. Additional conference listings are posted on their site.

Also, as discussed, check out **www.allconferences.com** for a comprehensive list spanning countless industries. Plus, *Shaw Guides* (**www.shawguides.com**) and *Craig's List* (**www.craigslist**), the venues we mentioned earlier as places to list your seminars.

Any published author is a good bet to speak at a writers conference, if you can make your case. Given that most conference programs are geared toward fiction writers, here's where the novelists might have a leg up. That said, many conferences will include sessions on creative non-fiction, poetry, children's books, and others.

I've spoken at a handful over the years, sending a "pitch letter" ([**e**]) to the organizer in advance, and following up. My topic (commercial writing) is an odd one for these conference folks. They're not sure what to do with me as it's certainly not a true "literary" topic, but they're often intrigued. Many others I never hear back from at all; it's just not a fit. No problem. I'm guessing self-publishing might strike a better chord.

What's the Pay?

Unless it's local, entailing no travel/hotel/food expenses, I don't do a conference unless they're willing to a) cover all expenses, b) pay me some kind of honorarium (minimum $400-500), c) allow me to sell books. And it has to be a reasonably cool location. If I was planning on visiting someplace anyway, I might be more flexible on those terms.

Generally speaking, don't look at conferences as places to get rich (though Katherine Gibson's story in Chapter Eleven shows the potential). Sure, you could come home $1000-1500+ richer (from fees and product sales), but look at them as fun outings, chances to boost your profile, add another brick to your "platform," and perhaps see another part of the country on someone else's nickel. Win-wins all around.

Affiliate Programs

As discussed earlier, affiliate programs can be great for making money, in two ways. In Chapter Five, we discussed implementing them to recruit others (who run related sites to yours) to sell your products on their sites, in return for a piece of the action.

Well, the reverse also applies. You could just as easily sell others' products on *your* site in return for a cut, something I've done a bit of over the years. When I decide to represent a product, I make sure it's reputable (get input from buyers), and a good complement to my offering. Start selling everything under the sun, and you end up like the guy with the trenchcoat full of watches (psssst!...Hey, buddy!).

Chances are, you start building a name for yourself, and those folks with similar offerings will find you, just like you should be doing with your products.

Just a few ideas for ways to fatten up your reputation *and* your bottom line. We're in the home stretch here! Let's turn to a few nifty tips and suggestions which didn't logically fit anywhere else, along with a nice indexed collection of those we *did* talk about so you can find them again fast...

Chapter 14

I've picked up a lot of great ideas over the years that have contributed nicely to my success as a self-publisher. What you'll find in this chapter are a few tips you haven't seen elsewhere in the book (seemed like a logical place to put them), along with shortened versions of a bunch more you have. They're listed here as a quick reference by broad category, along with page numbers in the book, in case you forgot where you saw them. You're welcome.

Marketing Tips

FOCUS ON MARKETING—HIRE OUT THE REST

Worth repeating: As a self-publisher, your #1 job is *Building the Demand for Your Book*. As such, I knew that any time I spent tied up with issues related to administration, web site, shipping, collections, etc. was time I wasn't devoting to doing that #1 job. Hire it out and stay focused. Remember: you might save a few bucks doing these things yourself, but it's the time you spend on them (and *not* on marketing) that truly costs in the long run.

GET "BOOK BUSINESS CARDS"

Wherever authors gather—book shows, conferences, writers groups, etc.—they'll be handing out glossy bookmarks and postcards about their book, featuring the book cover, "sell copy," testimonials, etc. Nothing at all wrong with bookmarks and postcards, especially the latter if you're planning on doing mailings (though I wonder how often they're actually mailed; I just see them handed out a lot). I say it's one of those things that authors just do without thinking: order their bookmarks and postcards.

Personally, I prefer "book business cards." ([e]) I put the book cover art in four-color on one side (URL at the bottom), and a bunch of info on the back (awards, book clubs, contact info, book vital stats, etc.), broken up nicely in blocked-off areas.

Given the bright, glossy, full-color look, they're always attention-getters. And I say they just make sense in this "business card world" in which we live and operate (oh, and it happens to make a fine bookmark, thank you very much...). As a rule, I give out two cards so that person can share one. Will people share bookmarks or postcards? Not likely. But business cards? Call them the "prevailing standard currency of networking." It's what everyone's used to. As such, why not work within that framework?

Every time I send a book out to someone, whether reviewer or purchaser, I always include three or four cards, and imagine them being shared with friends. Self-delusion perhaps (sometimes a self-publisher's best friend), but I also know that my books have been big word-of-mouth titles, and given how very cool these cards are, if someone really likes my books, it's an easy way to share it. I say that simply providing them will have people think about whom to share them with.

Two-sided cards with four-color process on one or both sides actually aren't very expensive these days—typically under $100 for 1000. Spend $20-30 more and you can probably get 2500, making it much easier to generously spread them far and wide.

The *Publisher Resource Recommendations* in Appendix A have some leads on the hefty, glossy varieties. Also, the PMA and SPAN newsletters feature ads from companies that do cards (and bookmarks, postcards, flyers, etc.). Ask for samples.

SEND THANK-YOU CARDS

Whenever a journalist does a story or mentions your book, a radio/TV host has you on their show, a conference organizer has had you present at their gathering, or anyone else has done something nice to promote you, send them a personal *snail-mailed* thank-you card. Thank-you notes just aren't all that common anymore. Do it and stand out.

I buy these striking handmade cards (colorful block printing) from an artist in Poulsbo, Washington. I met John Sollid at the Pike Market in Seattle a few years back, bought a few sets of cards, loved them, and have reordered many times since, for myself, and for gifts. He's got some beautiful floral designs (especially the tulips and irises), and a few less girly ones (sailboat/sun, totem pole, geese in flight). They run $7 for a pack of five (two-pack minimum). Not dirt cheap, but they stand out, and will be remembered. No web site, but contact him at j.sollid@att.net, 360/598-5886, or snail mail at P.O. Box 193, Poulsbo, WA 98370. Mention my name, and he'll ship 'em free.

TAKE ADVANTAGE OF FREE LISTINGS
Don't miss out on "freebie" book listing venues. (48)

AFTER JULY, NEXT YEAR'S DATE IS OK
Publishing after July? Use next year as a copyright date. (51)

VISIT A BOOKSTORE WITH YOUR COVER DESIGNER
Brainstorm covers with your designer by exploring your genre in the bookstore. While there, study good typesetting and see what you like. (38)

DELIVER A "PROMISE" WITH YOUR TITLE
Your title should tell readers exactly what's in it for them. (40)

DO AN EXPANDED TABLE OF CONTENTS
Make your table of contents into a selling tool that works hard for you. (52)

LOOK AT BOOKS AS "SEEDS"
Spread review copies far and wide and spread the word. (76)

THE "ONE-A-DAY" REVIEW COPY PLAN
A Good Plan: one review copy or five promos a day. (80)

NO CONTACT, NO REVIEW COPY
No review copy to anyone with whom you haven't communicated first. (81)

EMAIL "SIGNATURES" THAT EARN THEIR KEEP
Make email "signature" a dynamic "call-to-action," not a resumé. (93)

Ditto for your final "attribution" paragraph at the end of articles. (160)

PMA'S TRADE DISTRIBUTION PROGRAM
One-book publisher, but want a distributor? This could be the ticket. (109)

USE AMAZON MARKETPLACE TO SELL DINGED COPIES
And sign books for unfair advantage. (127-8)

USE DISCOUNT CERTIFICATES
Include coupons on other products with any customer book packages you send out, accessible through "side-door" links on your site. (128-9)

ASK FOR AMAZON REVIEWS
Ask happy readers who've emailed you to write a review (and send link). (131)

CREATE A "MEDIA RESOURCES" SECTION
Put together an "all-in-one-place" media link on your site. (147-8)

SCHEDULE BOOK SIGNINGS LATER IN MONTH
And get more promo time in store newsletters (and monthly pubs). (174)

SCHOOL BOOKINGS/AUTHORS & EXPERTS
www.schoolbookings.com (180) connects authors with schools for paying talks. It's a subsidiary of **www.authorsandexperts.com**, linking media folks with authors.

A BOOK AS A "BASE"
A book can lead to more lucrative income streams (even with low sales). (196)

DO "RELATED STANDALONE" EBOOKS
Package book-related content for free bonuses and extra income. (213)

Operational Efficiency Tips

TURN OFF YOUR EMAIL
Email is like "Death by 1,000 Cuts" on your time. Ever get to the end of your day and wonder where in the world the time went? Might just be the *Email Time Gobbler* at work. I got serious and went on an email crash diet. I check it once when I get up, again about noon, then around 4:00 p.m., and once more before I go to bed. And *shut it off between times*. Sure, not always possible, but you'll get much more done if you can. You'll quickly discover that few things are so pressing that they can't be dealt with a few hours later.

BUY A MICRO-CASSETTE RECORDER
Get one of these tiny recorders, and carry it with you whenever you leave the house. As self-publishers, the volume of detail we have to remember and act on is truly mind-boggling. Our job is never done. Not only will it ensure that nothing on your to-do list falls through the cracks, but it can help capture all the brilliant ideas that constantly occur to us for marketing, publicizing, and promoting our books. Plus, it could keep you alive (no more scrounging for a scrap of paper and a pen in a cluttered car at 75 mph). Oh, and if you forget to bring it one day and an incandescent thought hits you while you're on the road, call your home/office from your cell, and leave yourself a message.

ADDRESS FAQs & COMMON SITUATIONS WITH EMAIL "STATIONERY"
In the normal day-to-day email dealings with readers, you'll end up encountering both the same FAQs and common scenarios requiring the same answer.

I started saving these recurring replies in a file of their own, or if short enough, as an entry in my email "stationery." This feature allows you to create standard replies to common situations. When you get one, you simply do a *Reply With,* choose that answer, click, the message populates the email screen, add a name, and boom, you're done.

I shared this one earlier: someone emails me telling me how much he liked my book. I choose the "AmazomReviewRequest" stationery, and the screen is immediately populated with a quick note asking them if they'd go on over to Amazon to write a review, *and* I supply the link. Others? Product-specific purchase thanks, city-specific seminar enrollment thanks, link requests, ezine subscribe errors, and tons more.

ORGANIZE YOUR COMPUTER DIRECTORIES

Probably a no-brainer, but to keep order in your growing empire, organize your computer so you know where everything is. There's no right way to do this, just whatever makes sense for your operation. I have a main directory called TWFW (The Well-Fed Writer) and under that are sub-directories for:

1) Artwork—All the different graphic files and photos related to the book.

2) Articles—Every time I write an article for any purpose, I store it here and name it by the rough subject *and* word count. When I need an article of a certain length, I will often recycle the same one with minor alterations for web-based pubs, which just aren't as strict about printing previously published content as print pubs might be.

3) Promo Opps—All potential avenues for promotion, with sub-directories for contests, conferences, reviews, interviews, teleseminars, and more.

4) Seminars—All info related to my seminars: actual file clusters for each city, seminar outlines, testimonials, web content for my seminar link, press releases, etc.

5) Marketing Campaigns—Any concerted campaign I undertook to a particular niche market is here. Each file contains the email pitch I sent out to members of that group, plus a list of the entities and people contacted, along with follow-up results.

6) E-newsletter—All finalized issues of my monthly newsletter, plus lists of subscribers, and files full of possible content.

7) Ebooks—PDF ebooks, ebook reseller contacts, contracts, resellers marketing kits, etc.

You could have sub-directories for reader letters, distribution-related stuff, radio/TV interviews (information and databases) and anything else that warrants its own category.

NIFTY FORMATTING TIPS
Big time savers as you're assembling your manuscript:

Quote/Apostrophe Marks: From Straight to Curly
Whenever you cut and paste from emails, web pages, or other documents, quote and apostrophe marks can show up as straight, but ultimately, they should be curly. To change all of them at once, from your top task bar, click *Edit*, then *Replace*, then in *both* boxes, put the *same* quote or apostrophe mark. Because of the defaults set up in *Word*, you're actually telling it to change all the straight marks to curly. Click *Replace All*, and voila! You're all curly. Nyuk, nyuk, nyuk.

Sentence Spacing: From Two to One
A lot of writers still hit their space bar twice between sentences, even though one space is pretty standard these days. If you've got a long document of two-spacers, it's a snap to change all to ones at once. Again, from your top task bar, click *Edit*, then *Replace*, then in the first box, hit your space bar twice, tab to the second box, hit the space bar once, click *Replace All,* and, poof, you're suddenly running a much tighter ship.

FOR HASSLE-FREE SCHLEPPING
As an SP'er venturing out locally and beyond to do talks, seminars, conferences, etc., there are several convenient ways to haul around books, signage, credit card machine, business cards, tent cards, flyers, etc. For local jaunts, I picked up (from an office supply superstore) a most clever little contraption called a "Pack-N-Roll." Picture one of those hard plastic milk crates, but with wheels and telescoping handle, that neatly collapses down to attaché size; google the name, you'll see. Just as easy, and obviously preferable for out of town trips, is a small (22–26") wheeled Pullman.

YOU NEED GOOGLE™ DESKTOP
This is a way cool resource. When writing a book, you often find yourself trying to locate a particular passage. *Didn't I say this somewhere else?* Or, *I know I wrote this somewhere, but where?* And as we all know, the search function in Microsoft *Word*® is pretty useless. We've all looked for some snippet we absolutely *knew* was in there somewhere, put in a key word or phrase, and this idiot sniffing, tail-wagging dog function comes back saying, *Sorry, nothing there!*

Say goodbye to those days. Load up Google™ *Desktop* and it goes through your whole hard drive and tags everything (and keeps tagging new things as they're added). Yes, it can take a while to do (they say four hours, but it was more like 12 on my system), during which time your system is slower. Just start it some day after you finish working, and by morning, it'll be done.

Now, when you want to find something, just pull up a regular Google search box, type in what you're looking for, click Google Search, and the first things that come up (next to the Google Desktop icon) are the first few references on your own computer. Or click the actual *Desktop* link, and voila! In the time it takes you to say "Uh"(mazing), up pops every reference on your computer. It's fairly miraculous.

THE "DO-IT-YOURSELF" PCIP OPTION
See if a librarian can help you craft your PCIP info and save $150. (50)

CREATE AN ARTWORK "TOOLKIT"
Have your graphic designer create several sizes/resolutions of your cover artwork to handle any graphics requirement for print or online publicity. (39)

LESS COSTLY "CREATIVE" IS AVAILABLE
Get resourceful about finding less expensive creative resources. (39, 62)

HUNGRY INTERNS AWAIT
Use interns for the grunt work of identifying review copy prospects (and more). (87)

FREE PRESS RELEASE DISTRIBUTION
Check out **www.prweb.com** for an excellent free (or almost free) service. (137)

CREATIVE PRESS KITS
Print up extra book covers and use as press kit folders. (149)

CREATE "ARTICLE TOOLKITS"
Simplify article placement by using this formula to make up a bunch in advance. (157)

WRITE AN "ARTICLE-RICH" BOOK
Fill your book with bunches of Top 10 (or 7 or 12) lists that lend themselves to easy excerpting for articles. (158)

A FREE PDF-MAKING RESOURCE
(**www.PrimoPDF.com**) (216)

NEVER PAY FOR A REVIEW
(self-explanatory) (85)

CYA (Being Prudent) Tips

HIRE A CONSULTANT

As a naïve first-time, self-publishing author, one of the best things I did was hire a professional publishing consultant. A good one will make you money (not just save it) and help you avoid lots of mistakes and tons of heartache and hassles. As you know, (he said self-servingly), I offer this service. For more details, check out the *Mentoring* link at **www.wellfedwriter.com**.

PRINT LESS THAN YOU THINK YOU'LL NEED

Yes, you'll pay less per copy by printing 10,000 vs. 5,000, but not so much that it's worth the anxiety. Another reason to print less: if you have to make corrections or want to add, say, a new juicy testimonial or two to your extended blurb section in the front few pages of your book, you're not stuck until you move your "Mt. Book."

BACK UP REGULARLY WITH "THUMB DRIVES"

I say the cleanest and easiest way to back up data is a "thumb drive"—those "smaller-than-a pack-of-gum" gizmos with a USB port at one end. Ranging in size from about 128MG to 1G or more ($20-60, with rebates, for cheap piece of mind), they make it easy to back up your masterpiece every time you work on it. Get a small one just for your book and perhaps a larger one for everything on your hard drive.

ASK FOR REFERENCES

For every person planning on self-publishing a book, there's a long line of people waiting to take your money. Self-publishers get bombarded nonstop with every offer under the sun: places to list your book, ways to boost the visibility of your web site, programs to market your title, publicists to promote your title to the media, seminars that are "must-takes," and a zillion other offers. Of course, they all promise massive success if you buy their program, and total financial ruin if you don't.

Fact is, you don't need 95+ percent of them. But if you *are* considering parting with some cash, at least follow Joe Sabah's ("Mr. Radio Interview") invaluable advice, and ask: *Please supply me with the names and contact information of three people who are using your system successfully.* If they can't or won't, BIG red flag. Even if they do, as discussed earlier, know they'll be sending the best. Compare your book and approach with theirs when you talk to these folks. Ask yourself if it's reasonable to assume that you'll have a similar level of success.

Use "Registered" & "Trademark" Symbols

Whenever referencing proper names like Microsoft Word®, Kleenex®, Saran Wrap®, etc., always pay homage to registered trademarks by using the registered (®) or trademark (™) symbols (on your Word Tool Bar, *Insert*, then *Symbol*). If you mention the item several times in the book, you need only include the symbol the first time.

Get Permissions

If you plan on using any photographs, drawings, song lyrics, excerpts or anything else that doesn't belong to you, make sure you secure permissions to use them. A "cease-and-desist" letter hot on the heels of a major printing is a mighty frightening thought.

Don't Go "Book Blind"

Avoid the self-enamored "author" thing that can blind you from reality. (30)

Do a Book Proposal

Even if SP'ing, a book proposal can help clarify your thinking. (32)

The "6 x PPB" Book Pricing Formula

Your price should cover four to six times the cost of printing, paper, and binding. (57)

Galleys Should Look Final

Make your galley's editing and cover design look as close to the final edition as possible. (59)

Don't Forget Your "First-Line" Reviewers

This small group must see your book 90-120 days before OPD. (70)

Customer Service Tips

Be a Goodwill "Machine"

Make every effort to answer all reader email—and with more than one-line answers. Address questions. Give advice. I promise, they'll be blown away that they got an answer at all. Give them some attention and you'll have a friend for life. And friends talk. Most subject-specific communities just aren't that big, and people share good experiences. Getting a reputation as a nice, generous, and accessible author is a very good thing.

BE NICE TO EVERYONE

Get in the habit of projecting a friendly, helpful, accessible, humble, nice guy/gal persona. Sure, there are times when you're swamped and someone's just asked a *really* dumb question and you know how you'd *like* to respond. But be nice, and it will pay off.

KEEP CUSTOMERS HAPPY

Answer problem emails (*Where's my book...Where's my free bonus...My book's banged up...*) immediately and go overboard in making it right. It takes so little, in cold hard cash, to actually make someone happy. In my case, as a self-publisher, it takes about $5 total to send, say, a replacement book out. Spend the money, and they'll sing your praises to the rooftop, *and* tell a lot of other people how responsive you are, which will repay that meager investment over and over and over again.

I can't tell you how many times I've heard various and sundry versions of "Amazing that in this day and age, you deliver such a rare, refreshing, and positive customer service experience." Was I doing anything above and beyond? No. I was just responding promptly, keeping them abreast of the status of things, and treating them with respect because they opened their wallets to buy something from me. It's a testimonial to how lame most service is these days that it takes so little to make and keep people happy. They're starved for it! They just want what we all want: R-E-S-P-E-C-T.

SEND THE OCCASIONAL PERSONAL COPY

If someone who hasn't bought your book emails you with a question, answer it, suggest they order it from your site, and tell them you'll "pull it out of line" and send them a signed copy (as opposed to forwarding it to your shipping company for fulfillment). They'll be blown away that you replied at all, and hugely impressed. And blown-away, hugely impressed people tell others.

CREATE PERSONALIZED STICKY NOTES

Have some sticky notes custom printed (**e**) with your company name, maybe even a book cover graphic, your URL, and email address. Include them with review copies, the occasional "personal book send," and for other times calling for a professionally personal touch. I used Peerless Business Forms, Inc. (**www.peerlessbf.com**; 800-239-4670). A great site, where even a low-tech moron like me could easily design my note, order, and pay right on the site.

Whew! Guess what? We're just about done. Just a final wrap and a few thoughts to ease your mind about the exciting (but perhaps a bit scary) process that lies ahead...

Chapter 15

Every 100-story building begins with a hole in the ground and a blueprint. Every Super Bowl championship season kicks off with training camp and a goal. Every Tony award-winning Broadway production starts with a script and an empty stage. Every hot new product is born of an idea and drawings. And every successful self-publishing venture begins with an author and a story.

In each example above, a whole lot of things have to happen between conception and realization, and along the way, you break each mammoth undertaking into smaller bite-sized pieces. The big difference between most of the first four and the last one? As a self-publisher, you're in far more control of the outcome.

Healthy "Nearsightedness"

If this book has done nothing but make you wildly excited about the whole SP direction (my fond hope), wonderful. If however, you are excited, but that excitement feels suspiciously close to panic, then I'd invite you to look at your own personal self-publishing adventure through the lens of that old saying: *How do you eat an elephant? One bite at a time.* Looking at the BIG picture, and all that one has to do as a prospective self-publisher, can do a bang-up job of immobilizing you. It happened to me, until I regained a certain healthy measure of "nearsightedness."

While you need to understand the whole process and all the steps involved, for your own sanity, it's just smart to focus on each individual step, and get it done before thinking too much about the next. I promise it'll be a lighter, more joyful experience.

233

The Reality: "Triage"

Get clear in your mind the difference between two possible "to-do" lists. First, there's the non-negotiable to-do list that every SP'er has to follow in producing a book—hewing to certain rules, standards, conventions, deadlines, etc. Sure, some deadlines aren't mandatory in the sense that, if you don't do them, you can't put a book out. But they absolutely are if your goal is to maximize the financial potential of your title.

Second, there's the list of things you *could* do to promote your book, and the fact is, you simply *can't* do it all. As a self-publisher, it's all about "triage"— the medical term used to describe the process of treating the most seriously wounded first, even though there may be countless others needing attention. There were plenty of things I could have done—but didn't—to market my books, and it still ended up going well.

You don't have to do it all to be successful. Budgets and a 24-hour day will ensure the limits of your activity. Pick your battles, do your research, and choose the avenues that make the most sense for your book *and* your budget.

Natural Evolution

Then there's the whole issue of the myriad directions in which you eventually take your business. If, seven years ago, you'd showed me in your crystal ball where I'd be today with this mini-empire, I'd have scoffed, "No way." Well, way. In case that looks a bit intimidating, I want you to recall something I said earlier.

Back in Chapter Thirteen, I spoke about how arriving at this place I find myself today, with its exciting mix of income streams, was less about some rigid five-year plan mapped out way in advance, and far more about letting things unfold naturally when the time was right. I didn't force anything. *Geez, you're thinking, he wrote a pretty decent book, and in the home stretch he gets all flaky and "woo-woo" on us.*

Nope. Just pointing out that, whenever I headed off down a new path, it was because I wanted to (and sometimes readers had suggested it), I was ready, and if it involved a bit of start-up capital, I had it to spend. Not because it was mapped out way in advance.

A Compass, Not a Map

I recently came across a book with an intriguing title, *Goal-Free Living*, by Stephen M. Shapiro. Before I even cracked the book, I knew exactly what its premise was, as it was something that had occurred to me years back: religiously living your life by goal-setting can potentially leave you in a more or less constant state of anxiety, dramatically reduce your happiness level along the journey, and keep you from enjoying the ultimate realization of the very goals you've turned into your idol.

But, if you're thinking that Shapiro's book advocates sloth and a life with no direction, not so. Check out the first of his eight secrets: "Use a compass, not a map." Beautiful.

Those who use a map tend to have their face in it, so fixated on following a precisely planned route towards their goal that they end up missing a lot of scenery along the way. More importantly, they can miss potentially better routes, short cuts, and the lovely little waterfall just over the hill, but off *their* designated path.

Those who use a compass still stay on course. They know the general direction in which they're heading, but because they're not locked into a precise step-by-step plan, they're looking around, not down at their maps. Hence they enjoy the journey more, and stay open to interesting—and in the case of a business like ours—productive and profitable avenues along the way, ones that might not have been part of a more rigid blueprint.

Where Maps Work

Sure, when you're talking about the actual book production process, it's not a bad idea to stick to the plan set out here. It won't do to just blaze your own trail when creating a product for which there's a pretty rigorous checklist. But when it comes to expanding your business in different directions, grab your compass.

Know that there are maps out there if you need them, but just know this: if you set the wheels in motion, stay alert to opportunities, and do your homework (i.e., keep up with the industry, read books, listen to your readers, etc.), I promise you the right directions for your book will present themselves to you without your having to hunt too hard.

This is exactly how it happened for me. Looking back on my first book, I'm amazed at the tunnel vision I had, which was actually a good thing. In the early stages, I was focused on making sure the actual 6" x 9" baby I'd soon be rocking in my arms was the best it could be, and covering the early marketing and promotional bases. I gave little thought to the directions in which the book might eventually head.

Over time, each new step came to me as a, *Hmmm…I could do ebooks… I could do seminars…CDs…paid coaching…teleseminars* and so on. Everything in its time and place. Do I have a "to-do" list of things I think I should do? Sure, but I never let it turn into a serious anxiety attack. I just remember the evolutionary process that got me this far. It hasn't failed me yet.

A Business Plan?

Seems there's an over-abundance of talk out there in business circles about creating a "business plan." Of course, those making the suggestion usually just leave it at that, secure in the knowledge that they've offered up the quintessential piece of generic "Prudent Business Advice." Let's go a little deeper.

Funny story about business plans that I shared in my second book. A few years back, I was on a panel with several other commercial freelancers doing a university-sponsored workshop on writing. One of my fellow panelists went on and on about the importance of creating a comprehensive business plan. I was sitting next to a colleague who had just finished her first full—and successful—year in the biz and we exchanged puzzled looks.

My business plan was identical to that of my equally skeptical compadre: *Make zillions of phone calls and keep following up with those people until I have more business than I can handle. When it gets slow, just repeat until it's not slow anymore.* It was a good plan. After all, it worked in less than four months.

Keep It Simple

You could say the same thing here. As discussed in the introduction, if you follow the strategy I took, you focus on your *only* job (*Building the Demand for Your Book*), identify and zero in on the optimally targeted audiences for your book, and take massive action. Not a bad business plan.

That said, if your "inner bean-counter" craves something meatier, by all means go for it. In Chapter Three, we discussed creating book proposals, and later on I shared some sample book production scenarios. A combination of the former and some versions of the latter (adapted for *your* book) will go far in giving your budding venture some structure.

As for budgets, sure, sketch one out, but always remember that budgets are organic; as new information comes along, you adjust them. And remember, a lot of the numbers in your budget depend on how you tackle your promotional effort. Got a sales figure in mind? Great. How do you plan to achieve it? Enter your marketing plan. As you see in the case of mine described above, it doesn't have to be exceptionally complicated to be exceptionally effective.

Self-publishing is a big job, no question, but technology has made it *so* much more feasible than it's ever been before in history. Today, you truly *do* have the power to compete with far more established publishing entities, and do a *far* better job at just about everything they'd do for you (and a lot of things they won't!). Plus, if it's done smart, you'll make a lot more money than you ever could going the conventional route.

The best part of all this, as we discussed in the introduction, is that you can achieve this result even if you don't cover all the bases, and don't get it all right. It's not easy, but it doesn't have to be complicated either.

And, I'm here to tell you, the feeling you'll get from creating a book from nothing other than your vision, successfully bringing that book to market, and earning a handsome living in the process, is indescribably cool. I wish all that for you, and much more.

In Good Company

I'll leave you with this. Think you're a real trailblazer as a self-publisher? Well, you are…and you're not. All the literary lights below were originally self-publishers. You're in some pretty esteemed company, so be proud…

Henry David Thoreau

Walt Whitman

James Joyce

Elizabeth Barrett Browning

Edgar Rice Burroughs

Pat Conroy

e.e. cummings

Alexander Dumas

T.S. Eliot

Benjamin Franklin

Galileo Galilei

Lord Byron

Zane Grey

Thomas Harding

Nathaniel Hawthorne

Ernest Hemingway

Edgar Allen Poe

Beatrix Potter

George Bernard Shaw

Leo Tolstoy

Mark Twain

D. H. Lawrence

Anais Nin

Ezra Pound

Carl Sandburg

Upton Sinclair

William Blake

Stephen Crane

Rudyard Kipling

So, grab that knife and fork, plop that elephant down on your plate, and dig in. One bite at a time…

Appendix A

The following, while not necessarily an exhaustive compilation of resources for self-publishers, is a pretty decent list (though not all exclusively geared to folks like us). Readers of my second book may find a lot of the same entries here, and for good reason. Marketing is marketing, whether it's a writing business or your own books, and many of the same principles apply.

Books

The Self-Publishing Manual by Dan Poynter
The original classic on the subject, now in its umpteenth printing.

The Complete Guide to Self-Publishing by Tom and Marilyn Ross This industry "standard" (in it's 4th edition as of Spring 2002) was written by publishing veterans and founders of SPAN (See *Associations*).

Jump Start Your Book Sales by Tom and Marilyn Ross
Another gem by these authors, more for the book promotion end.

1001 Ways to Market Your Books by John Kremer
Another enduring mainstay of the field.

Building Buzz by Marisa D'Vari
Wonderful guide to maximizing your promotional reach in the media world.

How to be Your Own Publicist by Jessica Hatchigan.
Do-it-yourself playbook shares insider secrets for scoring positive publicity.

The Frugal Book Promoter: How to Do What Your Publisher Won't by Carolyn Howard-Johnson

Guerrilla Marketing by Jay Conrad Levinson
Guerrilla Publicity by Jay Conrad Levinson
Two standouts on creative marketing and publicity strategies.

1001 Ways to Market Your Services, Even if You Hate to Sell by Rick Crandall
A fun and wildly juicy marketing "thought-starter" with yes, 1001 one- or two-paragraph examples. **www.ForPeopleWhoHateToSell.com**

Writing.com by Moira Allen
While ostensibly for freelance writers, there's still tons of great info on using the 'net, which every author and self-publisher should get good at as well.

How to Publish and Promote Online by M.J. Rose and Angela Adair-Hoy
Tons of creative strategies to promote your book or ebook from two women who know what they're doing (plus advice from dozens of colleagues).

Buzz Your Book by M.J. Rose and Doug Clegg
Great advice and strategies for promoting your book online.

U-Publish.com by Dan Poynter and Danny O. Snow
Guide to publishing and promoting books using new technologies.

The 22 Immutable Laws of Marketing: Violate Them at Your Own Risk by Al Ries & Jack Trout (authors of *Positioning*)

From Book to Bestseller by Penny C. Sansevieri
Excellent guide on marketing and promoting your baby.

Grassroots Marketing for Authors and Publishers by Shel Horowitz
Comprehensive guide on promoting a book through bookstores, the Internet, special sales, publicity, and more
(**www.grassrootsmarketingforauthors.com**). Also from Shel: *Principled Profit: Marketing That Puts People First* (**www.principledprofit.com**).

Purple Cow by Seth Godin
Drives home the importance of differentiating your offering from competitors.

Zing! Five Steps and 101 Tips for Creativity on Command by Sam Harrison
Great guide to jumpstart your creative juices.

Don't Make Me Think by Steve Krug
Says one reader: "If you read just one book on web usability, make it this one." **www.sensible.com/index.html**

Web Word Wizardry by Rachel McAlpine
A must-have how-to for web content writing.

Reference Books

Simpson's Contemporary Quotations: The Most Notable Quotes Since 1950
By James B. Simpson

*Words That Sell: The Thesaurus to Help You Promote Your Products,
Services, and Ideas* by Richard Bayan

The Synonym Finder by J.I. Rodale
This nearly 1400-page beauty is, hands-down, the most often used reference
book on my shelf. Arranged like a dictionary for easy use.

Woe Is I: The Grammarphobe's Guide to Better English in Plain English by
Patricia T. O'Conner. Very practical, and delightfully written.

*The Grammar Hotline at Georgia State University's Center for Writing and
Research. 404-651-2906 and writing@gsu.edu.* Perhaps schools in other
markets have similar.

Web Sites

www.bookmarket.com—John Kremer's great site for book marketers. Lots of
free resources, "Top 101" lists, and signup info for John's *Book Marketing
Tip of the Week.*

www.publishingbasics.com—Ron Pramschufer's very cool site for
publishers. Lots of resources and an excellent podcast section.

www.parapub.com—Dan Poynter's (THE grandfather of self-publishing)
great site, chockfull of info and resources.

www.publishinggame.com—Fern Reiss (author of *The Publishing Game*
series) has put together a great site for authors seeking info on both
conventional and independent publishing.

www.selfpublishingresources.com—Tom and Marilyn Ross's
(authors and SPAN founders) site, offering a bunch of free resources,
services, and more.

www.publishingcentral.com—another great site with tons of free articles,
resource listings, and info on producing book-related products (CDs,
ebooks, ezines, etc.).

www.bookmarketingworks.com—Put together by sales pro Brian Jud, with
an emphasis on selling books through non-traditional outlets.

www.writing-world.com (formerly Inkspot.com)—The Writer's Resource; One of THE premier and most respected sites for writers: articles, links, resources, and networking.

www.yudkin.com—*Published!* and *Creative Marketing Solutions*, both by 25-year veteran freelancer and marketing pro Marcia Yudkin, offer dozens of useful articles on making a living as a writer and getting published. Subscribe to her *Marketing Minute* at **www.yudkin.com/markmin.htm**.

www.writersdigest.com—*Writer's Digest*, one of the world's leading pubs for writers.

www.writermag.com—*The Writer*, one of the world's leading pubs for writers.

www.writedirections.com—Classes, how-to articles, writing resources, coaching/consulting, and free newsletters loaded with tips, tools, and !eads!

www.writingcareer.com—ebook purveyors of the writing trade.

www.writers-editors.com—where editors, businesses, and creative directors can locate writers, copy editors, proofreaders, ad copywriters, ghostwriters and PR help.

www.amarketingexpert.com—Penny Sansevieri's great site with a focus on "Powerful Book Promotion Made Easy."

www.combinedbook.com—*The Combined Book Exhibit* is an exhibit and promotional service for publishers, allowing you to display your books at a host of state, regional, national, and international book shows.

www.freelancesuccess.com—The ultimate resource for established professional non-fiction writers. Newsletter, classifieds, classes, bookstore, writers' forums, and much more.

www.selfpublishing.com—The *Home Depot* for SP'ers. Printing bought in bulk and resold to SP'ers at prices normally reserved for major publishers. *Writers Digest* Top 101 sites for writers. Over 105 million books in print.

www.dobkin.com—the website for "Marketing Master" Jeffrey Dobkin, author of *How To Market a Product for Under $500* and *Uncommon Marketing Techniques*. A bunch of excellent (and free) articles on various aspects of the marketing process.

www.abraham.com—actionable strategies from marketing guru Jay Abraham to "grow your business beyond anything you ever expected or even hoped."

www.cargillsells.com—Gill Cargill, a top sales training professional, and according to one reader, "a fabulous resource for anyone who needs to market his or her business."

http://bartleby.com/141/—the perennial classic, The Elements of Style, by William Strunk Jr. (now it's free online!)

http://dictionary.reference.com—home of Dictionary.com

www.writerbeware.com—Who'd have guessed that the *Science Fiction and Fantasy Writers of America's* web site would keep a current database of over 600 agents, publishers, and independent editors who've earned black marks?

www.brainyquote.com—Excellent source for a good pithy quote from a famous notable, past or present; often just the ticket to spice up a book passage or article. Also see **www.quotationspage.com.**

www.idiomsite.com—the meanings and origins of zillions of common expressions such as "Doubting Thomas," "Chip on his shoulder," "Close but no cigar," etc.

www.prb.org—Population Reference Bureau: for all those obscure—but perhaps necessary for your research – people and population stats. For similar info, also check out **www.census.gov.**

www.authorsmarket.net—Interesting site for authors trying to sort through their various options; good ideas and straight-up honesty.

www.useit.com—Jakob Neilsen is a guru in the field of web usability. Go to **www.useit.com/papers/webwriting/** for links to numerous articles, books, and guides.

www.gerrymcgovern.com—Gerry McGovern, web content guru.

Associations

In the monthly publications of both the following, you'll find tons of advertisements and resource listings for all the book production category listings in the coming pages.

PMA, The Independent Book Publishers Association—www.pma-online.org
The world's largest non-profit trade association representing independent publishers. PMA offers tons of resources, cooperative marketing programs, the monthly *Independent* newsletter, their annual *Ben Franklin Awards* program, and much more.

SPAN (Small Publishers Association of North America)—(www.spannet.org).
Started by Tom and Marilyn Ross (authors of several SP books mentioned earlier), but under new ownership now, SPAN is smaller than PMA, but worth being part of. They publish a monthly newsletter, *SPAN Connection*.

Contests

The most popular contests for independent publishers are:

The Benjamin Franklin Awards
Sponsor: PMA
Web Site: **www.pma-online.org**

The IPPY Awards
Sponsor: Independent Publisher
Web site: **www.independentpublisher.com**

ForeWord *Magazine's Book of the Year Awards*
Sponsor: *ForeWord* magazine
Web site: **www.forewordmagazine.com**

Writer's Digest International Self-Published Book Awards
Sponsor: *Writer's Digest* magazine
Web site: **www.writersdigest.com**

For a larger list of competitions (including ones for conventionally published books), check out **http://www.writing-world.com/contests/index.shtml**.

Conferences

The April issue of *The Writer* magazine (**www.writermag.com**) provides a comprehensive listing of writers conferences (about 250 in any given year) across the country (by state), in Canada, and beyond.

www.allconferences.com (spans countless industries)

www.shawguides.com

www.craigslist.com

Writing/Marketing e-Newsletters

Book Promotion Newsletter (Every other Wednesday)
Editor: Francine Silverman
Web site: **www.bookpromotionnewsletter.com**
Focus: Book Promotion (Success Stories, Resources)

Book Marketing Tip of the Week
Editor: John Kremer
Web site: **www.bookmarket.com/tips.html**
Focus: Book Marketing

Marketing Matters Newsletters (Bi-Weekly)
Managing Editor: Brian Jud
Web site: **www.bookmarketingworks.com/**
Focus: Non-traditional Book Sales Outlets

Expertizing/Publishing Game (Monthly)
Editor: Fern Reiss
Web site: **www.PublishingGame.com/signup.htm**
Focus: Increasing Media Attention

The Publicity Hound's Tips of the Week
Editor: Joan Stewart
Web site: **www.publicityhound.com**
Focus: Effective Public Relations

The Marketing Minute (Weekly)
Editor: Marcia Yudkin
Web site: **www.yudkin.com/markmin.htm**
Focus: General Marketing, with an emphasis on writing

Marketing Sherpa [Email Sherpa] (Weekly)
Managing Editor: Anne Holland
Web site: **www.marketingsherpa.com**
Focus: Email Marketing

MarketingProfs Today (Weekly)
Editor: Ann Handley
Web site: **www.marketingprofs.com**
Focus: General Marketing Tips from Industry Experts

Publish for Profits (Bi-weekly)
Editor: Alexandria K. Brown (a.k.a. The Ezine Queen)
Web site: **www.ezinequeen.com**
Focus: Publishing Ezines

eNewsletter Journal (Monthly)
Editor: Meryl K. Evans
Web site: **www.internetviz.com**
Focus: Email Newsletters (Ezines)

My "A-List" Vendors

These are the folks I used in the various key stages of my book projects. You can't go wrong by doing business with them.

COVER DESIGN:

DiNatale Design—Atlanta, GA
Contact: Chris DiNatale
PH: 678-819-1303 (1305—Fax)
EM: chris@dinatalegraphicdesign.com
WS: **www.dinatalegraphicdesign.com**
Talented, strategic, creative; Chris designed all my book covers.

COVER DESIGN/ILLUSTRATION:

Xero Studios—Atlanta, GA
Contact: Debbie Rohde
PH: 404-432-9926
EM: debbie@xerostudios.com
WS: **www.xerostudios.com**
Excellent designer, 20+ years experience, very reasonably priced. AND very talented illustrator as well. Worked with me on miscellaneous book-related graphics projects.

EDITING/PROOFREADING:

Whyte ink—Gold Coast, Australia
Contact: Geoff Whyte
PH: 011-61-2-66795397 (total calling string from U.S.)
EM: geoff@whyteink.com.au
WS: **www.whyteink.com.au**
Brilliant, thorough, clairvoyant, insightful, thinks 10 steps ahead, amazingly reasonable.

EDITING/PROOFREADING:

Word Craft Services—Atlanta, GA
Contact: Mim Eisenberg
PH: 770-645-1166
EM: mim@wordcraftservices.com
WS: **www.wordcraftservices.com**
Awesome, eagle-eye editor at competitive rates.

AUDIO TRANSCRIPTION (TELESEMINARS, TALKS)

Word Craft Services—Atlanta, GA (see above for contact details)

TYPESETTER:

Michael Hoehne Design—Springtown, PA
Contact: Michael Hoehne (pron. Haney) or Angela Werner
PH: 610-346-6823
EM: michael@heyneon.com
WS: **www.heyneon.com**
Good people, great work; typeset first book, more "traditional" typesetting look.

TYPESETTER:

Contact: Shawn Morningstar—Short Hills, NJ
EM: shawnmstar@comcast.net
Joy to work with; very creative and reasonable; did this book (and #2); more fun, dynamic look.

INDEXER:

Contact: Diana Witt—Marietta, Georgia
PH: 770-575-0038
EM: diana.witt@comcast.net
Professional, fast, thorough, very reasonable

PRINTER/GALLEY PRINTER/DISTRIBUTION/FULFILLMENT:

BookMasters, Inc.—Mansfield, OH
Contact: Shelley Sapyta
PH: 888-537-6727; ext. 1130
EM: ssapyta@bookmasters.com
WS: **www.bookmasters.com**
Great job all around—friendly, thorough, reasonable, professional.

GALLEY PRINTER:

Publishers Graphics—Carol Stream, IL
PH: 888-404-3769
WS: **www.pubgraphics.com**

PUBLISHING CONSULTANT:

Peter Bowerman—Atlanta, GA
PH: 770-438-7200
EM: peter@wellfedwriter.com
WS: **www.wellfedwriter.com**
Visit "Mentoring" link at site above for details/rates/testimonials. Knowledgeable, friendly, thorough. ☺

WEB DESIGNER:
Marketing Masters, Ltd.—Atlanta, GA
Contact: Chris Papas
PH: 770-745-4695
EM: info@mm-ltd.com
WS: **www.mm-ltd.com**
Smart, highly technically savvy, nice guy.

PUBLICITY/MEDIA PROMOTION:
KSB Promotions—Ada, MI
Contact: Kate and Doug Bandos—
PH: 616-676-0758 (Fax: 0759)
EM: info@ksbpromotions.com
WS: **www.ksbpromotions.com**

NOTE: I use KSB for *KSB Links*, their thrice-a-year publication to 8,000+
media folks, and I tapped them for their contacts to publications serving the
Seniors market. *Professional, no-nonsense, delivers.*

MERCHANT ACCOUNT
Electronic Transfer, Inc.—Spokane, WA
Contact: Mike Knudtson
PH: 800-757-5453
WS: **www.electronictransfer.com**

Publisher Resource Recommendations
Who better (and more credible) than actual publishers to serve up their faves
for all manner of services? Here are the results of a survey sent out to a bunch
of "in-the-trenches" publishers. I've included comments and/or specific
contact info where it was provided. I've listed the categories roughly in the
order in which you'd need them. All were operating at press time, but things
do change.

Book Cover Design
Bookcovers.com (Winter Park, FL): **www.bookcovers.com**; 800-449-4095

Shu Shu Design (Madison, WI): **www.shushudesign.com**; 608-663-7638
*Contact: Peter Streicher; Our most recent book cover done by SSD has
gotten plenty of positive feedback. We couldn't be happier.*

Foster Covers (Fairfield, IA): **www.fostercovers.com**; 800-472-3953
Contact: George Foster; great reputation in the business.

Joss Paddock (Chelan, WA): *jossp@dogwise.com*; 509-682-7034

Brian Groppe; *bagroppe@bellsouth.net*

Norm Mayall (Emeryville, CA): 510-428-9251

Debra Warr (Abilene, TX): 325-677-0621.

Imagination Technology (Lafayette, CO): **www.imaginationtechnology.com**; 720-771-7274; *Contact: Robin Meetz; creativedirector@imaginationtechnology.com*

Inari Information Services (Bloomington, IN): **www.inarionline.com**; 800-536-5481 *Contact: Mike Kelsey; mikek@inarionline.com;*

TM Design (Bloomington, IN); 812-332-5269
Contact: Tim Mayer; timmayer@bloomington.in.us; great guy; used to be affiliated with Mike Kelsey at Inari. Has done a lot of work for Indiana University Press.

Bookwrights Design (Charlottesville, VA); **www.bookwrights.com**; 434-263-4818
Contact: Mayapriya Long; mayapriya@bookwrights.com; Mayapriya has won lots of awards for her covers.

Typesetters

(PB Note: I found my typesetter through my indexer, who posted a note on an industry billboard; the two fields are related and their practitioners communicate regularly.)

Lee Lewis (Tecumseh, MI), Words+Design: **www.Wordsplusdesign.com**; 888-883-8347

Shu Shu Design (Madison, WI): **www.shushudesign.com**; 608-663-7637
Contact: Jenny Green; excellent work, exceptional prices. Able to assist with some editing and proofreading.

Inari Information Services (Bloomington, IN): **www.inarionline.com**; 800-536-5481
Contact: Mike Kelsey; mikek@inarionline.com; Japanese translation and Asian language typesetting services available.

Indexers
US: **www.asindexing.org**

UK: **www.indexers.org.uk/**

Australia/NZ: **www.aussi.org/**

"The Index Lady" (Toronto, Canada): 416-762-6489
Contact: Elaine Melnick; reddot@cuic.ca; Easy to work with, super professional, really tries to understand the work.

Diane Worden: *Wordendex@aol.com*; 269-349-3624

Editors/Proofreaders
Diane Worden: *Wordendex@aol.com*; 269-349-3624

Joelle Steele; *joelles@juno.com*; 831-641-9316

Galley printers (Short-run)
Offset Paperback (Dallas, PA): **www.opm.com**; 570-675-5261

Fidlar Doubleday (Kalamazoo, MI): **www.fidlardoubleday.com**; 800-248-0888

BookMobile (Minneapolis, MN): **www.bookmobile.com**; 1-800-752-3303; ext. 126; *Contact: Nicole Baxter; nbaxter@bookmobile.com*

Sterling Pierce (East Rockaway, NY): **www.sterlingpierce.com**; 516-593-1170

Country Press (Lakeville, MA): **www.countrypressinc.com**; 508-947-4485

U.S. Book Printers
(PB Note: Visit **www.Printellectual.com** *to submit multiple quote requests at once.)*

Banta Corporation (Menasha, WI): **www.banta.com**; 920-722-7771

Whitehall Printing Company (Naples, FL): **www.whitehallprinting.com**; 800-321-9290: *Contact: Cindy Smith; product, price, and service all great.*

United Graphics, Inc. (Mattoon, IL): **www.unitedgraphicsinc.com**; 217-235-7161

DeHart's Printing (Santa Clara, CA): **www.deharts.com**; 888-982-4763

Kendall Printing (Greeley, CO): **www.kendallprinting.com**; 800-464-3538

Dickinson Press (Grand Rapids, MI): **www.dickinsonpress.com**; 616-957-5100
Specializes in bibles, dictionaries, children's books, and catalogs.

Malloy Incorporated. (Ann Arbor, MI): **www.malloy.com**; 800-722-3231
Contact: Lynn Rohlkohl or Patrice Smith (depends on region).

Thomson-Shore (Dexter, MI): **www.thomson-shore.com**; 734-426-3939
Contact: Maria Smith (depends on region).

Central Plains Book Manufacturing (Winfield, KS): **www.centralplainsbook.com**; 877-278-2726; *Contact: Becky Pate; consistently gives us the best prices.*

Petit Printing (Buffalo, NY): **www.petitprinting.com**; *716-871-9490 Contact: Rich Petit*

Sheridan Printing (Alpha, NJ): **www.sheridanprinting.com**; 908-454-0700

Graphic Image Group (Glen Ellyn, IL): **www.giginc.com**; 800-737-3393 *Contact: Jeff Link; small paperback orders up to 1,000.*

McNaughton & Gunn (Ann Arbor, MI): **www.bookprinters.com**; 734-429-5411 *Contact: Davis Scott; for larger, hardcover orders.*

Codra Enterprises (Huntington Beach, CA): **www.codra.com**; 714-429-0088 *Contact: Mike Daniels; miked@codra.com*

C&M Press (Denver, CO): **www.cmpress.com**; 303-375-9922 *Contact: Ken Malkin; ken1@cmpress.com*

Canadian Printers

PB Note: I've heard several comments about the possibility of saving decent money (given the favorable exchange rate) by going with a Canadian printer.

Transcontinental Printing (St. Laurent, Quebec, Canada): **http://transcontinental-gtc.com/en/index.html**; 514-954-4000 *One of the largest book printers in Canada; I use them for one- and two-color interior printing; they do many U.S. print jobs.*

Friesens (Altona, Manitoba, Canada): **www.friesens.com**; 204-324-6401 *Large printer; good for four-color interior printing; they match color proofs bang on (very important when printing food photos); do a lot of U.S. print jobs.*

"Collateral" printers:
postcards, business cards, bookmarks, flyers

Tu-Vets Corporation (Los Angeles, CA): **www.tu-vets.com**; *323-723-4569 Contact: Henry Ayala*

U.S. Press (Valdosta, GA): **www.uspressdirect.com**; 800-631-8506 *Prepay with credit card and shipping is free.*

Magnet Street (Blaine, MN): **www.magnetstreet.com**; 800-788-8633 *Magnetic business cards and other magnetized items.*

Modern Postcard (Carlsbad, CA): **www.modernpostcard.com**; 800-959-8365
The absolute BEST place for postcards; can't say enough about how good the cards look (four-color and one-color) and the turnaround time; great prices, too.

Online Print House (Tampa, FL): **www.onlineprinthouse.com**; 1-866-323-2400
Best deal on quality full-color bookmarks, glossy business cards, and more. Two-day turnaround, and cheap! I use the company all the time and they're excellent.

Morrell Graphics (Lafayette, CO): **www.morrellgraphics.com**; 303-665-4210
Contact: Jim Morrell; mail@morrellgraphics.com

Separacolor (Rolling Hills Estates, CA): **www.separacolor.com**; 800-779-1158
Contact: Dave Field

PSPrint (Oakland, CA): **www.psprint.com**; 800-511-2009

Quality Image Printing (Lakewood, CO); 303-988-1560

L'Impression Printing (St. Laurent, Quebec, Canada): **www.impression.net**; 877-735-7770

Peerless Business Forms, Inc.(Metuchen, NJ): **www.peerlessbf.com**; 800-239-4670 *Pre-printed sticky notes. Easy D-I-Y note designing.*

Fulfillment Companies
BookMasters (Mansfield, OH): **www.bookmasters.com**; 888-537-6727
Contact: Shelley Sapyta (x 1130); ssapyta@bookmasters.com

Fulfillco (Richmond, CA): **www.Fulfillco.com**; 510-232-6688
Contact: Joel Bernstein

BookWorld (Sarasota, FL): **www.bookworld.com**; 800-444-2524

A&A Quality Shipping Services (Hayward, CA): (No WS); 510-732-6521
Contact: Bill Armour;anaquality@rocketmail.com; small fulfillment company working mostly with small West Coast publishers.

R&L Warehouse Distribution (Emeryville, CA): (No WS); 510-547-3611
Contact: R. Michael Rypins

Web Design
EStreet Communications (Denver, CO): **www.estreet.com**; 877-ESTREET
Contact: Tim Otterbein; webmaster@estreet.com

Publicists

Planned TV Arts (New York, NY): **www.plannedtvarts.com**; 212-593-5820

BookPros (formerly Phenix and Phenix Literary Publicists) (Austin, TX): **www.bookpros.com**; 512.478.2028
Contact: Jennifer Berry; Got us coverage in The Christian Science Monitor, Philadelphia Inquirer, Toronto Star, Milwaukee Journal-Sentinel, Minneapolis Star Tribune, NPR, and many others. Delivered exactly what they said they would.

Marketing Companies

Marketability (Arvada, CO): **www.marketability.com**; 303-279-4349 or 888-55-TWIST
Contact: Kim Dushinski or Tami DePalma; twist@marketability.com

BookWorld (Sarasota, FL): **www.bookworld.com**; 800-444-2524

PMA, The Independent Book Publishers Association (Manhattan Beach, CA): **www.pma-online.org**; 310-372-2732; *cooperative marketing programs; trade show book displays, more.*

Combined Book Exhibit (Buchanan, NY): **www.combinedbook.com**; 800-462-7687; *Contact: Peter Birch; displays authors books at shows around the globe.*

Merchant Account Providers

Card Service International (Simi Valley, CA): **www.cardservice.com**; 800-456-5902

Shopping Cart Systems (with affiliate programs)

www.1shoppingcart.com; 1-888-255-6230

www.kickstartcart.com; 1-800-448-6280

www.fusionquest.com (standalone affiliate program)

Appendix B

Some time back, I was poking through my computer files and was blown away at the vast array of marketing, publicity, and promotional materials of every description that I'd created in the course of my book marketing campaign. "Wow," I thought, "Bet my readers would *love* to get their hands on all these things as they launch their own book campaigns."

Well, including all of it would have added 100 pages or more to the book, and that just wasn't feasible. But then I thought, "Why not include some of it in the book, and far more in a separate cut 'n pastable ebook?" Yes, I'm charging extra for that ebook ($29.95), but once you see what's in it, I'm guessing you'll think the toll is a steal.

More importantly, this represents the culmination of years of effort. I'm saving you from having to reinvent the wheel, and that's worth something. It's all in keeping with the goal of all my books so far: to spell out the real-world nitty-gritty detail, and leave the theoretical far behind.

This resource is valuable for several reasons: it shows you *what*, specifically, you need to have, and seeing it all laid out will undoubtedly have you realize that you didn't know you needed this, that, or the other. Just as importantly, it shows you *how* I crafted each piece. Not like my way is the right, best, or only way, but it got the job done. I encourage you to improve on it, but having a model to follow should make that job easier. Finally, by definition, you'll see the *when* and *why* of these pieces: the point at which you'd employ each one, and for what reason.

In the pages that follow, I've included a few pieces of the puzzle that I used to get things launched, and at the end, you'll see a longer list of what's included in the larger resource (which also includes the following pages). Enjoy.

Book Marketing Proposal

As mentioned in Chapter Three, even if you have definitely decided to go the self-publishing route, taking the time to do a book proposal (as if you were trying to woo a conventional publisher) is an exercise I'd strongly recommend. It'll force you to prove to yourself the fundamental viability of your book in the marketplace before you embark on what can be an expensive journey with no guarantee of profitability. Here's the book proposal I worked up for my first title. It might not be as comprehensive as one I'd put together for a publisher, but it covers enough of the important bases to be a useful undertaking. And as mentioned earlier, it's not a bad start to a business plan.

A couple of recommended books on the subject are:

Write the Perfect Book Proposal: 10 That Sold and Why (2nd edition), by Jeff Herman & Deborah Levine Herman (Wiley; 2001)

How to Write a Successful Book Proposal in 8 Days or Less, Patricia L. Fry (Matilija Press; 2004)

•   •   •

The Well-Fed Writer:

Financial Self-Sufficiency As a Freelance Writer In Six Months or Less

by Peter Bowerman

Introduction

We are in an age of redefinition—global and personal. Our world is changing dramatically and certainly not always for the better. More and more, we are becoming overloaded, overextended, overwhelmed. Many are reassessing their lives, taking a long hard look at how they spend their workday, and the stresses and tolls their careers are taking on them.

They find that their claim of the primacy of family and personal life is at odds with the reality of hours spent in pursuit of money, status, and titles, at the expense of family ties, health, and peace of mind. They want to reclaim those elusive components of "quality of life." For many, it means clearing the slate, starting over in a new business, and perhaps allowing themselves to believe that they can make a living pursuing a life of creative fulfillment.

The writing bug afflicts so many in our population. They become smitten with the notion of making a living—do they dare believe a *good* living?—with their words. But how to do it, given that the words *starving* and *writer* seem to be eternally joined at the hip? And do it quickly?

Enter *"The Well-Fed Writer: Financial Self-Sufficiency as a Freelance Writer In Six Months or Less"* (TWFW), an engaging, humorous, accessible, yet substantive game plan for achieving self-sufficiency as a freelance commercial writer—writing for corporate America—and landing accounts from the one-man shop to the Fortune 100 firm. And doing it within six months.

Drawing on six-plus years of personal experience building a successful freelance commercial writing business from scratch, along with an additional 15 years of sales/marketing experience, author Peter Bowerman provides a logical and detailed game plan for aspiring writers of every description and circumstance to build and maintain a lucrative freelance commercial writing business. I believe the title itself is strong enough to attract attention on bookshelves and in email marketing, press releases, and media appearances.

Who Will Buy This Book?

There are five key markets for this book, though in all likelihood, the first category is larger than the other four combined. See the *Back Cover Copy* (which will appear on my web site as well) for a closer look at how I will speak to my market, whether they're in a bookstore reading the jacket or visiting the web site.

1) ASPIRING WRITERS: By far the largest market is the literally many thousands of people who enjoy writing, feel they're good at it, are perhaps trying (and struggling) to make a go of it, and would love to figure out how to make a handsome living at the craft. I assert that this group defies demographic categorization—they are young, old, rich, poor, black, white, male and female.

2) SEASONED FREELANCERS: This book will also find a warm reception amongst experienced freelancers who perhaps, have focused on magazine freelancing, where the money is lower, and hassles higher. In the magazine writing field, it's all about flat fees and potentially vast open-ended commitments of time. By contrast, in the commercial writing field, you calculate fees based on healthy hourly rates ($50-125+) and *all time counts*. That should resonate nicely with writers used to far less attractive terms.

3) AT-HOME-MOMS: This group enjoys writing and may have once held jobs in PR, marketing, advertising, or a specific industry (i.e. healthcare, high-tech, retail, financial services, hospitality, etc.). With this book, they can leverage their professional experiences into a new, lucrative, flexible, "work-when-I-want-as-much-as-I-want" career.

4) JOURNALISTS: Consider this quote:

As a former award-winning journalist and current owner of a multi-media communications firm, I am struck by the scarcity of good writing these days. Professional journalists get a lot of practice at making ideas easy to understand. However, because of low pay and often terrible working conditions, most journalists want to make a career change within a few years of graduating. With their experience at expressing ideas in a clear, concise, *logical manner, they are very well positioned to escape the shackles of poverty and earn $50-$85+ an hour in the freelance commercial writing market. But regardless of your background, there is huge demand in the corporate arena for good solid coherent writing skills.*

Bob Hamilton
Multiple Associated Press Award-winner
President, In-Focus Communications
Atlanta, Georgia

5) CORPORATE STAFF WRITERS: Many writers working in-house for corporations (and often writing about one narrow area) dream of self-employment as a writer, where they can leverage their writing ability and experience into a higher income, a more flexible work schedule and a greater variety of work. TWFW is the detailed blueprint they need to make that transition.

6) RECENT COLLEGE GRADUATES: Short on overhead expenses but long on enthusiasm and energy, and perhaps unsure about the over-structured corporate world that awaits them, this group can find an attractive career alternative in these pages. Especially since the book emphasizes that a lack of contacts and industry experience (the author's story) is no obstacle to success.

Why Will They Buy This Book?

A FOCUS ON MAKING MONEY

A trip to the writing shelf of the local bookstore will turn up hundreds of books on writing just about anything: magazine articles, romance novels, cookbooks, children's books, poetry, science fiction, horror, and much more. Most focus on the writing with less emphasis on the business end of the equation. Creativity, not commerce, is the focus, which creates even more writers who live up to freelance writing's reputation as being largely the domain of struggling artists.

Starting with the title and maintained throughout the book, the theme of TWFW is about making money—good money—at the art and craft of writing. Not $15-25K a year, but more like $50-100K. (See *Back Cover Copy* for elaboration.) I assert that that focus will move people to action.

COMPETITION

The only book that I'm aware of that competes with TWFW is *Secrets of a Freelance Writer* by Bob Bly, the very well-written book that got me started in the business, and now in its second printing (1988 and 1997). While several other books devote perhaps a chapter to commercial writing, as part of a larger discussion of the writing profession, "Secrets..." is the only book geared solely to commercial writing.

Nonetheless, despite similar content, the tone of TWFW is worlds more fun, warm, humorous, and reader-embracing than "Secrets...", and truly sets it apart. In addition, my unique systems-oriented approach to the on-going business management reflects common sense and a healthy grasp of human nature (i.e. we're all basically lazy, and if it's not easy to do, we won't do it), with a consistent emphasis on enhancing the "do-ability" of the opportunity. In a larger sense, with only two books on the market dealing exclusively with this subject matter, the field can hardly be classified as overcrowded.

How Will I Market and Distribute the Book?

Master Wholesalers—to handle bookstore/library trade. I will support these entities' efforts with reviews as I receive them, along with press releases and info sheets as appropriate.

Book Review Campaign—I plan to send out 300+ books to select magazines, daily and weekly newspapers, and relevant web sites and online newsletters to garner positive book reviews and promote the book to their audiences. In addition to general audience publications, I will target publications geared to writers, mothers and journalists.

Web Site—I have reserved the domain name: **www.wellfedwriter.com**, which as a stand-alone advertising/promotional tool (with no additional copy), could make for an intriguing and inexpensive "teaser" link on a web site or in a small ad. I have hired a professional Internet marketing company to build, maintain and promote the site. The site will include a brief punchy sales presentation, a sample chapter, the book's table of contents, testimonials, back cover copy of the book and more.

Internet Marketing—I plan to contact hundreds of web sites geared specifically towards writers, at-home Moms, and home-based business seekers with requests to promote the book on their site through articles and marketing links, and will offer a 10-15 percent discount to their members/viewers.

Media Campaigns—Using email programs and media databases, I plan to send a mass emailed news release to thousands of media outlets. This will not only promote the book to that outlet's audience, but indirectly to another target market as well: the journalists themselves. With a book like this, I can also target career/work/business editors as well as those focusing on lifestyle.

Radio/TV Interviews—I plan to use Joe Sabah's "Radio Talk Show System," which includes a current database of over 900 radio programs that book guests. I will contact the ones whose program theme seems to be closest to mine, and market to them through both phone and email. I plan to have audio footage of a sample radio interview on my web site to make it easier for prospects to make a decision.

Projected "Breakeven" Point

With an initial marketing/printing budget of approximately $15,000 and a retail price of $19.95, yielding an average profit of $8 (by industry calculations), I will have to sell approximately 1900 books to break even.

• • •

Interested in seeing my actual Marketing Strategy Questionnaire submitted to Ingram (the large trade wholesaler), along with a real-world bookstore "pitch letter" sent by a self-publishing fiction writer? I invite you to consider investing in my 100-plus page *Well-Fed SP Biz-in-a-Box*. Full contents and purchase details are at the end of this appendix.

• • •

Sample Working Press Release
(See notes on this and other releases at end of release)

FOR IMMEDIATE RELEASE

CONTACT:
Peter Bowerman, Author
Fanove Publishing
3713 Stonewall Circle
Atlanta, Georgia 30339
770/987-6543
770/987-6542 (Fax)
peter@wellfedwriter.com
www.wellfedwriter.com

Bad Writing Skills: A Businesses' Nightmare,
A Freelancer's Dream.

ATLANTA, GA—July 12, 2005—As reported recently in *The New York Times**, American business is wrestling with the costs of poor writing skills of many of their workers. The May 15, 2005 Times article ("The Fine Art of Getting It Down on Paper" by Brent Staples) pointed out how a competitive business climate is demanding "more high-quality writing from more categories of employees than ever before."

But, that's good news for freelance writers, says Peter Bowerman, author of The Well-Fed Writer, and its companion volume, TWFW: Back For Seconds, two titles on the subject of "commercial" freelancing—writing for businesses, large and small, and for hourly rates ranging from $50-125+.

The Times article cited the 2004 report by the National Commission on Writing, which reported that only a third of the companies surveyed reported that only one-third or fewer of their employees knew how to write clearly and concisely.

Bowerman, whose first book was an award-winning Book-of-the-Month Club title, concurs: "Good writing is the engine that drives commerce, yet writing skills amongst many American workers, frankly, are atrocious. As companies see the bottom-line costs of this shortfall, it opens up tremendous opportunities for capable freelancers to step in and pick up the slack."

Sweetening the pot even more, says Bowerman, is the prolific downsizing of the past decade. He explains: "Many companies, of all sizes, are operating leaner than ever, yet good writing is still something that has to get done. Many have steady writing needs and the healthy budgets to outsource those projects—at handsome rates."

Veteran commercial freelance writer Bob Bly, author of 50+ writing titles, says of the field: "I know of no other arena of writing so lucrative yet so easy to get started in."

With no writing background, paid professional writing experience or industry contacts, Bowerman was paying all his bills through commercial writing in four months. He says, "If you're a decent writer and you dream of getting out of the rat race, working from home and having time for a life, this is a great option."

---

* The New York Times, May 15, 2005, "The Fine Art of Getting It Down on Paper, Fast" by Brent Staples; The New York Times, December 7, 2004, "What Corporate America Can't Build: A Sentence" by Sam Dillon

Media: Contact author for interviews or review copies. Visit www.wellfedwriter.com ("Attn: Media" link) for cover art, author pix, news "pegs", sample radio/TV interview footage, sample chapters, book reviews, "Attn: Moms" section for at-home Moms, and more. The book retails for $19.95 and can be purchased in bookstores, on Amazon, through www.wellfedwriter.com and at 800-247-6553.

• • •

The preceding release incorporates a wonderful set of *New York Times* articles—a great angle I could exploit. It gets away from talking about the book more than any other I used. The high-profile articles I use as reference points are just the sort of currency valued by media types, arguably giving it the greatest chance of resonating with this crowd or *any* potential reviewer. To see *The Amazing Evolving Press Release*, featuring four versions of a release (Ugly, Bad, Good, and Better), with an info-packed intro outlining six big mistakes often made in releases, I invite you to consider investing in my *Well-Fed SP Biz-in-a-Box*. Full contents and purchase details are at the end of this appendix.

SAMPLE EMAIL PITCH
(to Women's-Oriented Publication or Web Site)

A sample of a basic email pitch seeking exposure (i.e., reviews, blurbs, interviews, permissions to write articles, etc.). Arguably, I could shorten it but this basic template—tailored to different audiences—was effective in getting a response and generating a lot of activity. Note my inclusion of promotional email blurbs for possible use on their site. If you want people to do something, make it as effortless for them to help you as possible.

Ideally you have a name from hunting around on a web site but if not, you can substitute: "Greetings!" instead and include the following note at the top of the email:

(Wasn't sure exactly who to contact, but if you're NOT the right person, I'd be sincerely grateful if you'd forward the information on. Thanks so much!)

• • •

Hi Janet,

May I send you a review copy of my book?

Peter Bowerman here, best-selling Atlanta-based author (bio at bottom). I came across your web site and wanted to touch base with you about my book, which I believe could be an excellent resource for your members. Title: *The Well-Fed Writer: Financial Self-Sufficiency as a Freelance Writer in Six Months or Less*, an award-winning Book-of-the-Month Club selection.

Well-Fed is a very detailed how-to for quickly breaking into the lucrative and surprisingly accessible arena of freelance commercial (corporate) writing. As Corporate America has downsized, it has outsourced much of their creative needs, making this particular writing direction more viable and profitable than ever before.

Because of the freedom, flexibility and healthy income this career direction offers (*and the fact that the field is more than half female*), some key audiences I'm targeting are women, working moms looking to transition to a home-based career AND at-home mothers, looking to start a home-based career.

I've gotten a lot of wonderful reviews, including these:

> *"An excellent book worth every penny of the cover price, and written in a conversational style that makes you feel like you're talking over coffee. There's so much information here you could read it three times and come away with something different each time."*

> **Jerri L. Ledford**
> **www.momwriters.com**
> **Writer's Digest Top 101 Web Sites**

"Writing the Great-American-Novel isn't the only way for a writer to earn a living. If you love to write and want the flexibility of a work-at-home career, let The Well-Fed Writer and author Peter Bowerman guide you every step of the way with practical tips, straightforward advice, wit and honesty. I highly recommend this book."

Cheryl Demas, Editor
www.WAHM.com—The Online Magazine For Work-At-Home Moms
Author, *The Work-at-Home Mom's Guide to Home Business*

"The Well-Fed Writer is one of the best books I have read about making a living as a professional writer. Practical tips in a fun-to-read style."

Priscilla Y. Huff, Author
101 Best Home-Business Success Secrets for Women

I invite you to visit my web site (**www.wellfedwriter.com**), and especially the *Attn: Moms* link, which features interviews with at-home Moms making a go of this business (also in book).

If you feel this book would be of interest to your readers, I'd love to explore any opportunities to get the word out: book review, feature article (written by me), Q&A, a simple mention with link to my web site, or some combination. I have included three ready-to-use promotional blurbs below to use if you choose to, to make it easy for you to spread the word.

Shall I send a copy? If so, to whom and where? Thanks very much for your kind consideration and I look forward to hearing from you.

Sincerely,

Peter Bowerman
Fanove Publishing
3713 Stonewall Circle
Atlanta, GA 30339
770/987-6543
770/987-6542 (FX)
peter@wellfedwriter.com
www.wellfedwriter.com

•   •   •

Author Bio

Peter Bowerman has been a freelance writer and columnist in Atlanta, Georgia since 1993. His corporate client list includes The Coca-Cola Company, MCI, BellSouth, IBM, UPS, Holiday Inn, GTE, American Express, Mercedes-Benz, The Discovery Channel, Junior Achievement and many others. He has published over 250 columns and articles, leads seminars on writing, and is a professional coach on commercial writing start-up and self-publishing. His best-selling book, *The Well-Fed Writer*, has earned some key industry accolades:

- Second Place: ForeWord magazine's 2000 Book of the Year Awards (Career category)
- Finalist: Publisher's Marketing Association 2000 Ben Franklin Awards (Best First Book)
- Honorable Mention: Writer's Digest 2000 National Self-Published Book Awards

• • •

Promo Blurbs

Can you write? Interested in a lucrative, flexible home-based writing career? According to Peter Bowerman, best-selling author of the award-winning, triple-book-club selection *The Well-Fed Writer,* Corporate America outsources (thanks to downsizing!) an enormous number of writing projects, and at hourly rates of $50-125+! Get the details at **www.wellfedwriter.com**.

You CAN make a GOOD living writing! How? Corporate America is looking for freelancers and pays hourly rates of $50-125+. So says Peter Bowerman, best-selling author of the award-winning, triple-book-club selection *The Well-Fed Writer.* Get the details at **www.wellfedwriter.com**.

Love being an at-home Mom, but would enjoy a lucrative, flexible part- or full-time career that leverages your past work experience? Are you a decent writer? Well, according to Peter Bowerman, best-selling author of the award-winning, triple-book-club selection *The Well-Fed Writer,* Corporate America will pay handsomely ($50-125+/hour!) for your freelance skills. Get the details at **www.wellfedwriter.com**.

• • •

To see other examples of email pitches tailored to other groups, I invite you to consider investing in my *Well-Fed SP Biz-in-a-Box.* Full contents and purchase details follow.

"The Well-Fed SP Biz-in-a-Box"

Want to get your hands on virtually every piece of marketing material I created in the course of my successful book promotion campaign? Well, everything you see on the list below is in the separate "cut 'n pastable" ebook entitled, *"The Well-Fed SP Biz-in-a-Box."* We're talking about nearly 100 jam-packed pages of forms, pitch letters, releases, proposals, follow-up notes, thank-you notes, flyers, emails, certificates, and much more. All of which, I'd wager, might just save you a lot of time, money, and aggravation.

Visit **www.wellfedsp.com/spbinb.shtml** to purchase and immediately download your copy today (and for a paltry $29.95!). And get a jump on the marketing/promotion/ administration of your growing self-publishing empire!

- Book Proposal
- Book proposal
- Ingram Express Program: Marketing Strategy Questionnaire
- Sample "small press review" letter to major bookstore chain
- "The Amazing Evolving Press Release": Four versions
- "Background" release
- Sample press release cover letter
- Author bio (several versions)
- Sample email pitches (+ variations)
- Sample email pitch (seeking academic "adoptions" of book)
- Promo blurbs of varying sizes (for easy "cut 'n paste")
- "News pegs" web copy
- Book promo sheets (two versions)
- Mock book reviews (two versions)
- Combination review copy mailing labels/follow-up sheet
- Key review promo sheets (press kit enclosure)
- Book club promo sheets (press kit enclosure)
- "Good News" update letters to wholesalers
- Copyright page verbiage
- Galley insert sheet

- Galley copy cover letter sent to "blurbers"
- Seminar flyer
- Pre- and post-seminar e-mails
- Discount certificates (include with book for purchases thru special link)
- Amazon profile verbiage
- Amazon testimonials sheet (press kit enclosure)
- Amazon *Marketplace* thank-you notes
- Amazon review request (response to positive email)
- Autoresponder "thank you" after web purchase (with subscribe reminder and offers)
- Review copy cover letter (to first line reviewers)
- Review copy cover letter (to general audience)
- Email review copy pitch (sent by intern)
- New book pre-release email
- 55+ Pitch letter for marketing campaign
- 55+ Review copy cover letter
- Ebook reselling agreement
- Ebook promo copy (for "resellers promo kit")
- Ebook promo copy (for web site)
- Radio interview sample phone script
- Radio interview email pitch letter
- Sample suggested Q&A for radio host/producer
- Web links swap request
- Thank-you cover letter to CD set buyers
- Writers conference pitch letter
- Sample "book business cards" (back and front)
- Book package mailing labels
- Pre-printed sticky notes
- Event tent cards (with pricing/product discounts)

Appendix C

The following is a serviceable timetable for your own self-publishing adventure, drawn from my experience (*and* the mistakes I made). Certain production and review milestones are more rigid than others, but if you stay roughly on this course, you'll be in good shape.

Where applicable, I've included the page number in the book that discusses the step in more detail.

I. Before You Start Writing Your Book

1) Do a book proposal to make the case for the market viability of your book. (32)

2) Visit a bookstore to scope out what competition exists for your proposed topic. Is your topic or your approach unique or are there another 20 similar books out there? (31)

3) If your book has competition, give some serious thought to your USP (Unique Selling Proposition): how your book will be different and better than others. This can form a cornerstone of your marketing plan. (29)

II. Six Months Before You're Done Writing

1) Brainstorm your title and subtitle. (39). Once you have a few, run them past friends and colleagues. When down to a short list, verify that they're not taken on *Books-in-Print* (**www.booksinprint.com**; check "Forthcoming" titles, too) and on **www.Amazon.com**.

2) Line up a book cover designer. Ideally, visit a bookstore with him/her to scope out the competition, and which designs do and don't work. (38)

267

3) While exploring competitive (or similar) titles at the bookstore, get a sense of what's a reasonable and feasible price for your book. (57)

4) Secure your block of 10 ISBN numbers (**www.bowker.com**), and once received, assign one to your book. (46)

5) Decide on a name for your publishing company. NOT *Joe Blow Publishing*; you'll be instantly labeled as a self-publisher, and an amateur at that. Have simple, inexpensive business cards printed up.

6) Reserve your web site's domain name (I use **www.godaddy.com**; good service and low rates), and keep the registration info (and expiration date!) in an easy-to-find file. Make a note in your planner to renew; the companies don't always do so. (100)

7) Join both PMA, The Independent Book Publishers Association (**www.pma-online.org**) and SPAN, the Small Publishers Association of North America (**www.spannet.org**). (xxv)

8) As you work on the manuscript, pull out "excerptable" chunks that would make good standalone articles (e.g., Top Ten lists), and set them aside in their own file. (158)

III. Three Months Before You're Done Writing

1) After you've assigned your book's ISBN, register your title with Bowker's *Books-in-Print* and Ulrich's Periodicals (**www.bowkerlink.com**; register on the site first). (48) Secure your free listing with *ForeWord* magazine. (48)

2) Secure your Pre-assigned Library of Congress Control Number (LCCN) through the PCN program at **http://pcn.loc.gov**. (48)

3) Craft your PCIP information (49), either through a third party (50), or doing it yourself with the help of a librarian. (50) When you have the info in hand, input it on the copyright page of your work-in-progress, or if using a third party, you can forward the emailed file on to your typesetter for placement on the copyright page.

4) Finalize copyright page verbiage and copyright date; remember that next year's date is okay for books released after July. (51)

5) Secure your EAN bar code (**www.isbn.org/standards/home/isbn/us/index.asp**), and once the file is in hand, email it to your cover designer for back cover placement. (47)

6) Set up your publishing entity (i.e., sole proprietorship, partnership, corporation, etc.); contact a CPA (or EA: Enrolled Agent) or attorney to help.

7) Get a business license (call your county Business License division for details/fees). With license in hand, go to your bank and open up a business checking account.

8) Hire a web designer or start building your site yourself, adding content as you have it (table of contents, sample chapter, cover artwork, etc.). (100)

9) Get print quotes (at least five to seven) for both your short-run galley printing and your larger, final offset print run. BookMasters, Inc. (my printer) handles both. (60) Use **www.Printellectual.com** for getting multiple quotes. (60)

10) Nail down a good editor with proven skills in both editing and proofreading. Get references. If you're certain of your completion date, determine their availability for that time; if not, get back to them when you are. (52)

11) Ditto the above for a typesetter (see Appendix A for resources). Nail them down based on your editor's projected completion time. (54)

IV. When Your Book Is Done

1) Finalize your cover artwork, making sure you leave spaces for one blurb on the front cover and one or two on the back. Load the current image up to your web site. Have your designer create your "artwork toolkit" for various ongoing promotional needs. (39)

2) Send your manuscript off to your editor, and review changes when they're done. The editing/proofing process, on average, should take two to four weeks. In the meantime…

3) Start the ongoing process of crafting your book's promo materials, your "article toolkit" (157), and any other key written marketing components. Review all of Chapter Two to sharpen your marketing chops. If you haven't already done so, consider investing in *The Well-Fed SP Biz-in-a-Box* (Appendix B) **www.wellfedsp.com/spbinb.shtml**. (265)

4) Craft your back cover copy, understanding how crucial this piece is. (42)

5) Set up your home shipping center in advance of sending out your galley run. (275)

6) Get set up with the major wholesalers: Baker & Taylor and Ingram (either through a distributor or PMA's P/IWAP program) (104). Determine how you'll handle fulfillment, whether through a fulfillment company (114) or a distributor (107), and whether PMA's Trade Distribution Program makes sense for you and your book. (109)

7) If you plan to do your own accounting (vs. using a distributor or third-party fulfillment company), research and choose a D-I-Y book publishing software program. (118)

8) Make final printer selection for both your galley and offset runs, and get firm quotes in hand for the quantity print runs you've decided on. (60)

9) Put together your list of "blurb reviewers"—the folks to whom you'll send galleys for the testimonials that will appear on your front and back covers, and inside pages. (44) Think about authors and other "key influencers" in your subject area.

10) Line up an indexer for your book. Check out **www.asindexing.org** or see Appendix A for resources. (55) If you know precisely when your typesetter will be finished, lock the indexer in to a particular timetable. Or, to simplify things, have your typestter create the index if they can.

11) Have a designer or print shop design a 4" x 6" label (**e**) with your cover artwork on the front, for all future reviewer/purchaser book shipments. (276)

12) Get a "Review Copy—Not For Resale" stamp made up at your office supply superstore to stamp on the cut edges of all review copies. (277)

13) Research book clubs (and their submission guidelines) that might be a fit for your title. Check out *Literary Marketplace* or **www.booksonline.com** for ideas. Contact the acquisitions editors of the good candidates, pitch them, and offer to email sample chapters or send a galley when done. (118)

NOTE: As mentioned earlier, I'm using the outdated term "typesetting" here to describe the process of "interior book design," or "interior layout" to draw a distinction between "design" as it relates to your book's cover vs. its text.

V. When Editing Is Done

1) Send the edited, proofed manuscript off to be typeset, a process that should typically take three to four weeks. Provide your typesetter with cover artwork, and in addition to typesetting the manuscript for print, have them create your ebook version—a PDF with the cover artwork inserted. (209)

2) Make sure your typesetter leaves the first four to six pages of the book file blank as placeholders for testimonials with the words "(Blurbs Pending)" up top.

3) Figure out what customer payment system you'll use (e.g., third-party fulfillment company (114), your own merchant account (97) with shopping cart system (98), PayPal (98), etc.). If you've hired a web designer, get him or her involved in the process.

4) Start building your book's profile on Amazon.com, adding cover art, summary, author info and other salient info by joining and maximizing the Amazon Advantage program (**www.amazon.com/advantage**). (124)

5) Determine your "official publication date" (OPD) and make sure it's at least 90-120+ days after your "bound book date" (BBD), the date you have printed books in your hands (46). You'll use this period to get your book into the hands of key industry reviewers and to start building your grass roots buzz.

6) Identify potential resellers for the ebook version of your book, trying if possible to find resellers who focus specifically on your subject area. Start the process of creating ebook "reseller marketing kits." (210)

7) About six weeks before you have your galleys in hand (when your typesetter's about half done), email the folks on your blurb target list and secure their agreement to provide a blurb, and let them know to be on the lookout for a galley in 45 days or so.

8) For niche books, keep beefing up your "final book" review copy list (those who will get the final version) by hunting up web sites or web-based entities that mesh with your subject area. Shoot for having an initial list of 200-300 and grow it from there. Create a system for keeping track of your contacts. (**e**) Consider hiring an intern to help you with this process. (90)

9) For titles with more mainstream appeal, start making targeted pitches to relevant content editors of major magazines (six- to eight-month lead-times).

10) Continue the process of crafting marketing materials begun earlier (#3 in previous stage).

11) Craft chunks of your book (i.e., Top 10 Lists) into finished articles, perhaps of varying lengths, and add to your "article toolkit." (157)

VI. When Typesetting Is Done

1) Send the manuscript to your indexer, the final stage in your "content construction." Indexing should take roughly a week, two at most.

2) Make sure you have all necessary shipping materials in your home/office shipping center for your galley package mailing coming up. (275)

3) Verify with your galley printer the format in which they need to receive your text and cover files and alert your typesetter and cover designer.

4) Keep building your "final book" review copy list.

VII. When Indexing Is Done

1) Have your typesetter and cover designer send their files directly (and separately) to the galley printer (59). Verify with the printer that everything's in order. Galley printing should take two to three weeks, max. While you're waiting...

2) Assemble all your blurb reviewer packages, with written (preferable) or printed address labels affixed, cover letter written and copied, business cards ready, waiting only for books to arrive and assembly to begin.

3) Assemble packages for your "First-Line Reviewers" (the ones that need to see your book 90-120 days before OPD). This is your *only* window to reach these folks, so don't miss it. Visit their web sites and *follow their submission guidelines carefully.* (70)

4) Take a vacation. Seriously. As long as everything's kosher at the printer, there's nothing to do at this point but wait. It's about to get busy, so kick back while you can.

VIII. When Your Galleys Arrive

1) Assemble review copy packages for both your blurb reviewer list and first-line reviewers, affix galley insert sheets ($\boxed{\text{e}}$) on the inside front cover of the latter group's books, and send them all out.

2) Send galleys to any acquisitions editors of book clubs who expressed an interest in seeing the complete work.

3) Continue creating marketing materials and articles for placement.

IX. When Reviewer Blurbs Return

1) Edit any long blurbs down to roughly 35-40 words, and email the edited versions back to reviewers for approval.

2) Once all blurbs are finalized, choose the three biggest names, put one on the front cover and one or two on the back, then put the rest in order of notoriety in a list (with your cover stars repeated at the start) for placement on your opening pages.

3) Send cover blurbs to your cover designer to insert on the front and back covers.

4) Send the full blurbs list to your typesetter to insert on the four to six blank pages up front in the book. Make any final corrections to the manuscript that have been noted or brought to your attention since the galleys were printed.

X. Time to Go to Print!

1) Have your typesetter and cover designer send their final files directly to your printer, who will verify with you in 24-48 hours that all is in order. The printing process should take four to five weeks. Don't forget to print up 250-300 extra book covers to use as press kit folders (149). While you're waiting for your books…

2) Finalize your preliminary review copy list—the (ideally) 200-300 names you've been assembling, based on your research (or your intern's) into relevant web sites, associations, web- or print-based newsletters, or any other publication or entity that meshes with your subject. (73)

3) Assemble review copy packages (including press kit contents) for your main review copy mailing list, ready to add the books and the extra covers for your press kits.

XI. When Your Books Are Ready

1) Ideally, you've decided to use a fulfillment company or distributor, in which case, have your printer ship you 250-300 copies of your book.

2) Once you have books, finish assembling review copy packages and send them out.

3) Email the ebook version of your title to the ebook resellers you've chosen to work with (210), along with ebook "reseller marketing kits." (210)

4) Visit the U.S. Copyright site, download and fill out the copyright form, and send it in with two copies of your book. (50)

5) Send one copy to the Library of Congress as part of the PCN process. (48)

6) For titles with more mainstream appeal, start making targeted pitches to relevant content editors of major newspapers (one-month lead-times).

7) Keep the pressure on! Continue to identify new review copy targets, use mainstream media when appropriate (especially when making appearances), write and place articles whenever possible and keep doing everything else we've discussed. Most of all, have fun!

Appendix D

My *what*? Even if you, very wisely, decide to let an outside entity handle your order fulfillment, as I have, you're still going to be personally sending out a pretty steady stream of books from your home office: hundreds of review copies, and in my case, requested autographed copies from buyers off my site, and *Amazon Marketplace* sales (of my dinged copies).

Ideally, you have a small dedicated space to work with, perhaps a corner of the basement or garage or part of that spare bedroom or office. Get a cheap six-foot laminate table at an office supply store, or even better, a used office furniture outlet (where you'll likely pay $20-25). Doesn't have to be pretty—just sturdy and functional.

Also, a few years back, I went to The Container Store® (**www.containerstore.com**) and bought some of their InterMetro® rack shelving. In addition to being cheap and ridiculously sturdy, this stuff is completely modular: you buy the posts and the length shelving you want and put it together yourself in mere minutes (easy even for a dorkus mechanicus like me). It's a great way to organize books, mailers, packaging materials, your mini self-publishing library and anything else you need handy. Once you've got the basics in place, here's what goes in your packages…

275

Your Book "Package" Components

1) Books: Just seeing if you're paying attention. When I printed my first 5000, I had them send me 500 from that run. That first 500 are long gone, and every few months, I order another case or two.

2) Bubble Mailers: Buy them in bulk from a national packaging supply company like Uline (**www.uline.com**; 9000 items; 800-295-5510). I buy the Jiffylite #2 white padded bubble mailer—Model # S-5148, 8.5" x 12" (8.5" x 10.75" inside). It's just the right size to fit my 300-page 6" x 9" (or 8.5" x 5.5") book plus press kit. It'll even snugly accommodate two copies if necessary; if you want a bit more breathing room for two-book packages, go with the Jiffylite #4 mailer—Model # S-5149, 9.5" x 14.5" (9.5" x 13.25" inside).

A box of 100 of either will run you roughly $45-50 delivered, which is far cheaper than buying these mailers in packages of five or ten from the office supply store. (FYI, for single CDs, go with Uline's model # S-7759, 7.25" x 8" —about $65 delivered for 200).

I buy the white ones (not manila), which adds a bit of class. They're also blank, as in, minus the goofy pre-printed *To, From,* and address lines that scream "Office Supply Store!" I take care of that with...

3) Pre-printed Address Labels: (e) This was one of my better ideas, if I do say so myself. I had my print shop print 4" x 6" labels on bright yellow (for my first book, blue for my second, red for this one) "crack 'n peel" label stock, and in a boxed-off section to the left of the main address window on the label, I put "As Requested..." and a picture of the book on the label. It jogs the recipient's memory and lets them know they asked for this, as opposed to some unsolicited review copy, which we'd never send out anyway, right? At the bottom of the blank address box, I put my URL.

As for the book cover image I use on the label, remember discussing having your book cover designer provide various small, large, hi-res, and low-res versions of your cover graphic for various promotional uses? Here's one of those uses, and in this case, I had her create one that looks like a book lying down on a table.

The picture, coupled with the web address at the bottom, provides more free advertising. Okay, so I can't prove that countless postal workers have bought my books after seeing that intriguing book cover and the web address on the packaging. But, hey, it doesn't cost a penny extra to broadcast your message to all eyes that see it, so if you can make that packaging work for a living while it's traveling to its new home, why the heck not?

Finally, the bright yellow or blue (or other striking color) label on white packaging makes for a visually appealing package. Over the years, I've gotten plenty of compliments on the packaging. One woman who runs a prominent writing site, in her review of the book on her site, actually included a line about how the attractive and promotionally savvy packaging lent credibility to the author and the contents of the book even before she opened it. Loved hearing that.

4) Press Kit: *(contents discussed in Chapter Eight)*

If it's a buyer's book package, obviously lose the press kit, but you might want to include some...

5) Discount Certificates: In any purchaser packages I'm sending (Amazon dinged books, special requests, etc.), I include discount certificates, either like the "$4 BOOK-BUCKS OFF!" certificates I described in Chapter Seven (Amazon.com) or ones for discounts on other products (e.g., single teleseminar CDs). As mentioned earlier, I include "side-door" links on the certificate for purchasing the items, accessible from outside the site, but not visible from within the site, and which look identical to the normal-priced links except for price.

6) "Book Business Cards"—discussed in Chapter Fourteen. Put at least two in each reviewer package, maybe four or more in customer packages.

Stamp Them Before Sending

Go to your office supply store and have a stamp made that reads *Review Copy—Not For Resale*. Then before shipping out a review copy, stamp the book along the right-side cut edge of the closed book and perhaps even inside the front cover. Thanks to the *Amazon Marketplace* program (and other online booksellers' new/used book sale outlets), a bunch of my review copies sent out before I got my stamp have likely made their way into these resale outlets. My book gets sold and I don't make a dime.

USPS Rules

Keep in mind that any packages sent by the USPS (the logical shipping choice, given their Media Mail option, discussed ahead) that weigh over one pound have to be physically handed over the counter to a postal worker in a post office (under a pound can be dropped in any mailbox or left for a mail carrier to pick up when he delivers your mail). There are two exceptions to this "over-the-counter-drop-off" rule. The first is…

USPS Click-N-Ship Service®

All done online—calculate rates, print labels, pay postage and even get free delivery confirmation for Priority Mail packages. You can just hand your packages to your mail carrier or drop in any mailbox. More details at **www.usps.com** (under *Shipping Tools*, click *Print Online Postage*). The other exception is…

Pitney Bowes mailstation™

I've resisted getting a postage meter, but it's not a bad idea for an aggressive book marketer sending out a healthy volume of mail. It'll cost you roughly $20 a month through Pitney Bowes (**www.pitneybowes.com**), plus your postage, of course, but it can simplify your life dramatically. Using this option also allows you to just drop any one-pound-plus packages in any mailbox or leave for your carrier to pickup.

Going Postal

If you *are* going to make your own P.O. runs (I can hear the time management junkies howling), there's nothing too deadly about the mailing process, except the lines. Tips: Do it early or late, and avoid lunchtime and rush hour (for those sites that stay open past 5:00 p.m., like mine). Have your packages stamped and ready to go. Build a rapport with the folks who work there, so you can just hand off ones that already have postage, and avoid the lines.

If you're not going to go the Click-N-Ship or **mail**station routes, get a small scale to calculate and affix your postage in advance of your mail runs. Doesn't have to be an expensive digital one. Even a kitchen one will probably do the trick—ideally, one that goes up to a few pounds. Check **www.usps.com** for rate/weight details.

Media Mail (The Good, Bad & Ugly…)

Use Media Mail (a.k.a. Book Rate) for regular shipping. It's far cheaper than any other "regular speed" delivery service—about 50% of the cost of the brown company. The downside is that it can sometimes take 7-10 business days for packages to get delivered, and occasionally, a package sent Media Mail disappears into the USPS Bermuda Triangle. It's either never seen again or it actually surfaces a month or two after you've sent a replacement copy— usually in pretty beat-up packaging and sporting many exotic stamps chronicling its "scenic route" (suggest to your two-book recipients that they donate duplicate copies to their local library rather than returning it). Yes, those are frustrating moments, but do they happen often enough to warrant switching to a far more expensive option? No.

International Shipping

For you Americans shipping review copies internationally, become familiar with Global Priority Mail® (GPM) from your friendly folks at the U.S. Post Office. $9.50 (at press time) for a GPM Flat Rate Envelope to most places around the world (and $7.50 to Canada) in just 4-7 days. Small books (say, 4.5" wide or less)—or CDs—will fit nicely in the smaller GPM FRE for $5.25, $4.25 to Canada. I regularly get book orders from around the globe, and charge $10 extra for shipping. If they're buying both books, I still charge $10 as both will still fit in the FRE, which makes it a bargain.

By the way, whenever I'm using an expedited delivery flat rate envelope of any kind (USPS Priority Mail®, Express Mail®, or Global Priority Mail®), I still put the book(s) in a padded mailer before inserting in the envelope. I promise, they'll arrive in better shape and result in a happier—and more impressed—buyer than if you just threw them straight in the envelope. Being flat rate, it doesn't cost any more for the extra weight, and everything fits just fine.

Speaking of international, in our final appendix, we'll explore the whole exciting world of foreign rights. Passports, please…

Appendix E

Foreign rights. Sounds so exotic. Well, perhaps, but more importantly, if you play your cards right, it might just sound pretty profitable. While I didn't pursue foreign rights too vigorously on my book, some of it came looking for me. I sold the Chinese (simplified characters) translation rights to my book a few years back. Not a lot of money ($1200 advance and a sliding scale royalty of 6-8%), but it's that "found money" thing.

Since a single foreign rights deal doesn't exactly qualify one as an expert, I sought out one—and what an expert I found. Bob Erdmann has worked in the publishing industry for more than four decades. He's managed fourteen *New York Times* best sellers for one client. Wrote a marketing plan for a non-fiction book that resulted in $1 million in sales. Secured 65 foreign rights contracts for one book that turned into seven-figure royalty payments. See his web site (**www.bob-erdmann.com**) for more.

As a two-term past president of PMA, The Independent Book Publishers Association (the association I've mentioned about a bazillion times in this book), Bob created PMA's *Trade Distribution Program*, which has yielded more than $20 million in book sales for members. Bottom line, he knows the business, and is very good at what he does. One of his primary areas of expertise is foreign rights, as evidenced by his very successful *Frankfurt Foreign Rights Program*.

The Frankfurt Book Fair is the world's premier annual book fair, and, Bob has now made the trek to Germany almost thirty times on behalf of a select group of non-fiction authors to represent their works. Months in advance, he sends print and electronic catalogs to hundreds of publishers worldwide, resulting in back-to-back 30-minute meetings with foreign publishers for six straight days (and the catalog is posted on his site for a full year). So, who better to ask?

281

Based on years of experience, the books Bob represents (non-fiction only) are those he feels would translate well into a different language and culture, and as a result, are more likely to attract the attention of his foreign publisher network. Bob's basic cost for including a book in his *Frankfurt Foreign Rights Program* bookshelf is very reasonable, and customary commissions come into play as a percentage of successfully negotiated foreign rights contracts.

The following is an article from Bob covering the basics of this exciting direction. If you want to know more, give him a shout at bob@bob-erdmann.com or 209/586-1566, or visit his site at **www.bob-erdmann.com**:

Building a Foreign Rights Revenue Stream

As the world becomes smaller, foreign publishers have become increasingly aware of the abundance of excellent books by American publishers who, in turn, are discovering that foreign rights sales can contribute nicely to their bottom lines. A classic win-win.

Fact is, American publishers have content that's in demand by foreign publishers in nearly 400 countries—publishers willing to pay to acquire the rights. The best part? It will likely cost you nothing to start generating a foreign rights revenue stream.

A few years ago, a well-known client of mine published a best selling personal finance book. The book encouraged individuals to create as many sources of income as possible through diversified investment of their assets. What better strategy for profitability than viewing your book as a financial asset and broadening its base to create multiple revenue streams?

Bookstore revenues are an obvious stream, but an often-fickle one. So smart publishers also sell to catalog houses, educational institutions, museum stores, book clubs, periodicals, special sales outlets, mass merchandisers, *and* foreign rights buyers. What's the definition of a "foreign rights sale"?

The licensing of the right to a foreign publisher to reprint, distribute, and sell an English- or translated-language edition of a book for compensation to the licensor under stipulated terms and conditions.

The Hot Subjects

So, what are foreign publishers looking for? Psychology/self-help (always popular), business, personal development, personal finance, parenting, and anything with the word *success* in the title. There are thousands of books on these topics, so buyers abroad want books with unique angles, not just ho-hum, me-too titles.

"Will it travel?" is a common question we hear, meaning, *Is the content universal, or appropriate just for America?* Page count is also important. A 300-page book in American English would swell to more than 400 pages in German, and shrink to about 200 in most Asian languages.

Foreign publishers want easily translatable books with proven track records. The more work they need to do to make it a fit for their market, the less interested they become. Obviously, they prefer recently published books, with up-to-date content unlikely to become obsolete quickly (as would, say, travel and computer books).

How do you get started in building this foreign rights revenue stream? Either by being *proactive* (prospecting), *reactive* (participating in book fairs), or both.

The Proactive Process

Your best prospecting aid as you get started is *International Literary Market Place*. This directory, published by R.R. Bowker, is expensive, so first check to see if your library has it, but know that you can access it online on a fee basis (**www.literarymarketplace.com**). It lists virtually every publisher in the world by country, and each listing includes information on the kinds of books that entity publishes, along with contact information.

Pick the countries you feel would be most receptive to a particular book, remembering that what seems obvious may not be. For example, Germany and Japan don't want books about World War II. And, perhaps surprisingly, countries like China, Indonesia, Eastern European nations, and India are now active rights-buyers. Make a short list of the publishers you want to contact. You may also want to target foreign agents (who will charge a commission); they'll be listed separately in ILMP under "Literary Agents."

Create a detailed fact sheet for your title, with a small picture of the book's cover. List the elements most important to a foreign publisher: U.S. sales, author credentials, compelling features, countries to which rights have already been sold, quotes from important reviewers, trim size, page count, copyright date, etc. Be succinct, but thorough. Email the fact sheet to those on your list with a cover note asking them to contact you if they want to hear more. Interested publishers and agents will respond by asking for review copies.

The Reactive Approach

Proceeding reactively means participating in the book fairs best for foreign rights activity. Your best strategy is to target and research likely prospects before you go, and make sure you have a chance to talk with them while you're there.

The four main shows are:

Frankfurt International Book Fair: The granddaddy and most important one of all. Attended by 350,000-plus publishing people from every corner of the world, it's designed exclusively for buying and selling rights. If you can participate in only one fair, this is the one. **www.book-fair.com.**

London Book Fair: While primarily focused on British booksellers and the U.K. publishing industry, it has gained some importance for foreign rights. **www.lbf-virtual.com.**

BookExpo America: America's premier book industry trade show has a whole area for meeting with foreign publishers and agents. **www.bookexpo.reedexpo.com.**

Bologna Children's Book Fair: If you publish children's books, this is a place to be. **www.bolognachildrensbookfair.com.**

"Yes, We're Interested!"

Okay, so you've gotten a few nibbles from several foreign publishers and/or agents. They've requested review copies and likely asked for 90-day options while they study your books more closely (meaning that, for 90 days, that foreign publisher is given first right of refusal to pick up a book before you can let someone else buy those rights).

Your best, most cost-effective shipping mode is Global Priority Mail from the USPS. Though not nearly as expensive as FedEx, UPS, or Express Mail, its shipments will still arrive at most destinations within a week.

Include a cover letter, asking the publisher to confirm receipt by email. Then follow up regularly. This is critical. Don't be a pest, but keep in touch to prompt a decision, and maintain a status record of your follow-ups. I'm continually amazed at how many publishers go to the expense and effort of sending a book overseas, and then sit back and wait, complaining that they "never heard anything."

Follow Up, Follow Up, Follow Up,

If you haven't received confirmation that the book arrived after two or three weeks, follow up. Two or three weeks after you do receive confirmation, follow up again to see if prospects need more information, or perhaps to relay some good news about an award or accolade that can raise your book's stature a bit higher in their eyes. When their 90-day option hits the 30-days-left mark, follow up once more to make sure they know it's about to expire and to ask if they need more time. In other words, find legitimate reasons to keep in touch, while pressing courteously for a decision.

Your prospect's editorial staff will decide whether they think the book will "travel" and whether it can be translated easily. The production people will determine printing, paper, and binding costs for their edition. The sales and marketing people will make judgments about whether it will sell in their country. Finally, the financial people will determine whether they can make a yen, peso, euro, mark, dinar, schilling, franc, yuan, renminbi, rupee, or won, or two.

Responding to an Offer

Let's say a publisher decides they do want to acquire the rights to your book. At that point, they'll either make an offer or ask you for your terms. Ideally, you want them to make their offer first. Who knows? It might be better than you expected! Negotiating a deal that is good and fair for both sides can be confusing if you're inexperienced. The best advice is: Be realistic and know the norms.

First realize that value will vary from book to book, and from country to country. If you or your author isn't John Grisham, don't expect your book to be valued the same way his are. And don't expect a developing third-world country to value it the same way an established world power would.

How do you know whether an offer is fair and reasonable? Here's the rule of thumb: Multiply the total number of copies proposed for the first printing by the estimated retail price in that country to get the gross revenue; then multiply that by the royalty percentage (between 5 and 10 percent) to get a figure for a typical advance.

For example:

First printing: 5,000 copies
Retail price: $10
Revenue from 1st printing (gross): $50,000
Royalty percentage: 6%
Typical advance: $3,000

This formula will generally work for simpler transactions, but be aware of elements that can change the deal.

12 Tips For Making Foreign Rights Work For You

1) **Always use your contract, not one provided by a foreign publisher or agent.** But don't try to create your own. Have an intellectual property attorney who specializes in publishing draft one that suits your needs. *(PB Note: Bob has offered to assist authors in negotiating foreign rights contracts for his standard fee.)*

2) Stipulate the rights you are granting, and be specific. Know exactly which rights the publisher is seeking, as well as the language and country. Does the publisher expect book club, electronic, or other rights as well? If so, the value climbs for each of these.

Spanish-language rights, for example, might apply to many countries. Say you're granting rights to a publisher in Barcelona who's insisting on world rights. Find out whether the company has adequate marketing and distribution in Central and South America (and possibly the U.S.). If so, world Spanish rights would be worth more than rights only for Spain, and you should get more money. If the publisher only wants rights for Spain, then you won't make as much, but you could make additional rights sales to Spanish-language publishers in Central and South America (and, again, maybe the U.S.).

3) Define the advance. Always try to get the entire royalty from the first printing as the advance, using the formula above.

4) Set a term. Three to five years is a typical term for a grant of rights to a foreign publisher. Occasionally a publisher will ask for seven, eight, or ten years. If you agree to such an extension, the publisher should sweeten the offer.

5) Defer to the publisher on format. Maybe you published your book as a hardcover or an 8" x 10" trade paperback. In some countries, a hardcover would necessitate a prohibitively high retail price, and an 8" x 10" can't be produced. The foreign publisher wants its edition of your book to succeed even more than you. Let them make the right choice for their market.

6) Set a schedule for accounting. Reporting of sales and resulting royalty payments should be every six months, although more and more foreign publishers insist on reporting annually. I don't consider this a deal breaker, but if a publisher insists on annual reporting, then you should insist on a higher advance to cover the longer period between royalty payments.

7) Specify payment currency. Payment should always be in U.S. dollars.

8) Be aware of the "flat-fee" agreement. This interesting concept allows a foreign publisher to pay you a one-time flat fee, and no more, for printing a certain number of copies. The amount of the fee is usually determined by the formula I used earlier. If you agree to a flat-fee agreement, specify that it terminates whenever the inventory is depleted or after a specified period (less than the normal three to five years), whichever occurs first. Or provide a clause that allows reprints under the same payment terms, or provides for re-negotiating terms for future printings.

9) Consider artwork. If a book includes illustrations, photos, or other artwork, it may have higher value for a foreign publisher. But before you grant artwork rights, be sure you're in a position to do so. They may have been granted to you by another party for your use only, and granting those rights to a third party may require permission and compensation to the artist, illustrator, or photographer.

10) Charge for providing a CD. Foreign publishers who wish to use your cover (or other artwork) may ask you to provide it on a CD. And English-language foreign publishers (in the U.K., India, and Singapore, for example) may also ask for a CD, which would greatly simplify production for them. You are entitled to compensation for this, either in the form of a separate CD-use fee or an increased advance and royalty payments.

11) Factor in taxes. Some countries may require their publishers to withhold taxes, which can be from five to 20 percent of payments due to you; others may not. Ask and plan negotiations accordingly. If an Indian publisher is paying you a $500 advance and withholding 20 percent, you're netting $400. If you're paying a 10 to 20 percent agent's commission on top of that, you won't have enough left to go to Starbucks.

Some countries are participants in a treaty with the United States to "avoid double taxation." Those will require you to submit an Internal Revenue Service (IRS) Form 6166 to them, obtainable from:

Department of the Treasury
Internal Revenue Service
U.S. Residency Certification Unit
P.O. Box 16347
Philadelphia, PA 19114-0047
215/516-7135;
fax 215/516-1035, 215/516-2845

Request a Form 6166 for each specific country you're dealing with, and allow four to six weeks.

12) Respect cultural differences. There are nearly 400 countries in the world, and each has its own way of doing things. The world doesn't march to the beat of our drum. Sending a letter to a Japanese person on gray stationery carries a very upsetting message. Bargaining is expected in many countries, but insulting in others. Try to learn about the cultures of the various countries with which you may be dealing.

I have made some incredible lifetime friendships with people from all over the world as a result of foreign rights activities, people I never would have met otherwise. Negotiating foreign rights deals can be fascinating and rewarding in many ways that go beyond the obvious.

Index